Behind the Veil

Also by Anindita Ghosh:

POWER IN PRINT: POPULAR PUBLISHING AND THE POLITICS OF LANGUAGE
AND CULTURE IN A COLONIAL SOCIETY, c.1778–1905

Behind the Veil

Resistance, Women and the Everyday in Colonial South Asia

Edited by

Anindita Ghosh
Lecturer in Modern Extra-European History,
University of Manchester

South Asian edition first published 2007 by

PERMANENT BLACK
'Himalayana' Mall Road, Ranikhet Cantt
Ranikhet 263645
perblack@gmail.com

This edition published 2008 by
PALGRAVE MACMILLAN

Palgrave Macmillan in the UK is an imprint of Macmillan Publishers Limited, registered
in England, company number 785998, Houndmills, Basinsgtoke, Hampshire RG21 6XS.

Palgrave Macmillan in the US is a division of St Martin's Press LLC, 175 Fifth Avenue,
New York, NY 10010.

Palgrave Macmillan is the global academic imprint of the companies and has
companies and representatives throughout the world.

Palgrave® and Macmillan® are registered trademarks in the United States, the United
Kingdom, Europe and other countries.

ISBN-13: 978–0–230–55344-6 hardback
ISBN-10: 0–230–55344-3 hardback

This book is printed on paper suitable for recycling and made from fully managed and
sustained forest sources. Logging, pulping and manufacturing processes are expected
to conform to the environmental regulations of the country of origin.

A catalogue record for this book is available from the British Library.

Library of Congress Cataloging-in-Publication Data

Ghosh, Anindita, 1967-

    Behind the veil: resistance, women, and the everyday in colonial South
    Asia/ [edited by] Anindita Ghosh.
    p. cm.
    Originally published: Delhi: Permanent Black, 2007.
    Includes index.
    ISBN-13: 978-0-230-55344-6 (alk. paper)
    ISBN-10: 0-230-55344-3 (alk. paper)   1. Feminism—India—History.
    2. Women—India—History. 3. Women—India—Social conditions. I. Title.
HQ1742.B44 2008
305.48'8914—dc22   2008015067

10 9 8 7 6 5 4 3 2 1
17 16 15 14 13 12 11 10 09 08
Printed and bound in Great Britain by
CPI Antony Rowe, Chippenham and Eastbourne

CONTENTS

ACKNOWLEDGEMENTS

The idea for this volume originally sprang from my earlier work on print and popular culture in nineteenth-century Bengal, where I was consistently confronted with the problem of 'fitting' women into my overall study of subaltern groups. When trying to tackle the issue I realized how often and easily women were appended as 'just another' group to larger studies of the subordinated, unless there was a specific feminist perspective at work.

Further research on women's reactions to the modernizing regime of the Bengali bhadralok, and emerging work on the subject, made me convinced that the story of women in colonial India had only been half told. An isolated chapter in my book on Bengal was not enough. Similar evidence for the rest of India had to be brought together. A conference I was able to organize in the summer of 2004, in Manchester, enabled me to achieve this. There was much heated discussion on the subject of 'resistance', but all the participants agreed that the project should be taken forward from extant histories of organized, 'successful' movements by women, and examine the overwhelming evidence—writings, rituals, and symbols of deviance and subversion in women's lives.

I am grateful to the Society for South Asian Studies, British Academy, and the University of Manchester for funding the conference. Nadeem Noor's one-man team was amazing in managing the event. Sukumar was extremely helpful with the posters. Many thanks to the contributors for their patience and to Rukun for being so extraordinarily efficient.

As always Partha provided steadfast support and encouragement.
Finally, this book is for my mother, whose silent but staunch everyday resistance to dominating regimes—even benevolent ones—has proved inspiring.

NOTE ON CONTRIBUTORS

Padma Anagol teaches modern Indian history at the School of History and Archaeology, Cardiff University. She has published widely in gender and women's history of India and is the author of a monograph titled *Feminism, the Politics of Gender and Social Reform in Colonial India 1850–1920*. She is on the Editorial Committee of *South Asia Research*; *Cultural and Social History*; *Women's History Review* and a consultant for *BBC History Magazine*.

Clare Anderson is Senior Lecturer in the School of Historical Studies, University of Leicester. She holds a personal research fellowship from the Economic and Social Research Council, working on 'British penal settlements in Southeast Asia and the Indian Ocean, 1773–1906'. This is her main research interest, though more recently she has become interested in prisons in early colonial India and Mauritius. She is the author of several chapters and articles that discuss these themes, as well as *Convicts in the Indian Ocean: Transportation from South Asia to Mauritius, 1815–53* (2000) and *Legible Bodies: Race, Criminality and Colonialism in South Asia* (2004).

Geraldine Forbes is Distinguished Teaching Professor of History at the State University of New York Oswego. Her first book, *Positivism in Bengal* (1976) was selected for the prestigious Rabindra Puroskar awarded by the West Bengal government. Among her publications on the history and lives of Indian women are *Women in Modern India* (1996) in the New Cambridge History of India series, *The Memoirs of Dr Haimabati Sen* (with Tapan Raychaudhuri, 2000), *Manmohini Zutshi Sahgal, An Indian Freedom Fighter Recalls Her Life*

(1994), *Shudha Mazumdar, Memoirs of an Indian Woman* (1989), and *A Historian's Perspective: Indian Women and the Freedom Movement* (1997).

Anindita Ghosh is Lecturer in Modern History at the University of Manchester. Her published work in the form of journal articles and contributions to edited volumes focuses on the commercial vernacular book market in Bengal, and the social history of print in colonial India. Her monograph based on these themes is *Power Print: Popular Publishing and the Politics of Language and Culture in a Colonial Society, 1778–1905* (2006).

Siobhan Lambert-Hurley is Senior Lecturer in Modern History at the Nottingham Trent University. The primary focus of her research is the emergence of a Muslim women's movement in South Asia from the late nineteenth century, with a particular eye on Bhopal. Within this framework, she has written widely on education, social and political organizations, the culture of travel, missionaries, and personal narratives, including (edited, with Avril Powell), *Rhetoric and Reality: Gender and the Colonial Experience in South Asia* (2006), *A Princess's Pilgrimage: Nawab Sikandar Begum's 'A Pilgrimage to Mecca'* (2008), and *Muslim Women, Reform and Princely Patronage: Nawab Sultan Jahan Begam of Bhopal* (2007).

Nita Varma Prasad obtained her doctorate in South Asian and Middle Eastern history from the University of California, Berkeley. She is Assistant Professor of History at Quinnipiac University in Hamden, Connecticut.

Tanika Sarkar is Professor of Modern History at the Centre for Historical Studies, Jawaharlal Nehru University, New Delhi. She has published several monographs, including *Bengal 1928–1934: The Politics of Protest* (1987); *Words to Win: The Making of Rashsunadri Debi's 'Amar Jiban'* (1995); and *Hindu Wife, Hindu Nation: Religion, Community, and Cultural Nationalism* (2001).

1

INTRODUCTION

ANINDITA GHOSH

The overwhelming image of Indian women during the colonial period has been of passivity, of a group silenced doubly—first in nationalist discourses and second in the more recent post-colonial scheme of things. Far too often, we see woman as a silent shadow, veiled and mute before her oppressors, and unquestioningly accepting a discourse that endorses her subordination. As has been pointed out, for the colonial state this was part of a strategy to per-petuate domination: helpless and weak Indian women in need of protection provided one moral justification for colonial rule.[1] Later, historians showed how the Indian woman became the site for nation-alist constructions of tradition and cultural authenticity in the quest for self-identity from the late nineteenth century onwards. Faced with defeat and humiliation in the political and material world, Ind-ian men constructed their women as the repositories of all that was pure and worthy in their own culture.[2] In both perspectives, women

[1] Lata Mani, 'Contentious Traditions: The Debate on Sati in Colonial India', in K. Sangari and S. Vaid (eds), *Recasting Women: Essays in Colonial History* (New Delhi: Kali for Women, 1989); Rosalind O'Hanlon, 'Issues of Widowhood: Gender and Resistance in Colonial Western India', in Douglas Haynes and Gyan Prakash (eds), *Contesting Power: Resistance and Everyday Social Relations in South Asia* (Berkeley and LA: University of California Press, 1992).

[2] Partha Chatterjee, 'A Nationalist Resolution of the Women's Question', in Sangari and Vaid, *Recasting Women*.

emerge as unresisting, inert, and passive objects of defining discourses, as people without any control over their lives. On the other hand, where women are discovered in assertive roles, they are either participants in larger mass struggles under the tutelage of their male peers and guardians (women activists in the nationalist movement),[3] or unusual eruptions within a conventional social fabric (Tarabai Shinde, Binodini Dasi, Pandita Ramabai).[4]

But such representations by no means exhaust the possibilities of defining subjecthood among women in colonial India. We need to grasp the dynamic of hegemonic discourses on the one hand, and women's subjectivity and agency on the other. There seems to be little recognition of the multiplicity of strategies for constructing selfhood that women have been adept at in South Asian contexts. Far from representing themselves only in ways dictated by males, this book argues, women often imaginatively scrutinize and critique the social world that they experience, and give voice to it in subversive expressive traditions or actions, some more overtly dissident than others.

Studies on women and resistance in colonial India have generally tended to waver between the achievements of the exceptional and educated few—against a presumed backdrop of ignorance and helpless passivity—on the one hand, and radical activities on the other. Among recent compilations of essays dealing with women's agency in India, only a few are relevant here. While volumes such as those by J. Krishnamurty, Bharati Ray, and Meera Kosambi have made valuable contributions towards increasing the visibility of women in historiographies of the nineteenth and twentieth centuries, other more critical and questioning works have opened up debates on resistance and agency underlying gendered regimes of power.[5] A noteworthy exploration of the issues under scrutiny here emerges in a

---

[3] See e.g. Geraldine Forbes, *Women in Colonial India*, New Cambridge History of India, vol. IV.2 (Cambridge: Cambridge University Press, 1996).

[4] Rosalind O'Hanlon, *A Comparison between Women and Men: Tarabai Shinde and the Critique of Gender Relations in Colonial India* (New Delhi: Oxford University Press, 1994); Rimli Bhattacharya (ed.), *Binodini Dasi, My Story, My Life as an Actress* (New Delhi: Kali for Women, 1998).

[5] J. Krishnamurty, *Women in Colonial India: Essays on Survival, Work and the State* (New Delhi: Oxford University Press, 1999); Bharati Ray (ed.), *From the*

parallel study by Nita Kumar that sets out to recover women as 'subjects' in South Asian history.[6] But while the essays in that volume are principally concerned with the recovery of agency, the present collection aims to problematize the very conditions out of which this agency is constituted. In addition, it knits together a more cohesive narrative of resistance by throwing an exclusive spotlight on the issue.

In some ways, this project picks up the threads of that seminal publication, *Contesting Power* (1992), and uses the methodology evident there in the field of women's history. We argue here against the traditional emphasis placed on violent confrontational struggles in social and political history writing because of its tendency to ignore everyday negotiations of power that go on between the dominated and dominant on a more sustained basis.[7] Before this, Scott and Adas had studied non-violent forms of resistance among the oppressed that stopped far short of open rebellion, and their significance for power relations in peasant societies in South East Asia.[8] *Contesting Power* extended the model—although not entirely uncritically—to look at everyday resistance in more diverse social situations in South Asia.[9] As the editors, Haynes and Prakash, pointed out:

> Rather than insist that one form of resistance is more significant than the other, these essays establish the 'everydayness' of struggle in yet another sense: by placing all forms of resistance within the ordinary life of power . . . the authors study the ways in which the social relations of daily existence are enmeshed in, and transfigured by, resistance, both extraordinary and 'everyday'. . . . Social structure, rather than being a

---

Seams of History: Essays on Indian Women (New Delhi: Oxford University Press, 1995).

[6] Nita Kumar (ed.), *Women as Subjects: South Asian Histories* (Charlottesville and London: University Press of Virginia, 1994).

[7] Haynes and Prakash, *Contesting Power*.

[8] Michael Adas, 'From Avoidance to Confrontation: Peasant Protest in Precolonial and Colonial Southeast Asia', *Comparative Studies in Society and History*, vol. 23, 1981; James Scott, *Weapons of the Weak: Everyday Forms of Peasant Resistance* (New Haven: Yale University Press, 1985).

[9] The volume disagrees for instance with Scott's critique of the Gramscian notion of hegemony.

monolithic, autonomous entity, unchallenged except during dramatic instances of revolt, appears more commonly as a constellation of contradictory and contestatory processes.[10]

But in more fundamental ways our volume challenges the present understanding of women's struggles in colonial India. It does so by offering a backdrop of 'invisible' but consistent gendered resistance against which to map the more well-known outbursts of the organized radical feminist movement, or of outstanding female public figures.

In trying to reconceptualize women's resistance in South Asia, the contributions of the Subaltern Studies collective in the 1980s, which studied the underprivileged in colonial India, seem another logical correlate. But a closer look reveals that women did not figure very prominently in that framework.[11] The reason for this is not hard to find. As a few Subalternists later admitted, in their eagerness to highlight elite oppression of the underprivileged, the collective tended to favour analysis of the more violent and spectacular forms of protest by exploited groups.[12] To radically confront existing notions of mass inertia in popular struggles, this seemed the most obvious focus. Women, who mostly appeared only in non-combative roles in such works, could not constitute the preferred subject matter. It is not without ground, therefore, that scholars have criticized the virile assumptions underlying most such writings on resistance.[13] Undoubtedly, therefore the exclusion of more 'peaceful' moments of resistance was a shortcoming. Later historians writing for the series softened the stance by looking at a range of conflicting attitudes—such as insubordination and even collusion—alongside open revolt.

[10] Haynes and Prakash, *Contesting Power*, pp. 2–3.

[11] Not until the fifth volume did women figure as 'subaltern' actors in their own right.

[12] David Arnold, 'Gramsci and Peasant Subalternity in India', *Journal of Peasant Studies,* vol. 11, 1984; Sumit Sarkar, 'The Conditions and Nature of Subaltern Militancy: Bengal from Swadeshi to Non-Cooperation, *c.* 1905–1922', *Subaltern Studies, III* (New Delhi: Oxford University Press, 1984).

[13] Rosalind O'Hanlon, 'Recovering the Subject: Subaltern Studies and Histories of Resistance in Colonial South Asia', *Modern Asian Studies*, vol. 22, no. 1, 1988; Veena Talwar Oldenburg, 'Lifestyle as Resistance', in Haynes and Prakash, *Contesting Power*, p. 25.

The idea of resistance fashioning everyday social relations is relatively new. James Scott's study of peasant society in a Malaysian village in the 1970s was path-breaking in highlighting the presence of resistance in everyday life. The constant struggle between prosperous ruling groups on the one hand, and powerless labourers and smallholders on the other, Scott argued, was sustained by a series of seemingly innocuous behaviour such as footdragging, false compliance, pilfering, slander, and sabotage, often without any explicit intention to rebel. This placed serious limitations on coercive structures and diluted their ability to extract resources from the oppressed.[14] In his later work Scott developed his thesis by exploring what he called the 'hidden transcripts' in power relations. He described these as the conscious statements of insubordination by the lower classes, made in safety among confidantes and accomplices—proof of a consciousness that has been able to escape the effects of total domination—even while scrupulously maintaining structures of deference and obedience in the presence of authorities.[15] Where unable to find more open expression, such moods of resentment and discontent survived more covertly, in the public discourse of dominated groups: 'we might interpret the rumours, gossip, folktales, songs, gestures, jokes and theatre of the powerless as vehicles by which, among other things, they insinuate a critique of power while hiding behind anonymity or behind innocuous understandings of their conduct.'[16]

Surveying a wide range of situations across historical contexts, from slave to caste societies, Scott sees how the weak have always expressed discontent using multiple strategies and avenues. From small 'inoffensive' acts in the presence of the dominant to louder pronouncements of disquiet in congenial surroundings, the dominated have consistently critiqued the conditions of their subordination. The apparent harmony between oppressors and the oppressed is merely a masquerade as it conceals deeper and ever-present roots of disquiet and change. Closer home, Ramanujan's work on old women's tales, both bawdy and imbued with a sense of fun, 'expressing

---

[14] Scott, *Weapons of the Weak.*

[15] James Scott, *Domination and the Arts of Resistance: Hidden Transcripts* (New Haven and London: Yale University Press, 1990).

[16] Ibid., p. xiii.

their point of view' and 'ranging from the tragic to the ludicrous', can be seen to be pointing towards the potential recovery of precisely such a domain.[17]

Such an approach can be immensely rewarding when analysing women's lives in India, where, given the discursive trappings, even close readings of the historical and archival evidence does not offer much beyond hegemonic narratives of power relations. What has been systematically excluded from accounts of women's struggles is the everyday realm of social relations in which power is constantly and relentlessly negotiated. While some of the essays in the present volume address this sphere, others, inspired by the general shift away from the spectacular and the successful, explore small acts of rebellion and lone struggles on the fringes. In this sense, we have widened the interpretation of 'everyday' to include not just the quotidian, but also the marginal.

There is another difference with the Scott models. Unlike him, we look into the multiplicity of power relations, highlighting not just resistance but also the *active* complicity of the subordinated within the structures of their own domination. While gender is acknowledged as an immensely important factor of social ordering, other equally contingent praxes—e.g., class, caste, and colonialism—are seen to render the narrative more complex.

II

There are obvious problems in trying to recover the woman as 'subject' in a South Asian context. To begin with, it would seem un-historical to see women as the possessors of essential qualities that characterize them beyond conflict and history. Besides, there remains the sticky issue of resistance itself. How far can we label these hardly visible struggles as 'subversion' or 'resistance', given that women not only continue to operate within dominant structures, often as colla-borators, but also have no vision of an alternative social order? And finally, which women are we talking about? Is it right to treat 'women'

---

[17] A.K. Ramanujan, 'The Indian Oedipus', in Lowell Edmunds and Alan Dundes (eds), *Oedipus, A Folklore Casebook* (New York: Garland Publishing Company, 1983), pp. 234–61.

as a homogeneous category, ignoring the trappings of power that come with wealth and status?

While the importance of uncovering outstanding opposition to gendered regimes of power is beyond doubt, the underlying complexities that frame these structures are often ignored. In fact, as some studies have shown, the lines of battle are much more ambiguous than we would like to imagine.[18] Women who dissent do not always emerge only as 'victims', but often as 'perpetrators' in upholding repressive orders. And, as such, their compliance with patriarchy must be placed alongside their resistance in order for us to fully grasp these struggles. This is a contradiction that lies at the heart of women's experiences in India, and partially explains the woman's complex position, like that of her subaltern male equivalent, as both resisting agent and collaborator.[19]

These are, in fact, some of the issues that we put to the test in order to try and make sense of this vast and indisputable fabric of unsystematic and unorganized activity among women that have only begun to be tapped by historians. The significance of undertaking such a project cannot be underestimated. What Oldenburg says in her chapter on the courtesans of Lucknow in the Prakash and Haynes volume is relevant in this context: 'Their [the courtesans'] struggle obviously cannot be a collective, revolutionary "class struggle" for the gender divisions are vertical, not horizontal, and cut through class lines. [However,] the validity of their struggle cannot be refuted on the grounds that it is engaged in at a private, unobtrusive level. Their will to resist existing gender relations and reproduce the radically ordered social relations within their ambit is as self-conscious and intractable as it is undeniable.'[20]

The elements of a gender critique are self-evident in the essays

<hr>

[18] O'Hanlon, 'Issues of Widowhood', in Haynes and Prakash, *Contesting Power*.

[19] For an inspiring study outlining similar complexities in lower-caste resistance in Bengal, see Ranajit Guha, 'The Career of an Anti-God in Heaven and on Earth', in Asok Mitra (ed.), *The Truth Unites* (Calcutta: Subarnarekha, 1985).

[20] Oldenburg, 'Lifestyle as Resistance', in Haynes and Prakash, *Contesting Power*, p. 51.

collected here. Even though not matched by any practice articulate and strong enough to turn the world upside down, they register genuine distress and the desire to overcome it. If these stories of resistance are not recorded for fear of their inability to contribute to a history of women's struggles in any real sense, we risk their erasure from historical memory. The small rebellious acts of Bengali women would thus be forever frozen, like images behind a camera, were it not for the intervention of scholars such as Geraldine Forbes. Her interrogation, as seen in her essay here, prompted stories not self-evident in the women's photographs themselves, bringing to life long-lost memories of struggle, and making in the process valuable contributions to the narrative we are trying to knit together.

Most importantly, we note, occurrences of resistance do not themselves always imply pure forms of autonomy or escape from dominant structures. But in treating gender as a site where power is constantly fractured and reshaped by the struggles of subordinate groups, it is possible to see this as part of an ongoing negotiation between the dominant and dominated to condition the material, social, and political structures in which they exist. Dramatic confrontations and resultant radical dislocations, in that sense, are to be regarded as only the visible façades of this continuum. By an extension of this logic, struggle resides in the everyday, even where it is seemingly contradictory, least dramatic, and least visible.[21]

The move against totalizing conceptualizations of cultures and subjectivities has been witnessed in recent times in Indian anthropological and folklore studies. In exposing the many points of closure and openness, pluralities and contradictions, in the textual and ethnographic domains, scholars have underscored the heterogeneity of mental worlds, as in women's tales from South India.[22] In two separate anthropological studies, singing women from both high

---

[21] See M. de Certeau, *The Practice of Everyday Life* (Berkeley: University of California Press, 1984).

[22] A.K. Ramanujan, 'A Flowering Tree: A Woman's Tale', paper presented at the conference, 'Language, Gender and the Subaltern Voice: Framing Identities in South Asia', University of Minnesota, April 1991, cited in Ann Grodzins Gold and Gloria G. Raheja (eds), *Listen to the Heron's Words: Reimagining Gender and Kinship in North India* (Berkeley: University of California Press, 1994), p. 24.

and low castes are seen as subverting dominant male regimes in their own innocuous ways, while continuing to subscribe overall to local patriarchal structures.[23]

The essay by Tanika Sarkar, on the ways in which widows in nineteenth-century Bengal reconstructed their selfhood by borrowing from prevalent dominant discourses on marriage, love, and conjugality, brilliantly highlights precisely this tension between the subordinated on the one hand and hegemonic discourses on the other. It demonstrates how ideologies of resistance can be bred within strongholds of power, and how women make strategic use of dominant discourses to improve their position in society. Sarkar's concern is echoed in some other contributions. While discussing ties of gendered solidarity among women in the Bengali *antahpur*, Anindita Ghosh is thus aware that they are not just bound in ideal sisterhood. Kinship and marital status, among other things, pit them in antagonistic positions in many situations—as between the wife and mother-in-law/sister-in-law; a widow and a married woman, and others. Siobhan Lambert-Hurley's work also highlights how elite Muslim women in Bhopal, while negotiating gendered colonial medical discourses, were simultaneously reinforcing the divide between themselves and their less fortunate sisters.

In their inspiring volume on women's songs in North India, Raheja and Gold argue that social relationships are constructed within not one but multiple discursive fields. Women's apparent compliance in one thus needs to be juxtaposed against their opposition in another, and relative conclusions drawn. Images of Indian women as repressed and submissive can be misleading in that 'submission and silence may be conscious strategies of self-representation deployed when it is expedient to do so, before particular audiences and in particular contexts.'[24] For Kumar too, even though their location within and acceptance of structures of subjugation—apparent from their half-silent and seemingly invisible voices—pose problems, the persistent struggle by women from within structures

---

[23] Gold and Raheja, *Listen to the Heron's Words;* Fernando Franco, Jyotsna Macwan, and Suguna Ramanathan (eds), *The Silken Swing: The Cultural Universe of the Dalit Women* (Calcutta: Stree Publications, 2000).

[24] Gold and Raheja, *Listen to the Heron's Words,* see Introduction, p. 11.

cannot be ignored. Just because such resistance is on the 'inside, private, hidden and silenced', it does not give the struggle less currency.[25]

For us what is interesting is the conscious and tactical use of various ideas and identities on both sides of the power spectrum that women make. The social and symbolic splits in their identities are in fact mutually reinforcing, and can offer forceful and critical commentaries on some dominant discourses of gender and authority.[26] None other than women themselves are more painfully aware of their dual roles—as wife and sister, or wife and mother. Competing identities and competing perspectives, when put to creative use by singing women in North India, make for interesting narratives. The bold and strategic juxtaposition of their discrepant roles in the songs, argues Raheja, illustrates a reflexively ironic and acute awareness of the duality in women's social positions. [27]

What O'Hanlon has to say on subaltern resistance and the subjectivity of the subaltern may be relevant here.[28] The problem with the subaltern, she points out, is that he emerges as a 'self-originating, self-determining individual, who is at once a subject in his possession of a sovereign consciousness . . . and an agent in his power of freedom'.[29] Such unproblematic premising of the subaltern's agency means that his inescapable and simultaneous location within dominant discourses has been largely ignored. 'The demand for a spectacular demonstration of the subaltern's independent will and self-determining power', she goes on, has led to inadequate documentation of the limits of subaltern resistance.[30]

---

[25] Nita Kumar, *Women as Subjects*, p. 21.

[26] Lynn Bennett's work on the split roles of wives and sisters, played out by women in Nepal, is relevant here. See Lynn Bennett, *Dangerous Wives and Sacred Sisters: Social and Symbolic Roles of High-Caste Women in Nepal* (New York: Columbia University Press, 1983).

[27] See Gloria Goodwin Raheja, 'On the Uses of Irony and Ambiguity: Shifting Perspectives on Patriliny and Women's Ties to Natal Kin', in Gold and Raheja, *Listen to the Heron's Words*.

[28] O'Hanlon, 'Recovering the Subject'.

[29] Ibid., p. 191.

[30] Ibid., pp. 213, 219.

The classic problem of historians of social protest and resistance—having to contend with the idea of autonomy *versus* hegemony—remains in the current literature. Even though it is now recognized that conflict is an integral and necessary part of hegemony, with struggles commonly occurring not outside but inside the realm of power, there has been no sustained attempt to grapple with the problem. Prakash and Haynes marked a departure from Scott's hypothesis in offering a reasoned critique of subaltern autonomy, but not all contributors were agreed on its precise parameters. On the theme of gender and resistance, in particular, O'Hanlon and Oldenburg differed over the position of women as visible historical and social actors. While Oldenburg discovered women's agency in clandestine acts in the heart of patriarchy among the courtesans of Lucknow, O'Hanlon was hesitant to accept even a full-blown critique of men in Tarabai Shinde's rhetorical pamphlet as evidence of free will.[31]

The essays in the present volume revisit the vexed issue, some tackling the question more directly than others. Critics who believe that collective ritual, or lonely, unorganized acts of resistance lack serious social intent will find some of the contributions provocative and thought-inspiring. The survey of women's resistance in colonial Maharashtra by Padma Anagol puts 'intention' at the centre. In the cases she explores, women are seen acting consciously to redress injustice. In this, their response is almost invariably gendered and targets patriarchy, Anagol suggests, even if deeper entrenched socio-economic and political structures are contributory. Nita Verma Prasad's startling study of widows in North India, fighting law suits either as claimants or defendants to retain property rights, also reveals women as determined agents who can use the legal system to further their own ends (although they are usually assisted by male relatives and their cases are fought by male pleaders). Without pushing the contention of agency too far, she concludes that their actions reveal gaps within patriarchy and the colonial legal system which women manoeuvre to their own advantage. Clare Anderson's essay on incarcerated women in the penal colonies of Burma, Mauritius, and South East Asia attempts to painstakingly recover, in the absence

---

[31] O'Hanlon, 'Issues of Widowhood', Haynes and Prakash, *Contesting Power.*

of audible 'voices', fragments of female convict experiences from 'cracks in the colonial archive'. Her examination leads her to conclude that the highly unstable gendered boundaries of penal regimes were being negotiated by female convicts through everyday resistance, much to the consternation of jail authorities. Anderson is understandingly much more cautious in attributing agency to such acts taking place under highly repressive structures, seeing in them a representation of both the power and powerlessness of such women.

One of the more daring situations in which the question of agency arises is that of the upturned world order, as expressed in customary traditions. Singing women in domestic situations, indulging in seemingly dangerous role reversals, thus present an intriguing facet of power relations in Bengal in the nineteenth century, as shown in the essay by Ghosh. The contribution of safety-valve theories is undisputed. But other studies on rituals of reversal have shown how such practices, while renewing and reinforcing established hierarchies in certain ways, also had an imaginative spillover into everyday life. Comic sexual and ritual inversions of gender hierarchies in pre-industrial Europe, argues Natalie Zemon Davis, can thus be seen as not only strategies of accommodation to systems of power but also ways of nurturing alternative thoughts on family structures.[32] The 'hidden transcripts' within such carnivalesque worlds keep alive ideas of social rebellion until they actually manifest themselves in overt action. Dramatic instances of role reversals, such as the acts of poisoning and murder that Anagol describes, thus appear less remarkable and more meaningful when traced back to a potent undercurrent of simmering discontent. A similar study of reversed worlds, visible in more sober expressive traditions in recent times, also demonstrates women inserting the philosophy of their songs into their practical, everyday lives.[33]

As Scott points out, it would be a mistake to think that 'the absence of actual knowledge of alternative social arrangements produces automatically the naturalisation of the present, however hateful that

[32] Natalie Zemon Davis, 'Women on Top', in *Society and Culture in Early Modern France* (Stanford: Stanford University Press, 1975).

[33] See *Listen to the Heron's Words*.

might be.'[34] Besides, the assumption of inability on the part of sub-ordinate groups to imagine a counterfactual social order is ill founded. They do imagine both the reversal and negation of domination. Printed images of the world turned upside down we know have been replicated in the actions and utterances of insurgents during rebel-lions.[35] The challenge to cultural discourses encoding female subordi-nation can thus be a more immediate and real threat than hitherto appreciated. Such cultural practices, in fact, free actors 'to experiment with alternative, normally hidden, views of personal worth and power relations'.[36] Turning to Haynes and Prakash again, 'Resistance, we would argue, should be defined as those behaviours and cultural practices by subordinate groups that contest hegemonic social formations, that threaten to unravel the strategies of domination; *"consciousness" need not be essential to its constitution.* Seemingly innocuous behaviours can have unintended yet profound conse-quences for the objectives of the dominant or the shape of a social order' [emphasis mine].[37]

What is also fundamental to these acts, we would like to add, is the constitution of a moral discourse in which gender identities are constructed, represented, negotiated, and contested in everyday life. The intervening gaps between spectacular protests, we often forget, are not as barren as they seem, and provide crucial succour and agenda to succeeding upheavals. It is impossible to ignore the culture of resistance that lurks beneath a veneer of utter supplication. For, as Scott points out, the greater the power of the dominant, the more convincing the masquerade of normality among the dominated.[38] Similar observations have been recorded for South Asia. Songs sung

[34] Scott, *Hidden Transcripts*, p. 80.

[35] This can be seen happening in both the Reformation and the subsequent Peasant War in Europe. See David Kunzle, 'World Upside Down: The Iconogra-phy of a European Broadsheet Type', in Barbara A. Babcock (ed.), *The Reversible World: Symbolic Inversion in Art and Society* (Ithaca: Cornell University Press, 1978), pp. 63–4.

[36] David Parkin, 'The Creativity of Abuse', *Man*, vol. 15, 1980, p. 62.

[37] Haynes and Prakash, *Contesting Power*, p. 3.

[38] Ibid. See, for instance, pp. 27, 33, 35.

by untouchable Paraiyar women, it has been suggested, could constitute socially meaningful action as they have the potential to instigate changes in local cultural patterns.[39] Household proverbs offering a picture of gendered domination, the 'small acts of rebellion' remembered and recalled on revisiting family albums and photographs, and the refusal by female convicts in the Indian penal colonies to engage in certain types of labour all demonstrate how subordinates in large-scale structures of domination can maintain a fairly extensive social existence outside the immediate control of the dominant. It is in such sequestered settings that, in principle, a shared critique of domination may develop.

In all the cases discussed in this volume there is a larger hegemonic structure that binds the lonely acts of resistance, a structure which is unquestionably dominant, powerful, controlling. However, as we argue, power exercised by the dominant is contingent on its relationship with the dominated. As such, paradoxically, part of that power is vested in the latter. The methodological leap we have to make is to envision how 'even the weakest and most muted of efforts assert themselves within such structures of power by posing alternative models. For, to speak in an alternative voice is already to assert a subjectivity'.[40] As Ranajit Guha points out in a remarkable analogous study of resistance among low castes, the absence of overt acts of defiance and even conscious mimicry of the material aspirations of higher castes do not conceal the central theme of social antagonism in the religious beliefs of certain castes and tribes. The elements of a critique are evident, even though not matched by any practice articulate and strong enough to turn the world upside down. This is a contradiction that lies at the heart of lower-caste religiosity, he contends. Both these tendencies—i.e. to conform and to dissent—constitute the social reality of the lower castes in India.[41]

Even if resistance in this case does not contribute to any real, discernible, or immediate social change, we believe it constantly realigns power relations. It establishes that dominant power structures,

---

[39] Margaret Trawick Egnor, 'Internal Iconicity in Paraiyar "Crying Songs"', in Stuart Blackburn and A.K. Ramanujan (eds), *Another Harmony: New Essays on the Folklore of India* (Berkeley: University of California Press, 1986).

[40] Kumar, *Women as Subjects*, p. 20.

[41] Guha, 'The Career of an Anti-God'.

far from being autonomous and monolithic, are being constantly fractured and rearranged by struggle. The whole spectrum of protest must therefore be seen as part of the same structure of power that creates the dominant discourse. Only then can we understand the role of women as both agent and collaborator in these struggles, and see how 'they are (in that sense) simultaneously, like subaltern male subjects, both empowered and powerless, active and passive, constituted and constituting.'[42]

Nita Kumar's work offers some insightful analyses of women's subjectivity in South Asia. In her Introduction she argues that the Cartesian dichotomy between subject and object that privileges knowledge as an abstraction created by an autonomous being has been challenged by postmodernist writings that see all knowledge, and hence power, as constituted of both subject and object working collectively and discursively. But for feminists, the current questioning of subjecthood seems a luxury, for 'in order to announce the death of the subject one must first have gained the right to speak as one'.[43] The choice, for those like Kumar, therefore, has to be a political rather than philosophical one. But in pointing out the androcentric and patriarchal nature of discourses on femininity she does offer a polemic—'a feminist modification of postmodernism', as she calls it. If the constitution of 'man as the subject, the rational knower' is a power ploy, 'so must the constitution of woman as subject be seen to be.'[44] Simply reinstating the dominated to centrestage does not help for it reinstates alongside the hierarchy from which the confrontation sprang in the first place. So, 'to develop an account of the world that treats our perspectives not as subjugated or disruptive knowledges, but as primarily and constitutive of a different world' seems the way forward.[45]

Resistance offered by women in their everyday life for us, then, is only a trope, a means of anchoring more complex and multilayered

[42] Kumar, *Women as Subjects*, p. 21.

[43] Rosi Braidotti, 'Envy: Or With Your Brains and My Looks', in Alice Jardine and Paul Smith (eds), *Men in Feminism* (New York: Methuen, 1987), p. 80.

[44] Kumar, *Women as Subjects*, p. 9.

[45] Nancy Harstock, 'Foucault on Power: A Theory for Women?', in Linda Nicholson (ed.), *Feminism/Postmodernism* (New York: Routledge, 1990), pp. 166–7, cited in Kumar, *Women as Subjects*, p. 10.

struggles for power taking place in society. It is by no means our wish to claim that the instances discussed in this volume possess the force and resolution of wider, organized movements by women that seek to improve their position: they are far from that. However, in the surreptitious and often insidious ways in which they operate (as in Bengali homes and penal colonies), in their firmness of purpose (as in the case of widows in North India and Maharashtra asserting their right to property), in their sturdy imagination of alternative value systems (as in the case of Bengali widows in the nineteenth century), and in the constitution of critical moral discourses on patriarchy (as in the memories of Bengali women surrounding photographs—albeit in different degrees), there is an unmistakable social, political, and moral agenda.

III

The vision of the woman making conscious, ordered, rational choices aimed at wresting a better life for her lot continues to plague the question of women's agency in South Asia. The interplay of silence, collaboration, and protest clouds the issue. In almost all the cases discussed here there is partial alignment with dominant structures, so that autonomy is never complete, often ambiguous, and not probably always desired.

But neither power nor knowledge is the prerogative of those in control, for the battle lines are never conclusively drawn. Women's discourses therefore must be read as 'their alternative knowledge and also as necessarily exercising power as well, presently or potentially.'[46]

This volume thus collectively aims at re-examining the issue of everyday resistance through essays that explore its significance for gender and power relations in South Asian history and society. Resistance here is not an identifiable thing or object to be retrieved, much less a coherent one. Rather, it is to be understood as a strategic articulation of power relations among social groups, including women, working at multiple discursive levels and involving diverse identities. The intervention that the volume more specifically seeks to make here is against a historiography that has consistently eliminated the

---

[46] Kumar, *Women as Subjects*, p. 20.

possibility of assertive action and critical assessment by ordinary women in their everyday lives of the patriarchies that dominate them. As Gold's timely reminder alerts us, 'South Asian women are too often perceived as veiled figures acting out graceful pantomimes of submission and debasement.'[47]

Some of the explorations into the idea of both resistance and agency in the volume might give an indication of the kind of rethinking that is underway. Almost all contributors agree that gender is just one of the various strategies of power struggle in society, wielded alongside equally potent ones of class and colonialism. Lambert-Hurley thus demonstrates how elite women in Bhopal were negotiating both socially stratified and gendered regimes of colonial health and medicine to assert their own space; Prasad and Anagol highlight the overarching nature of the oppressive structures framed by colonial law and indigenous patriarchy; the women remembering photographs with Forbes were as much opposed to colonialism as to the nationalist patriarchies which dictated their lives; while the gendered regimes of the penal colonies, Anderson points out, were overlaid with other colonial categories of race and criminality.

The problem that we encounter endlessly in describing such examples as acts of resistance is similar to those faced much earlier by scholars of 'history from below'. Historians like E.P. Thompson and Christopher Hill, who were pioneering in their attempts to retrieve a history of relatively low-key people's movements in the 1970s, had to contend with the strident contemporary academic climate that favoured the documentation of organised working-class struggles.[48] Thompson and Hill were attacked for their valorization of people's movements that had little by way of either a coherent political ideology or a definite plan of social action. Most were not even successful, it was claimed.[49] The prerogative of being deemed

[47] Gold, in *Listen to the Heron's Words*, p. 33.

[48] E.P. Thompson and Christopher Hill's works collectively embody evidence of this *passim*.

[49] The literature that can be cited here is prodigious. For a start, see the contributions by Raphael Samuel, Stuart Hall, Richard Johnson and E.P. Thompson in the section 'Culturalism: Debates Around the Poverty of Theory', in Samuel,

struggles of resistance, it seemed, only accrued to politically conscious, radical, successful movements.

Very much the same difficulty besets scholars of feminism today. In advancing its very definite political ideology—with its inevitable attachment to liberalism, rationality and progress—feminism seeks to highlight women as either radical achievers or victims.[50] Fudging those binary positions, recovering intermediate situations, and unearthing role reversals are seen as retrograde, unexplainable, embarrassing. The intervention that we seek to make is thus also one of methodology. By reopening the debate from a different angle and reinstating the woman as subject in seemingly conflictual and fractured positions, we hope to have gone some way in understanding the ambiguous nature of such resistance in South Asia. The essays here do not claim to offer any glimpse of a sublime sovereign feminine consciousness untainted by complicity in conditions that perpetuate oppression; ours is an unidealizing appraisal of both the potential and the limitations of women's everyday struggles.

The essay by Forbes uncovers hidden stories behind frozen images from family albums in early-twentieth-century Bengal. While at first glance the photographic project to capture familial moments seems to reinforce patriarchy, the study demonstrates that in fact photographs do not simply fix identity. When women (born *c.* 1899–1914) who took strong stands on political and social issues showed Forbes their family photographs in more recent times, they often recalled 'small acts of rebellion', instances when they defied authority and/ or social convention behind the photo shoots. Forbes focuses on these

---

ed., *People's History and Socialist Theory* (London: Routledge and Kegan Paul, 1981), pp. 375–408; John Clarke, Chas Critcher, and Richard Johnson, eds, *Working Class Culture: Studies in History and Theory* (London: Hutchinson, 1979).

[50] See e.g. Gail Omvedt, *We Will Smash This Prison: Indian Women in Struggle* (London: Zed Press, 1980) for the former position, and Kumari Jayawardena and Malathi de Alwis (eds), *Embodied Violence: Communalising Women's Sexuality in South Asia* (New Delhi: Kali for Women, 1996), and S. Anandhi, 'Representing Devadasis: "Dasigal Mosavalai" as the Radical Text', *Economic and Political Weekly*, Annual Number, March 1991, for the latter.

tellings and raises questions about the nature of resistance and its significance for women's history.

Prasad's study relies on the court records of the Allahabad High Court from 1875 to 1911 to show how widows systematically pressed for their claims in inheritance disputes involving their deceased husbands' property. We see widows suing their in-laws boldly and audaciously over their right to receive regular maintenance payments, their right to effectively manage their late husbands' estates, and even challenging financial abuses such as the usurpation of property. Sarkar too throws a spotlight on widows: her entry point is the 1856 Act legalizing the remarriage of Hindu widows. This is studied in the context of colonial Bengal where reformist agitation for widow remarriage was first initiated. The various debates and controversies in the Bengali public sphere in the wake of the Act—where liberals and the orthodoxy engage in reinterpreting scriptural sources, customary discipline, gender norms, and the nature of Hindu female love and desire, throw up deep fractures in the older discipline of widowhood and conjugality. Sarkar concludes with a brief speculation about the ways in which the limited and rather ineffective law generated discursive shifts in the ideology of gender relations, with conjugality emerging as a terrain for talking about rights and equality. Significantly, women themselves participated in this debate.

The Ghosh and Anderson essays both look at hidden spheres registering discontent in the face of seemingly stable gender regimes. Ghosh's essay looks at a world hidden away in the inner courtyards of Bengali homes in the nineteenth century—of religion and ritual, resolute domesticity, and sisterhood—which bound women together in strictly gendered ways and marginalized men in their lives. Anderson, on the other hand, turns her attention to a much neglected group, Indian female convicts, and reads their 'voices' and 'silences' in the colonial archive in a specific historical context—their transportation to colonial penal settlements across the Indian Ocean. Their sudden appearance as a 'disciplinary problem' in colonial records after the 1840s, Anderson suggests, represented not only a discursive shift within local power regimes but also the active role played by convict women in reshaping the boundaries of their incarceration. From accounts left by prison officials and the repertoire of punishments meted out to them, it is clear that female convicts were engaging in everyday resistance against their prison regime.

The essay by Anagol introduces us to the various strategies of individual and collective assertion and resistance deployed by women in late-nineteenth and early-twentieth-century colonial Maharashtra. By analysing representations of symbolic gender inversion in women's literature and theatre, the ways in which women used appeals and complaints to assert their rights to property and productive resources in law courts, as well as some acts of husband-killing, the study demonstrates how women were negotiating the everyday domain of power relations. Not just patriarchy, but also the custom-bound, class–caste nexus of colonial India, it is apparent, played a role in shaping the specific nature of these struggles. Lambert-Hurley too is keen to underscore the various axes along which women participating in colonial medical discourses in Bhopal were reconfiguring themselves, including those of class and gender.

By concentrating on certain specific instances when resistance emerges as a dialogue with hegemonic discourses, an assertion of rights, an invocation of moral obligations, a form of violence, or a sign of freedom—as the case may be—many of the essays here offer more complex, conflictual, and counterintuitive narratives on gender struggles and their social ordering. As such, the volume is as much about resistance as the conditions that produce it. At the same time, 'everyday' and 'small' (even failed) rebellions are shown as complementing larger meta-narratives of more successful women's movements, reopening and enriching questions of agency in the process. Far from turning away in embarrassment from such seemingly contradictory and ineffective fragments, their significance is both celebrated and interrogated by the contributors to this book.

2

FROM THE SYMBOLIC TO THE OPEN: WOMEN'S RESISTANCE IN COLONIAL MAHARASHTRA

Padma Anagol

In the 1970s social historians from the British Left inaugurated a refreshingly new way of uncovering histories of dispossessed and marginal classes made famous in the opening remarks of E.P. Thompson, who declared his intention to rescue the poor labourer and the factory worker from the 'enormous condescension' of history in his classic *The Making of the English Working Class*.[1] Historians of Asia in search of new models to explain peasant resistance found punditry in the works of Eric Hobsbawm, Christopher Hill, E.P. Thompson,[2] and later James Scott, who adapted the Thompsonian concept of the 'moral economy'.[3]

My thanks to Anindita Ghosh, Raka Ray, Patrick McGinn, Geraldine Forbes, and Andy Wood for help in shaping this essay.

[1] First published in 1968, see E. P. Thompson, 'Introduction', The *Making of the English Working Class* (Harmondsworth: Penguin, 1968), pp. 76–136.

[2] E.P. Thompson, 'The Moral Economy of the English Crowd in the Eighteenth century', *Past and Present*, vol. 50, February 1971.

[3] The most influential have been his trilogy: see in chronological order, James C. Scott, *The Moral Economy of the Peasant: Rebellion and Subsistence in*

Innovative ways of looking at women's resistance are in evidence as early as the early 1970s. The earliest, and some of the most influential, texts in understanding how patriarchy works and the ways in which women resist abject domination have issued from mainly anthropological but also to some extent historical work steeped in micro-studies of the minutiae of women's lives in the Nepalese, Pakistani, Sri Lankan, North Indian, and Bangladeshi communities.[4] Many of these works either pre-date James Scott and the 'history from below' approaches or have worked independently of them by applying tools culled from the social sciences, women's studies, and feminist theory to unravel women's dissent and protest. Understandably, these were regarded as more appropriate than the use of models stemming from exclusively male working class and male peasant histories either of Britain or Malaysia. Without necessarily labelling them 'everyday forms of resistance', yet locating them in everyday social relations, anthropological and historical works have analysed the subcultures of women's protest which have included acts such as

---

South East Asia (New Haven: Yale University Press, 1979), and *Weapons of the Weak: Everyday Forms of Peasant Resistance* (New Haven: Yale University Press, 1985). In his most recent statement on everyday resistance Scott has extended peasant behaviours to other sections of society and provides a more sophisticated theoretical framework of the official or elite domination termed as 'public transcript' and the routine nibbling away of power by the underclass as 'hidden transcript'. See *Domination and the Arts of Resistance* (New Haven: Yale University Press, 1990).

[4] The field is vast but some representative examples of female resistance outlined in various Asian contexts are L. Bennett, *Tradition and Change in the Legal Status of Nepalese Women, Parts I and II* (Kathmandu: Tribhuvan University, 1979); J. Arens and J. van Beurden, *Jhagrapur: Poor Peasants and Women in Bangladesh* (Amsterdam: Third World Publications, 1977); C.M. Pastner, 'The Status of Women and Property on a Baluchistan Oasis in Pakistan', in L. Beck, and N. Keddi (eds), *Women in the Muslim World* (Cambridge, MA, Harvard University Press, 1978), pp. 439–49; H. Papanek and G. Minault (eds), *Separate Worlds: Studies of Purdah in South Asia* (Delhi: Chanakya Publications, 1982); Neera Desai, 'From Articulation to Accommodation: The Women's Movement in India', in L. Dube (ed.), *Visibility and Invisibility of Women* (Oxford: Oxford University Press, 1986), pp. 287–99; Meredith Borthwick, *Changing Role of Women in Bengal* (Princeton: Princeton University Press, 1984).

feigning sickness to stave off work; threatening to return to the natal home in gross cases of injustice; refusing sex to disloyal or recalcitrant husbands; learning to read and write in secret; and utilizing vows of silence and non-communication as strategies of withdrawal to bring attention to themselves within the home. Collectively and individually these suggested the everyday efforts of women to gain some control over their lives. Whilst subaltern historians of modern India have utilized and reaped harvests from the theoretical and conceptual advance in agrarian history, and in many cases shifted and advanced these models of explanation,[5] scholars of gender and women's history of India have been either slow or—a fairer assessment would suggest—reluctant to utilize the broader developments in social history. Some of this reluctance can be easily explained. In the few works that engage with Scottian or the Subaltern Studies models there has been a tendency to acknowledge some of the uses of 'everyday forms' of resistance, but also and mainly to critique these models for the obvious lack of negotiation with gender relations in the making of power structures and the failure to see the extreme heterogeneity of the category 'woman'.[6]

In the early 1990s the poststructuralist obsession with delineating women as 'sites' for the play of dominant discourses ebbed and gave way to posing the question of women's subjectivities and how they are constructed. The shift in focus which now emphasized the subjecthood and agency of women launched a whole new series of works, some of which have been extremely valuable contributions to the subject of Indian gender and women's history. Looking at women's lifestyle as resistance was an astoundingly original method inaugurated by Veena Talwar Oldenberg,[7] who applied it to subaltern classes

---

[5] For an excellent revisionist work on subaltern resistance as applied to Indian peasantry, see David Hardiman, *Feeding the Baniya: Peasants and Usurers in Western India* (New Delhi: Oxford University Press, 2000).

[6] Several impressive works have appeared in the recent past and they include the Introduction in D. Haynes and G. Prakash (eds), *Contesting Power: Resistance and Everyday Social Relations in South Asia* (Delhi: Oxford University Press, 1991); and Bina Agarwal, *A Field of One's Own: Gender and Land Rights in South Asia* (Cambridge: Cambridge University Press, 1994).

[7] See her 1990 article titled 'Lifestyle as Resistance: The Case of the Courtesans of Lucknow, India', *Feminist Studies*, vol. 16, no. 2, Summer 1990, pp. 259–87.

of women such as the courtesans of Lucknow and the idea of looking at the interiority of traditional women's lives—something as conformist as the religious life of a housewife—as embodying non-conformism was inaugurated in a brilliant reading of Rashsundari Debi's autobiography as a genre of rebellion by Tanika Sarkar.[8] For western India, Rosalind O'Hanlon translated Tarabai Shinde's treatise,[9] and provided an introductory statement to it demonstrating how one could read it as a project of a widow's protest against contemporary Maharashtrian socio-political relations. Equally, such defiance and subversions were read in song, poetry, folktale, myths, and movements of self-education by a group of scholars in a collection appropriately named *Women as Subjects* edited by Nita Kumar.[10]

Theoretically and methodologically, however, it was with the appearance of *Contesting Power: Resistance and Everyday Social Relations in South Asia* (1991) that a more nuanced understanding came about of how everyday forms of resistance are enmeshed in social relations of day-to-day existence; and, more importantly, how power is constantly fractured by the struggle of subaltern groups—both male and female—as well as conditioned by it. In other words, the contentious concept of the 'autonomy' of the subaltern was no longer the issue. Instead, how 'insurgent consciousness is simultaneously conditioned by, and conditions, the structures of domination' was given precedence over claims to a pure form of agency for the peasantry—as earlier peasant studies had suggested through the delineation of dramatic moments of resistance.[11] Haynes and Prakash also proposed a definition of resistance, arguing that it 'should be defined as those behaviours and cultural practices by subordinated

---

[8] See her 1993 article titled, 'A Book of Her Own, A Life of Her Own: Autobiography of a Nineteenth Century Woman', *History Workshop Journal*, 36, Autumn 1993, pp. 35–65.

[9] See O'Hanlon, *A Comparison between Women and Men: Tarabai Shinde and the Critique of Gender Relations in Colonial India* (Madras: Oxford University Press, 1994).

[10] Nita Kumar (ed.), *Women as Subjects: South Asian Histories* (Calcutta: Stree, 1994).

[11] See Introduction, Haynes and Prakash, *Contesting Power*, especially pp. 2–9.

groups that contest hegemonic social formations', and further that '"consciousness" need not be essential to its constitution. Seemingly innocuous behaviours can have unintended yet profound consequences for the objectives of the dominant or the shape of a social order.'[12] If 'consciousness' is divorced from the resister's act/s, then it appears that instinct and intuition and karma (if defined loosely as accidental happenings in this life or otherwise) come into play, leaving the structures of power untouched. In this sense, the Haynes and Prakash definition of resistance stays close to the Scottian model which allows for 'hidden transcripts' to be safely expressed in the comforting atmosphere of the plebeian community, transcripts that are usually never 'enacted'.[13] In other words, do footdragging, spitting, flared nostrils, guarded speech, and feigned ignorance have any kind of impact on power relations and their modification or reversal?[14] In the many fine studies of women's resistance within Indian history, outlined earlier, marking and celebrating the projects of women's resistance has been accomplished but the project of conceptualizing women's resistance has not yet commenced.[15] Is 'change' envisaged and heralded in the many acts of women's subversion? Are possibilities for transformation and a more equitable life envisioned and made

[12] Ibid., p. 3.

[13] See Scott, *Domination and the Arts of Resistance*, p. 16.

[14] The Scottian models have been enthusiastically reclaimed and also critiqued for methodological shortcomings in European contexts: see H.R. Kedward, 'Resiting French Resistance' in *Transcations of the Royal Historical Society*, vol. 9, 1999, pp. 217–82; also H.R. Kedward and Nancy Wood (eds), *The Liberation of France: Image and Event* (Oxford: Berg, 1995); and for early modern Europe, see Andy Wood, 'Seditious Speech, Popular Agency and the Social Logic of Betrayal in Tudor England', unpublished paper given at the North East Conference on British Studies, Yale, October 2002.

[15] For example, despite the 'modified postmodernism' model adopted in the volume *Women as Subjects*, the editor argues that 'she is neither free, nor autonomous, nor necessarily an agent with the power to act', and the 'larger implications of this for normative discourse do not add up to revolt and the overthrowing of authority.' The transformative abilities and the functions of the project of women's resistance remains in doubt here. See Kumar, op. cit., p. 13.

possible by women? Some of these issues can be better answered if we begin to define 'women's resistance' and also if the right kind of questions are asked of women's resistance and these lie in the context/s and conditions of her being; the role of the resister, the deliberation of her action and its impact, to which I will turn to now.

Conceptualizing Women's Resistance: Conditions and Circumstances

'Throughout historical time, women have been discriminated against and disadvantaged politically, economically, sexually and legally', is Gerda Lerner's well-considered statement.[16] The monopoly of knowledge (via philosophical and theological systems of thought) and education, alongside the control of female sexuality, by men is commonly observable in societies all over the world. Equally, the circumstances of living under these male-dominated conditions have generated and shaped women's resistance quite differently from that of men. However, if we agree with the commonplace assertion that if patriarchy is everywhere, then resistance to it could be found everywhere too, a logical extension of this statement would suggest that almost any and every act of a woman could be categorized as resistance. However, can we merit every act and utterance of a woman as potentially subversive or expressive of dissent and capable of addressing gendered power relations effectively? The 'function' of resistance is a moot point here. If resistance and power are locked in a *karmic* cycle of sorts, shaping and being shaped by each other endlessly, then where is the scope for change? At what juncture does the historian understand that change has occurred? Or, as Raka Ray has argued, the '*capacity* to act' has to be considered as well as the distinction between 'interest in resisting and capacity to resist.'[17]

[16] Gerda Lerner, *The Creation of Feminist Consciousness: From the Middle Ages to the Eighteenth Century* (New York: Oxford University Press, 1993), p. 280.

[17] She provides a thoughtful study in the context of the creation of counter-cultures by schoolgirls in Calcutta: see 'Conformity and Rebellion: Girls' Schools in Calcutta', in B. Ray (ed.), *From the Seams of History: Essays on Indian Women* (Delhi: Oxford University Press, 1995), p. 151.

Certainly, there are varieties of female resistance, some of which are extremely capable of bringing about change. However, we need to pose a new set of questions. Some of these would include—Whom is the resister addressing and what means and methods of resistance is she utilizing? How does she intend to impact on the condition of subordination or oppression that she is facing?

I would, therefore, like to begin my essay by looking more closely at the concept of resistance, keeping in mind the circumstances of the subordination of women and the conditions in which resistance may be generated. The term 'resistance' is wide ranging, encompassing many acts and extending its sweep from the private sphere of the home while also implying the public/political arena. By *resistance* we mean the ability to limit, nullify, or overturn structures of power. As such, women's resistance is a conscious act and is characterized by intention arising within conditions of unequal relations of power within society, and is often generated (although not exclusively) by the imbalance of power between the sexes.

A feature common to all women who engaged in resistance in late-nineteenth- and early-twentieth-century Maharashtra was their experience of functioning within the colonial context; but apart from this their circumstances varied vastly and caste and class affected their life chances in crucial ways. Consequently, their access to and forms of resistance differed greatly, depending on their conditions of existence and familial circumstances. Thus, a *sardar* lady—i.e. an elite woman from a landed family—experiencing oppressive conditions would not necessarily resist in the same fashion as a *malin* (female gardener) working her estate lawns. Literacy and access to resources, such as to legal and political institutions, also played a large part in determining the modes of resistance sought. In these practices of resistance evolved by women much care, planning and thought is evident, and this deliberation is directly connected to the stakes, these being much higher and more risk-laden in patriarchal societies where one inappropriate move could result in dire consequences for the woman concerned.

In the exciting social reform phase of the mid- and late nineteenth century, Maharashtrian women had begun a self-authorization movement encompassing all walks of life pertinent to them—be it the home or the world.[18] The beginnings of the feminist movement in Maharashtra were accompanied by the questioning of patriarchal modes of thought, as manifest in the Indian classics and literature; women's disadvantage in education; female subordination in socio-cultural practices, e.g. the ban on widow marriage, the prevalence of child marriages, and women's lack of access to the resources created by the new colonial economy. Inevitably, their modes of resistance, both individual and collective, were aimed not only at installing their position as 'subjects' within the home, as seen in the call for domestic reform, but also in the creation of a more just and humane society. Many of the modes of resistance fashioned towards transforming Maharashtrian society were therefore accompanied by 'purpose' and 'intention'. There were also instances where domestic and conjugal relations were marked by oppression at its most extreme, calling for more direct and open forms of resistance by women. Hence, I seek to show the varied modes of resistance evolved by women—from symbolic to open resistance—all seeking to bring about change either in their individual lives or within society as a whole. Three modes of resistance, chosen for the purposes of this volume, appear in the ensuing three sections.[19]

Nature and Significance of Symbolic Resistance

Amongst the diverse forms of resistance practised by women, conveying protest through literature was perhaps one of the most powerful in the social arsenal. Such acts of symbolic resistance were widely expressed in Maharashtra by women during the late nineteenth and early twentieth centuries. The medium of expression was predominantly a specific genre of writing within which a symbolic inversion of roles dominated the plot of the novel, short story, play, or a folk song. Barbara Babcock, editor of an important monograph on

---

[18] See Padma Anagol, *The Emergence of Feminism in India, 1850–1920* (Ashgate: Aldershot and Burlington V.T., 2006).

[19] For obvious reasons of space I have not been able to cover the entire gamut of the modes of resistance evolved by Maharashtrian women, but readers are directed to my book (ibid.) for a more detailed discussion of women's resistance in the nineteenth century.

'symbolic inversion', has broadly defined this as 'any act of expressive behaviour which inverts, contradicts, abrogates, or in some fashion present an alternative to commonly held cultural codes, values, and norms be they linguistic, literary or artistic, religious, or social and political', and it is in this sense that I analyse role reversals.[20] The reasons for the popularity of this genre of writing among women was probably because the expression of repressed desires could emerge in their narratives as creations of fantastic or utopian worlds—a medium acceptable to male censors.[21] Equally, sexual inversion and role reversals as literary strategies brought home the injustices and exploitation of women in a subtle and sophisticated manner.

One example of this is a play by Girijabai Kelkar, the first woman playwright of Maharashtra.[22] In 1912 she wrote a five-act play entitled *Purushanche Band* (Men's Rebellion).[23] Although there are other novels written during the same period by women which have similar plots, this play seems particularly representative of this variety of subversive writing.[24] It is representative first because it fits well into

[20] For a study of a variety of symbolic inversions in Western societies, see Barbara Babcock (ed.), *The Reversible World: Symbolic Inversion in Art and Society* (Ithaca: Cornell University Press, 1978).

[21] Susan Friedman has convincingly analysed the way 'the return of the repressed' takes effect in women's narratives in keeping with censorship rules through the study of a cluster of texts by Hilda Doolittle: 'The Return of the Repressed in Women's Narrative', *Journal of Narrative Technique*, vol. 19, 1989, pp. 141–56.

[22] Girijabai was already well known as a novelist, essayist, and social commentator by the time this play was enacted. A prolific writer, she promoted Marathi language and literature. She wrote and lectured extensively on all aspects of women's lives and rights. She was President of the All India Hindu Mahila Parishad in 1935. She held complex views on the nature of women's oppression expressed in her literary works, such as *Purushanche Band* (Men's Rebellion) and *Striyancha Swarga* (Women's Paradise). For more detail, see Anagol, *Emergence of Feminism*, Appendix.

[23] Girijabai Kelkar, *Purushanche Band* (Men's Rebellion) (Mumbai: Indu Prakash Press, 1913). I use the second edition of 1921, published by Girijabai in Jalgaon.

[24] For examples of other writings in this genre by women, see the novel

the conventions of symbolic inversion through complete role reversals and use of parody, irony, and paradox—core elements of this genre of writing. Second, it poses a challenge to social control and attacks the established order by situating it in the context of the problems of the women's movement in Maharashtra at the time.

Given that I have honed my definition of women's resistance as conscious and purposeful, thus demarcating my work from earlier studies, it is imperative that the motives of Girijabai Kelkar be made clear in writing this play. Girijabai, we should note, was already adept at essay and short-story writing and had also written advice manuals for women. So why did she choose an unfamiliar genre such as the 'prose play' for her new work? In her Preface she clearly lists her reasons: 'I started reflecting on the state of our society after I got interested in reading and writing. It struck me on several occasions as to why the instrument of drama that is widely utilised as a means of leisure alone should not be used to produce an impact on society, as a play is bound to produce a powerful and beneficial effect.'[25] She goes on to delineate how the content of the play had to be radically overhauled too, because the theatre-loving public in Maharashtra was, according to her, held in thrall by historical/mythological topics, which only attracted the religiously-minded as the well-informed middle classes rather than the masses. So she picked the genre of drama, but with a highly hybridized format, imbuing it with a traditional location and plot (a kingdom with kings/subjects) and a contemporary content, including the debates raging on moral and social issues.

Thus the themes in *Purushanche Band* bring out a great number of the tensions in Maharashtrian gender relations, reflecting the anxieties, resentments, and hopes of women at the time. Issues such as women's higher education, the need for economic independence from men, the freedom to work out one's choices in life, sexual rights

---

Palkicha Gonda (The Tassel at the Centre of the Palanquin) by Kashibai Kanitkar published in 1928 but which appeared serially in the popular Marathi journal *Navayug*, in 1913.

[25] Girijabai Kelkar, 'Preface'. My translation throughout, p. 1.

including the recognition of rape within marriage, the need to embrace modernity and blend it with tradition—all these form the bulk of the play's concerns. All the events take place in a kingdom, the location of which is revealed as a 'place somewhere in Hindustan', ruled by a king called Sadhu Singh, who drives out all women from his realm, forcing them to form their own parallel kingdom. An important theme in the play is that women do *not* turn the world upside down. Things turn topsy-turvy when the king comes under the influence of Vikarananda, a misogynist monk-adviser who incessantly harangues him with arguments that essentialize women as wicked and evil. Eventually, the king appears to be persuaded by Vikarananda's exposition on the 'nature of women' and decrees that no man in his kingdom will get a job or be allowed to practice any profession unless he leaves his wife. Except for one *sardar* (nobleman), the entire male population signs a contract stating it will have nothing to do with the female sex, and then the wives are driven out. What follows is a state of anarchy in the kingdom of men: utter lawlessness and chaos ensue. Chandrakant, heir to the throne, receives many petitions by cloth merchants, goldsmiths, and other such tradesmen who complain bitterly about great losses to their enterprise, since their main clientele were women. More significantly, men in all professions seem now to work inefficiently, and the author shows what ensues: without their womenfolk, most men bear the dual burden of tending to household chores as well as to business. What contemporary feminist activism has striven in vain to demonstrate, Girijabai almost a century earlier astutely proves through her characters that even the most ambitious multi-taskers (in this case, men) are quickly worn out by the 'dual burden'. This unfolds when the angry king demands an explanation from his head gardener on the unkempt appearance of the palace gardens, with the latter retorting impatiently: 'How can you expect a man who spends most of the night baking bread and looking after four children to work well throughout the day?'[26]

If the kingdom inhabited by men is dystopic, what is happening among the women? The women gather around their leaders for

---

[26] Ibid., p. 56.

direction and support. The female protagonist is a remarkable single woman, Saraswati Devi, who is depicted as a *puranika* (woman-preacher learned in Hindu scriptures) as well as being Western-educated. She convinces the distraught queen to take the reins of the women's kingdom in her hands. Working as a collective, women are now able to organize a large number of welfare schemes and embrace modernity under the patronage of the queen. In no time, women assume all responsibilities and manage the mercantile, banking, and manufacturing sectors. The women's kingdom prospers and appears utopic.

Here it seems appropriate to ask—what is the function of this sexual inversion? The answer seems to be that when women reverse roles and act like men they prove themselves as good or better than men in public life and therefore as deserving in social status as men. A second function served by role reversal is to contest men's arguments about women's inferiority in intellect, reasoning, and administrative ability. In Saraswati Devi's rhetoric this translates as 'women being equals to men, and if there is difference to be found between the sexes it is merely one that nature endows us with'.[27] In a world without women—a world turned upside down—there is disorder and inefficient administration, which is the creation of men alone. The rebellion of men instigated by the king's decree serves other 'consciousness raising' functions too. Whilst women leaders such as Saraswati Devi and Kumudini already have a feminist vision the other women in the kingdom do not. Women who upheld patriarchy and were themselves bastions of conservatism are forced to rethink issues of dominance, power, and resistance.

This transformation in women is best observed through the intellectual growth of Janakibai, wife of a Brahmin priest. Initially, she is portrayed as a traditional woman who believes in the Hindu notion of a *pativrata* (the perfect wife who worships her husband as God). Janakibai therefore condemns strongly nonconformist single women like Saraswati Devi and Kumudini. However, Janakibai's world crumbles when the raja's decree leads her husband to kick her out of the house without so much as an explanation. We hear Janakibai's sarcasm as she tells her husband while leaving, 'Now your true colours

---

[27] Ibid., p. 124.

are out. You are a fine man, indeed! What great depths you show in your love for your wife! What returns for the many years of service!'[28] She then plunges wholeheartedly into the emancipatory programmes of the female leaders.

While women like Janakibai have arrived at a feminist view of the world through painful experience, there are others who were never as naïve or trusting of their husbands yet had no opportunity to prove that they could manage well on their own.

The function of role reversals is also to provide outlets for women from the lower classes to protest and change their lives, which in normal times was denied to them through the male exercise of sheer brute force. Thus, the wives of the soldiers, cooks, and gardeners are not too unhappy about their husbands abandoning them. This feeling is echoed by the malin, who says:

> See, we women work so hard. A lot harder than men do. I am the one who plucks the flowers and makes the garlands. Only when it comes to grabbing the salary and spending it on liquor—it is only this area that he [referring to her husband] specializes in. And if I protest he beats me . . . Serves him right. Now not only will I earn but I will keep it too. I will be rich enough to make my own jewels too.[29]

This woman gardener is a fine example of a resister born out of observing and experiencing everyday forms of oppression. The disrespect shown to her in earlier days by her husband through wife-beating, appropriating her salary, and denying her the right of leisure are all dealt effective blows by the new arrangements in the women's kingdom. Girijabai also uses literary techniques from comedy to draw out themes of sexuality and question patriarchal notions of ownership of a woman's body. There are several amusing scenes which actually carry serious reflections on these issues. One such incident takes place in the dead of night, when a neighbourhood is woken by a woman's screams for help. Several policewomen on patrol arrive and handcuff the thief despite his protestations to the effect that he has committed no crime for he was in his own house

---

[28] Ibid., p. 32.
[29] Ibid., p. 50.

and the woman who screamed for help was his wife. When the bewildered patrol officer questions her, she replies that since her husband had broken the marital bond by signing the king's contract, he was a stranger to her and she regarded his entry into 'her' house as illegal and his demand for sexual intercourse as 'molestation'.[30] The wife's perspective that this is tantamount to rape within marriage was upheld within the justice code of the women's kingdom and proved by the enraged husband's imprisonment.

The oldest and universally prevalent assumption that has governed gender relations that make the woman subordinate to the man has been the system of thought that has privileged men with 'reason' and women with 'feeling' or 'emotion'. Fundamentally, the function of role reversal in Girijabai's play is to demonstrate the falsity of this position, especially in the light of nineteenth-century Maharashtrian hate literature against women at the height of the nineteenth-century social reform movements, such as in *Stricharitras* (Portrait of Women).[31] The resolution to these 'separate' worlds of men and women takes place when the heir apparent Chandrakant's life is saved by a female doctor in the kingdom of women, which then leads to a confrontation between Saraswati Devi and Vikarananda, the monk who has misled the king.

The debate between them is conducted at several levels. First, both opponents fall back on scriptural injunctions on the rights and duties of the sexes, and Saraswati Devi ably matches Vikarananda's learned rendering. For every example he cites—in which women spell doom for men's path to salvation—she provides ten to the contrary. At another level she compares and contrasts administration in the men's kingdom to that in the women's, and demonstrates how inefficient was the former. Here we notice the function of the dystopia (men's kingdom) versus Utopia (Women's Kingdom). She lets the men know that every woman in the kingdom 'prefers complete

---

[30] Ibid., pp. 78–83.

[31] A very thoughtful discussion of this misogynist literature is provided by Rosalind O'Hanlon in her Introduction to *A Comparison between Women and Men: An Essay to Show Who's Really Wicked and Immoral, Women or Men?* (Madras: Oxford University Press, 1994), pp. 38–47.

independence' to following men, who are under the influence of a rogue like Vikarananda. There is a twist in the plot at the end, when Saraswati Devi exposes Vikarananda as her own irresponsible husband who had absconded from his marital duties, leaving behind a child-bride to fend for herself. The king is now completely convinced of his own folly and that of Saraswati Devi's wisdom: he begs forgiveness, and so does Vikarananda. The social message of Girijabai is conveyed via Saraswati Devi's final words of advice to the heir apparent: 'God created the sexes and He treats them as equals. They are blessed with equal intelligence and equal rights. If one sex tries to rule the other it will end in chaos.'[32] To this advice the heir to the throne replies that he will try to ensure that no injustice will take place against the female sex in future.

Thus, by role inversion, women help to clarify problems in their society. The play also extends behavioural options for women when, through formal means, they are able to exercise power and protest against an unjust social order. It is significant that the reversal of roles by women does not entail mimicking men and male conduct in society, but pointing out to men that society can be a harmonious place with both sexes sharing equally the joys and sorrows of life. Girijabai's belief in the complementary roles of the sexes in this sense anticipates the views held by members of the later women's movement led by prominent nationalists such as Kamaladevi Chattopadhyaya, who also adhered to the theory that men and women were 'equal, but different'. Thus we find the perspectives of late-nineteenth-century Indian feminism percolating and affecting the making of twentieth-century Indian feminism.

Symbolic resistance, as expressed in Girijabai's play, possessed the potential to effect changes in society by forcing people to think and act. Her motive in choosing to write a play rather than a treatise was much shrewder than that of her predecessors, such as Tarabai Shinde. Girijabai's choice of this genre allowed her to step from symbolic to open resistance because of a play's potential to create an impact in Maharashtrian society. This fact is impressed upon us when it is observed that her play was enacted many times on stage by some of

---

[32] Girijabai Kelkar, p. 116.

the best-known Marathi theatrical companies. These performances were not only in big cities like Mumbai and Pune, but also in smaller towns and villages such as Jalgaon, Nasik, Sholapur, and Bhagur.[33] Many reactions and responses, negative and positive, were expressed. Even the negative press said her play had fuelled people's appetite to see it enacted again and again. One such adversarial review grudgingly admitted that the play had succeeded in conveying that 'the men's rebellion' was futile precisely because it had 'set itself the impossible and foolish objective of dethroning women from their rank led by men's acts of pure self-delusion.'[34]

In this sense, literature that subverts authority can at times possess more than a 'steam valve' effect for subordinated peoples.[35] It also suggests the maturity of the feminist movement in early-twentieth-century Maharashtra, and the fact that this consciousness went beyond those engaged directly as activists for the advancement of women.

Assertion as a Mode of Resistance

I turn now to the second mode of resistance practised by Maharashtrian women, namely assertion. Assertion is, of course, an act of resistance, but it is useful to distinguish it from other forms of resistance. Assertion refers to those actions by women that demanded recognition of their claims or rights, whether to property and inheritance, conjugal relations, mobility, livelihood, remarriage or divorce, and education. As such, women's assertion usually took the form of recourse to the courts set up by the British state, or of the mode of

---

[33] The Bharat Drama Troupe performed the play in Jalgaon and Nasik. Premier Women's Societies and Schools hired the services of Nutan Maharashtra Drama Company and the Sulochana Musical Play Co. for the enactment of such plays. See Kelkar's 'Preface', op. cit., pp. 2–3, and Saraswatibai Kirloskar, *Amrita Vruksha* (Immortal Tree, or the Institutional History of Saraswati Mandir on its Seventy-fifth Anniversary) (Pune: Kirloskar Press, 1971), p. 90.

[34] S.K. Kolhatkar's Introduction to G. Kelkar, op. cit., p. 9.

[35] A classic formulation of the 'steam valve' effect through rites of rebellion is to be found in Max Gluckman, *Order and Rebellion in Tribal Africa* (New York: 1963).

petitioning and writing memorials to the government in order to influence and persuade it to intervene in the empowerment of women. The importance of petitions and memorials in Indian political life long before the Indian National Congress was formed has been noted and studied by mainstream Indian historians. The Moderates, under the leadership of Ranade and Gokhale, had impressed on the state the aspirations and discontent of the educated classes through petitions and meetings. Equally, we find that middle-class women, and to a lesser extent lower-class women, had begun to access this benign form of asserting their rights.

One of the most assertive acts of Maharashtrian women related to their control or ownership of property. This could involve houses or businesses, agricultural land, and even farms and livestock. Contention over property meant that these women came from wealthy, and in many cases upper-class, backgrounds. In the early part of nineteenth century, the establishment of colonial courts of law as well as the right to appeal to executive authorities opened a venue for the successful assertion of women's property rights. Sandra Rogers has already shown that Hindu women were pioneers of property rights in the city of Bombay in her study spanning the years 1875–84.[36] And in my work on the emergence of feminism in western India I have demonstrated how the daughters and widows of landed elites (*sardars*) in the Bombay Presidency appealed against the onslaught of the Watandari Bill (or Bill of Hereditary Offices Act of 1874). By Regulation XVI of 1827, the government had declared that a female could not inherit a *watan* and further claimed that the ruling was in 'complete harmony with the feeling of the watandars themselves'[37]— what we witness here is the happy marriage between various forms of patriarchies, Indian and Victorian, made visible in land-administration policies in nineteenth-century Maharashtra. An impressive

[36] Sandra Rogers, 'Hindu Widows and Property in Late Nineteenth Century Bombay', in Gail Pearson and Lenore Manderson (eds), *Class, Ideology and Women in Asian Countries* (Hong Kong: Asian Studies Monograph Series, 1987).

[37] Cited in the Second Reading of the Bill No. 2 of 1885, a Bill to amend Bombay Hereditary Offices Act III of 1874, vol. 24, Bombay Legislative Council Proceedings, hereafter BLCP, 1886, V/9/2802, p. 91 (Oriental and India Office Collections, hereafter OIOC).

sixty-one sardar ladies, all widows, are listed as managing the administration and running of their estates (*inam* villages and *jagirs*) in western India.[38] In the beginning, landed women found loopholes in the law and resorted to adoption or appointed deputies to perform estate-management services. The number of successful cases by which women began to control watans by resorting to the High Court was so great that case-made law led the government in 1886 to bring in further amendments in the Hereditary Offices Act (1874), which plugged these loopholes. As the century progressed, and further readings of the Watandari Bill took place, the Bombay government tried in 1904 to place stricter control over female successors of estates and revenue-yielding villages by the establishment of a Court of Wards on the ground that women practising purdah could not manage their own affairs. Although it was pointed out by Indian members of the Council that not very many Maharashtrian women were in fact in purdah and females who were landholders had often proved able administrators, the state insisted that 'a female subject to the customs which prevail in the country [in this case purdah] may be on that account unable to manage her estate with any efficiency'.[39] The same Bill empowered the District Collector to declare a female landholder incapable of managing her property 'on grounds of sex', and this was 'to apply mainly to purdah ladies'. The right to appeal was also withdrawn and such women could not adopt or make wills after their disqualification. What is clearly evident in the successive amendments of the Watandari Act is how the erosion of women's power took place—firstly by the colonial invitation to indigenous groups to represent the proper sphere of Hindu women's duties, and then by these groups being empowered by the state on the basis of these representations of womanhood.

In spite of the alarming restrictions on their powers, women from the landed classes were still able to protest successfully against the

---

[38] 'List of the three classes of and widows of Sardars', vol. 84, Comp. no. 1150 (Judicial Department), hereafter JD, 1890 (Maharashtra State Archives), hereafter MSA.

[39] Bill No. 1 of 1904 (A Bill to establish a Court of Wards in the Bombay Presidency), BLCP, 1904, V/9/2806, vol. 23, p. 139, OIOC.

arbitrary decisions of the state, especially in the day-to-day management of their estates. Their assertions included the right to retain armed guards, and for tax relief and facilities that would substantially help them to better the administration of their estates. In precolonial times watandars had their own military retainers to guard standing crops.[40] After the Rebellion of 1857 the government had ruled, for security reasons, that watandars could not bear arms beyond a certain limit. Several sardar women argued against this regulation and were successful in getting a sanction for more arms. Umabai Saheb Purandhare, a widow of Class I Sardar, complained that she was obliged to take out licences for certain old arms which were heirlooms of the family and which served no purpose other than ornamentation.[41] Her complaint arose from the fact that aristocratic families resented the curtailment of such privileges and, more significantly, because the Arms Act operated as a tax on such family property. On the complaint of several such widows, the Governor-in-Council exempted sardars of all classes from the necessity of taking out licences for old family heirlooms.[42]

Other petitions by sardar widows that were granted were usually concerned with tax relief and for facilities that would substantially help them to manage their estates.[43] A fine illustration of the success of the petitioning method is the case of Umabai Bivalkar, widow of Class I Sardar of the Deccan, who stated that her estates produced a revenue of Rs 10, 002 a year, of which she paid Rs 6000 in taxes to the state. In order to protect and guard her standing crops, she employed 43 sepoys, each armed with a weapon. However, the District Magistrate of Thane had seized 35 of these weapons and she requested them back on the ground that she could not administer her estates

[40] H. Fukazawa, 'Maharashtra and the Deccan: A Note', in T. Raychaudhuri and I. Habib (eds), *The Cambridge Economic History of India, Vol. I, c. 1200–1750* (Cambridge: Cambridge University Press, 1982), p. 194.

[41] Appeal by Umabai Saheb Purandhare, 25 August 1880, Bombay Judicial Proceedings, hereafter BJP, 1880, vol. P/1591, no. 2254, OIOC.

[42] Resolution of the Governor of Bombay BJP, ibid., OIOC.

[43] For tax refunds, see petition of Class I sardar, 6 April 1881, BJP, 1881, vol. P/1796, no. 858, OIOC.

efficiently with unarmed guards.[44] The government allowed her to reclaim 16 of the weapons. However, not all appeals were answered satisfactorily in view of the tightening restrictions on the claims of aristocratic women, and quite a few petitions were rejected which related to subjects of inheritance and adoption. Where conflict was generated between the aristocratic claims of indigenous men and women, it was likely that the state sided with the interests of men— as the highly publicized cases of Anandibai Daphle and Bayjabai reveal.[45]

A greater degree of success in asserting rights over property was achieved by women who came from less wealthy backgrounds than the landed aristocrats described earlier. An analysis of these women's petitions over property disputes reveals a great variety of claims, ranging from suing for damages caused to their houses or belongings, reclaiming *stridhan* (women's wealth), special appeals for the maintenance of agricultural land, and reclaiming goods stolen from their property. Several women successfully sued the municipality of Bombay for damages caused to their property through illegal orders by municipal authorities. Janubai and Pilubai were awarded Rs 2120 as compensation for land confiscated under the City of Bombay Improvement Act of 1898 and were also successful in reclaiming a further Rs 897 from the Court of the Tribunal of Appeal, Bombay, which had been taken from them as agricultural tax.[46] Likewise, Mulibai claimed a sum of Rs 501 from the municipality in a suit for damage caused to her home.[47] There are cases when women successfully intervened in the management of their property. Gangubai

[44] Memorial by Umabai Bivalkar, 24 September 1881, BJP, 1881, vol. P/1796, no. 2682, pp. 1016–17, OIOC.

[45] Lakshmibai and Anandibai Daphle's petition to adopt an heir to the throne of the state of Jath was turned down in favour of a male relative. In *Bodh Sudhakar*, 17 September 1892, *Native Newspaper Reports*, hereafter *NNR*; see too the case of Bayjabai, wife of an *inamdar*, who lost her entire estate in Kolhapur to Appa Saheb Jadav, *Induprakash*, 31 January 1881, *NNR*, OIOC.

[46] Proceedings of the Court of the Tribunal of Appeal appointed under section 48(3) of Bombay Act IV of 1898, BLCP, 1907, P/8032, no. 40, OIOC.

[47] *Gujarati*, 9 June 1883, *NNR*.

Shinde, for example, was able to prevent her father's creditors from demanding a lump sum payment by the sale of her father's property by appealing to the High Court; she thereby secured the right of administration of the estate and this enabled her to deal directly with the creditors. She went to the length of publishing a 'notice' in local newspapers to the effect that she 'alone has the right of effecting a settlement of the claims of the mortgagee and redeeming the property'.[48] Likewise, Danawa, a widow deprived of her moveable and immoveable property by the illegal actions of village officers, who had allowed her husband's property to pass on to her husband's sister's son in her absence, appealed successfully to the government to file a suit in the name of the state on the ground that the village officers' conduct was irresponsible.[49] A large number of petitions by widows during the latter half of the nineteenth century addressed to the government relate to rights of special appeal in the High Court for suits over landed property.[50] In many cases women who felt threatened by intrigue and duplicity from members of their extended family or friends over property disputes sought the protection of the government, and in cases that came from princely states the government normally directed these petitions to the Political Agent or to local authorities for redress.[51]

We find women among the rising middle classes resisting the onslaught of poverty brought about by the peculiar conditions of the colonial economy. Here I am referring to the specific partial industrialization that drove thousands of Maharashtrians from the hinterland to urban areas to seek work. As middle-class women's writings of this period show, they lost the cushioning provided by

[48] *Vritt Sudha*, 23 September 1893, *NNR*.

[49] 19 December 1884, BJP, 1884, P/2423, no. 3485, OIOC.

[50] BJP, 1884, P/2423, no. 3366, OIOC; and BJP, 1884, P/2423, no. 2248, OIOC.

[51] Petition of Assa, 12 August 1870, BJP, 1870, P/442/4, no. 194, OIOC. Such cases were regularly reported in the vernacular press too. For details see Padma Anagol, 'Vasahatkaleen Bharatatil Marathi Madhyamvargiya Streeyanche Gharagutee Bugget' (Thrift and Household Budgeting in Middle-class Maharashtrian Women's Writings in Nineteenth-century India), *Marathi Samshodhan Patrika*, vol. 53, no. 1, October–December 2006, pp. 23–32.

the extended family left in the villages.[52] For example, the financial hardships of middle-class women were starkly depicted in their attempts to claim pensions for the services of their husbands who had died a few months before becoming eligible for pension rights. In many cases, the magistrate forwarded the petitions to the governor recommending the 'case as a hard one'. Special exceptions were made, especially when the widowed mother or wife had a large family of children, and depending on the number of years served by the petitioner's son or husband.[53] Many middle-class men in professions like teaching had left their villages for good and, in times of distress, their wives could no longer depend on either the natal or marital home. The family of Kero Lakshman Chhatre, a well-known professor of mathematics of Fergusson College at Pune, was a good example. His widow's appeal was successful in securing a pension worth Rs 100 per month, which prompted other widows to quote her case in arguing their own.[54]

Utter helplessness in the face of dire poverty caused by the death of the head of the household is recorded in women's petitions to the government. Between 1880 and 1890, women pleading for compassionate allowances, gratuities, or employment sent hundreds of petitions to the government. The nature of the problems differed from case to case but the overriding link was destitution created by the dependence of urban-based professional classes on single-salaried incomes. For example, in 1884 Mai explained how her husband, a constable working for the Satara police, was discharged from service due to sickness with a gratuity of Rs 50. She took a job as a domestic help and 'has struggled since then to maintain herself, her sick husband and four children with difficulty, but is now quite broken down by

[52] For details, see Padma Anagol, '"*Kat Kasar*": Thrift and Household Budgeting in the Writings of Indian Middle Class Women of the 19th Century', in *Bhasha ani Jeevan: Journal of History, Literature and Society in Maharashtra* (Marathi), Spring issue, 2005.

[53] Petition of Gajah Mannugiri, n.d., BJP, 1883, vol. P/2177, no. 1899, OIOC; and petition by Parbutee, n.d., BJP, 1884, vol. P/2423, no. 3161, OIOC.

[54] E.g., Parvatibai Kunte's petition, 22 December 1888, Bombay Education Proceedings, hereafter BEP, 1889, vol. 3559, no. 164, OIOC.

her hard labour to support her family.' She requested employment for her eldest son 'who knows to read and write Marathi and is quite willing to do any menial work'.[55] Doolumbee, on the other hand, whose husband had died after putting in twenty-three years' service in the Satara police department, petitioned for an allowance because she was 'childless, and alone and quite destitute for the means of support'. Quite a few petitions were by women demanding compensation for the loss of their husbands' lives in the execution of public duties—for example while trailing rebellious Bhils or dacoits or from accidental killing by European soldiers. These speak volumes for the assertion by women and their awareness of compensatory rights. Compensation was usually demanded either in the form of money or employment for a family member who had agreed to look after the widow in return. There are several instances when the state granted up to Rs 300 as compensation or agreed to employ the eldest son in the department where the widow's husband had worked.

One of the remarkable trends in women's search for a livelihood during this period was the bid made by lower-class women for survival. These women faced new forms of harassment in towns and cities. The vernacular press reported the harassment of vegetable vendors, mat-makers, and fish-sellers by police officials.[56] Often, such women sought the help of the vernacular newspapers in publicizing their grievances. Parvati Navar, a fish-seller, wrote a letter published in *Vengurla Vritt* asking for protection against the police patel oppressing vendors like her who did not sell their goods at the prices dictated by him.[57] A mat-maker complained that a police constable had threatened her on a trifling issue and extorted a bribe of Rs 10 from her, while a newspaper from Chikodi carried a complaint from a vegetable vendor who was assaulted by two police officials when she had refused to leave her wares in a spot directed by them.[58]

[55] Petition by Mai Bor, 4 June 1884, JD, 1884, vol. 96, Comp. no. 1201, MSA.

[56] E.g., *Dnyanodaya*, 10 February 1877, *NNR*; *Dnyan Prakash*, 21 April 1877, *NNR*.

[57] *Vengurla Vritt*, 17 November 1883, *NNR*.

[58] *Samsher Bahadur*, 17 February 1877, *NNR*; *Chandrakant*, 24 November 1894, *NNR*.

Corrupt practices and harassment by police officials were everyday experiences of lower-class women. These came about at least partly due to the speed with which new legislation brought new taxes, and partly due to the lack of awareness of the illiterate masses. A great number of vendors in towns and cities were unaware of the fact that licences were required by municipal authorities for practising their trade as well as new taxes introduced on professions like wood-gathering and salt-making. For instance, in 1878, in the town of Nandgad a uniform levy was introduced on fuelwood, the chief means of livelihood in that area.[59] Many women who defied the new taxes were fined. When such acts of defiance by women were noticed, their cause was sometimes fought for at higher levels of the administration. In 1887, the constant complaints of female hawkers and vendors reported in the vernacular press were taken seriously by Indian elites and sub-section (2) of section 314 of the Municipal Law, which prohibited 'hawking articles of human food without a licence from the commissioner', was revoked through the efforts of K.T. Telang and Pherozeshah Mehta.[60] Some of the more prominent Maharashtrian social reformers such as K.T. Telang, M.G. Ranade, and Pherozeshah Mehta, who were elite representatives on legislative bodies, were in a position to influence and bring about change in the laws governing urban civic life. They used their influence to mitigate hardship among the lower classes.

Typically, we find women arguing and appealing for other rights too, such as the right to divorce and to remarry, and the right to mobility, especially with the new-found phenomenon of 'eve-teasing' rampant in urban areas of Maharashtra.[61] In many of the instances detailed above it is observable that women of all classes—upper, middle, or lower—resisted the encroachment of their menfolk or/ and the state where they perceived it to be unjust and actively made claims.

[59] *Native Opinion*, 9 March 1878, *NNR*.

[60] See the proceedings of the Bill No. 4 of 1887, 'A Bill to Consolidate and Amend the Law Relating to the Municipal Government of the City of Bombay', BLCP, 1887, vol. 25, pp. 44–5 and the final reading and passing of the bill, BLCP, 17 March 1888, vol. 26, pp. 133–4, OIOC.

[61] See chs 3 and 4 of Anagol, *Emergence of Feminism*.

Open Resistance

Finally I turn to the third mode of resistance practised by Maharashtrian women, namely open resistance. One of the more significant trends during this period was aggressive resistance by women over notions of self-respect and respect for others, dignity of life, self-worth, love, and passion that typically arose over differing conceptions of conjugality and marital rights between the spouses. Acts of 'open' resistance arose when constitutional methods of agitation, such as petitioning, had either failed or were considered to be wholly ineffective. These actions were also located in circumstances of extreme oppression, reflecting women's deep unhappiness. Here I analyse crimes of passion, resulting from marital dysfunction, which include killing of husbands and co-wives or their children by Maharashtrian wives.

Acts of open resistance by women were inspired when gross injustice had been committed against them, either by their natal or adopted families (their in-laws) in the collective sense or by individuals closest to them—their husbands. To a large extent, the social position of a wife depended on her ability to win the affection and sympathy of her husband. This was the case whether it was a question of maintaining a balance in power relations with a co-wife or mother-in-law, or even to command respect within the marital home and the community at large. Consequently, the happiness felt by wives when they received love and affection from their spouses, as well as the accompanying anxieties and neurosis if they failed to do so, disproportionately fill the pages of Marathi fiction, treatises that examine gender relations and women's magazines meant for female consumers.[62] Folk tales and women's songbooks depict the sadness and stress of the unlucky women who failed in love.[63] These are the circumstances

---

[62] For an analysis of the Marathi Women's Press, see Anagol, *Emergence of Feminism*.

[63] (Compiler unknown) (n.d.) *Striyan va mulikarita sangeet sundar gani* (Songs of Women and Girls), Ratnagiri: Damanskar, pp. 100–1; Vishnu Parashuram Shastri Pandit (ed.), *Strigayansangraha athava bayakanchi ganyi* (A Collection of Women's Songs) (Bombay: Indu Prakash Press, 1882), pp. 128–9.

behind the many cases of accidental poisoning of husbands by wives. The belief that a husband's love could be re-kindled by administering aphrodisiacs in their food quite often had tragic consequences. Basavi, who had asked her father to give her 'some medicine which would bring back the love of her husband', was supplied with some poisonous substance. Her husband survived but she was sentenced to five years' rigorous imprisonment.[64] While some women were given sentences of a few years in prison, reflecting the lack of murderous intent on their part, others received harsher treatment. Akku for example, received a sentence of transportation for life. She appealed against this, stating that the real circumstances of her misfortune were as follows:

> I did not knowingly administer poison to my husband. As my husband did not like me I mentioned the circumstance to a neighbour named Ramu bin Babaji who told me that he would give some substance to me and that if I administered the same to my husband with food, my husband would start to like me. . . . Had I known that the powder was a poison and that it was injurious to life, I would not have done so.[65]

Although the colonial authorities did not believe her innocence, as witnessed in the rejection of her petition, with hindsight we are able to understand the circumstances in which 'accidental' killing of husbands took place. Instances of women unwittingly poisoning their husbands in an attempt to cure them of some malady by administering 'magic powders and potions', which they had procured from quack medicine men and priests, are narrated in advice manuals written by women during this period.[66]

The use of chemicals such as arsenic and lead, or curative drugs in the form of herbs and seeds, came through knowledge of medicines passed on through generations. Reproductive rituals, even in contemporary India, reveal the knowledge and recommend the use

---

[64] See JD, 1885, vol. 38, Comp. no. 764, MSA.

[65] Akku's petition, 20 November 1890, JD, 1890, vol. 70, Comp. no. 174, MSA.

[66] Pandita Ramabai, *Stri-dharma niti* (Prescribed Laws and Duties on the Proper Conduct of Women) (Kedgaon: Mukti Mission Press, 3rd edn., 1st edn. 1882, rpnt 1967), pp. 74–5.

of a range of kitchen-based herbs and dietary items to enhance fertility.[67] Women's songbooks refer to the cycle of reproduction with an amazing accuracy of detail and precision as well as give advice on parturition and other topics pertaining to reproduction.[68] In rural communities knowledge of folk medicine was transmitted orally. The trial of Veni illustrates the widespread use and practice of folk medicine. Veni mixed some herbs with her husband's food to cure him of epileptic fits. When this resulted in his becoming ill she was tried and sentenced to five years' rigorous imprisonment.[69] The petition of Savitri, mother of the victim in this case, is particularly illuminating. She had given her daughter some medicine to help rid her of syphilis and thus save herself from disgracing her in-laws. However, in her anxiety, she had forgotten to tell her daughter to apply it externally, and having swallowed the medicine the daughter was poisoned. Even though the daughter recovered her mother was transported for ten years.[70]

In the emerging women's movement, Maharashtrian feminists did concern themselves with the ignorance and naiveté of women and sought to tackle illiteracy and superstition through education programmes.[71] Traditional legal systems, such as caste panchayats and village councils, had shown flexibility and understanding in such circumstances. The erosion of such institutions meant that, before the work of reformers had made an impact, women had to feel

[67] Seetha Anagol, 'When Treatment Fails', in Kanthi Bansal (ed.), *Practical Approach to Infertility Management* (Delhi: Jaypee Medical Publishers, 2004); for Bengal, see Supriya Guha, 'The Unwanted Pregnancy in Colonial Bengal', *Indian Economic and Social History Review*, vol. 33, no. 4, 1996, pp. 404–7.

[68] 'Gane garbhakhand varnan' (Songs of Pregnancy and Birth), in (Compiler Unknown, n.d.), *Songs of Women and Girls*, pp. 67–70 and pp. 74–81. Also songs on 'Dohale' (The Longings of Pregnant Women) and 'Palan' (Child-birth Rites) in Shamrao M. Naik (ed.), *Strigeetmala athava striyanchi manoranjak gani* [Collection of women's songs or songs for women's leisure] (Bombay: Jagmitra Press, 1982), pp. 62–77.

[69] Proceedings of the case of Veni *vs* Dew Ramji in JD, 1881, vol. 46, Comp. no. 793, MSA.

[70] *Imperatrix* vs *Savitri*, JD, 1884, vol. 46, Comp. no. 1352, MSA.

[71] Anagol, *Emergence of Feminism*, particularly chs 1 and 2.

the full weight of the British judicial system. These are the circumstances behind the many cases of accidental poisoning of husbands by their wives. Whilst constraints of space do not allow me to wax lyrical on accidental poisoning of husbands, suffice it to say that winning the love of one's husband and keeping his 'roving eye' from roaming—as Tarabai Shinde repeatedly pointed out—was uppermost on a nineteenth-century Maharashtrian wife's mind.

While some women had been unwitting killers of their husbands, in others the intent was clear and unmistakable. Elsewhere, I have demonstrated how social restrictions on women's autonomy in marriage matters had tightened due to changes in the shape of the criminal justice system, which endeavoured to make caste panchayat power ineffective.[72] Some women, especially child-wives, poisoned husbands or killed their own offspring in acts of extreme protest against their natal and marital family when forced into disagreeable marriages.[73] Extra-marital liaisons were also behind many cases of the killing of husbands by wives. Divorce was not permitted among higher-caste Hindus, and among lower castes consent by the husband to separation was rarely forthcoming. Many Hindu women who had found ways of acting as free agents in redressing their marital problems were prevented from doing so by the interference of the colonial courts. The following cases illuminate the processes by which their agency took effect, as well as the heavy-handed power of the state in curbing it.

Bhagi, a Hindu woman, was convicted and sentenced to three months' imprisonment for having married a second time during the lifetime of her first husband. She argued that she had good reason to do so because her first husband had not only ill-treated her but had left her and remarried, thus depriving her of support.[74] Bigamy

---

[72] Ibid.

[73] Some instances of such extremely aggressive behaviour against their own infants can be found in Padma Anagol, 'The Emergence of the Female Criminal in India: Infanticide and Survival of Women under the Raj', *History Workshop Journal*, vol. 53, Spring 2002, pp. 73–94.

[74] *Bombay Chronicle*, 22 July 1882, *NNR*. A very similar case was that of Abai, *Jame Jamshed*, 9 August 1884, *NNR*.

had been outlawed but the courts in their effort to strengthen the British judicial apparatus, had refused to recognize the authority of a caste to declare a marriage void or give permission to a woman to remarry in the absence of the consent of her husband.[75]

Ganga, a Hindu woman, had converted to Islam before marrying Kasim, but the court ruled that Hindu law did not consider a marriage dissolved merely by apostasy, and without the consent of her Hindu husband her second marriage was illegal. Ganga was imprisoned for three years thereafter.

Many women who, on the authority of a caste panchayat, had obtained permission to divorce and remarry faced various terms of punishment for repudiating British laws. A woman belonging to the tailor caste had petitioned the High Court to grant her judicial separation from her husband, but Justice Candy dismissed her case on the ground that Hindu law did not allow the severance of the matrimonial bond. In another case a woman was convicted of bigamy even though she argued that she had the authority of her caste panchayat to remarry when she produced reasonable evidence to show her husband's inability to fulfil conjugal duties.[76] Due to its reliance on and adherence to scripture-based legal texts, British law, in effect, upheld the theory that a Hindu woman was not an agent in her own right. What is out of the ordinary about the above case studies is that they describe the very process in which women refuted the state's text-based mythology that Indian women could not be agents in their own right.

This process of appealing to the government is well illustrated in the case of Benibai, who had been married to Ranchhod when she was a year and a half. It was obvious when he grew up that he was mentally handicapped (the petition says 'simpleton') who did not understand the obligations of a marriage. Her father-in-law would not consent to her remarriage, to which she had a customary right according to her caste rules. She had appealed twice, once to the

---

[75] See the cases *Regina* vs *Bai Rupa* and *Regina* vs *Shambhu Raghu*, quoted in judgment of *Imperatrix* vs *Ganga*, 29 January 1880, JD, 1880, vols 17 and 18, MSA.

[76] *Subodh Patrika*, 17 November 1894, *NNR*.

District Magistrate, who directed her to apply to the Governor. Pointing out her youth, she begins the petition by saying she is 'only twenty-six years old' and that it had dawned on her that—

> There is not the least chance of receiving a bit of worldly enjoyment from Ranchhod. . . . Now I leave it for His Lordship to consider how am I to pass the bloom of my life with a lunatic who can afford no sort of worldly enjoyment. I request His Lordship to relieve a distressed, wretched woman ordering Ranchhod to divorce me, his wife and allow me to perform a *Natra* (contracted marriage deemed lesser than the first marriage) with another man according to our caste custom.[77]

The widow's desire for sexual fulfilment is eloquently expressed here by her pointed suggestion to the British officials to sympathize with the needs of someone her age. Nineteenth-century writings on widowhood by widows themselves speak volumes regarding the biological and emotional needs of widows. In fact, Tarabai Shinde's entire treatise is a refutation of the central concepts of Hinduism, namely *Dharma* (Right Conduct of Men) and *Stridharma* (Women's Duties), on the basis that the latter was an impossible ideal to follow, for widows were equally governed by biological and physiological needs, and because their need for physical and emotional succour, love, and care led them to seek the company of married men (in the absence of access to remarriage), ultimately resulting in the birth of illegitimate children and the crime of infanticide.[78] Benibai's petition expresses powerfully her yearning for sexual realization which, she argues, is her legitimate right within the marriage contract. Benibai's situation was that in the absence of caste authority she was forced to appeal to the government in order to avoid a case of bigamy as defined by colonial laws. Abandoned or neglected wives or child-wives whose husbands were on life terms petitioned for the annulment of marriages on grounds of 'unnatural widowhood'. This happened once they realized they could not circumvent the centralized control of British law courts, but usually without success.[79] The colonial

[77] 19 April 1883, JD, 1883, vol. 115, Comp. no. 683, MSA.

[78] For a feminist interpretation of Tarabai Shinde's treatise, see Anagol, *Emergence of Feminism*.

[79] Petition of Yemmenne, 17 November 1880, JD, 1881, vol. 48, Comp.

courts tried to establish greater control over female sexuality, but the large number of cases that reached the courts in which rules had been defied shows the extent of resistance put up by women. It is certainly clear that, in the latter half of the nineteenth century, widows asserted the right of marriage both in and out of courts precisely to avoid the ultimate fate of being hanged or transported for the crime of infanticide, as Tarabai Shinde's text illustrates. Women in unhappy conjugal unions were left with few options. Those who wanted to enter a relationship with another man had no means of redress and sometimes resorted to extreme measures. More often, however, when women attacked their husbands it was in response to the brutality meted out to them.

Crime as resistance is most strikingly revealed in these violent acts by women against their spouses. Culturally as well as physically, women were conditioned not to fight back using violent means. Reflecting the unequal balance in physical strength, it was by stealth rather than open confrontation that women were forced to carry out resistance. Administering poison in food or by sprinkling small amounts of powdered glass over a period of time were the methods most commonly resorted to, however, occasionally, brutal husbands were attacked while they slept.[80] Ambi kom Dhavji struck fatally at her husband with a sickle while he was sleeping.[81] She was hanged despite her protest that she had been driven to protect herself against her husband's constant cruelty. As well as reflecting the repressive nature of social custom, this particular offence discloses the extreme imbalance in power relations between the sexes. Often, acts of violence by men, such as cutting off the noses of wives, branding and

----

no. 305, MSA; Jaya's appeal, 11 December 1887, JD, 1887, vol. 49, Comp. no. 112, MSA.

[80] The act of administering powdered glass in food was favoured over all other methods for its advantages: it was the cheapest and least detectable as most Hindu married women wore glass bangles. It was also the hardest of all crimes of passion to establish as the resulting injuries occurred over days and sometimes weeks whilst the powdered glass ripped intestinal walls causing internal bleeding in the stomach.

[81] Ambi kom Dhavji's case is reported in detail in *Mahratta*, 27 July 1895, *NNR*.

wife-beating, drove women to retaliatory acts of violence against husbands: killing the husband was more usually a desperate attempt by women to save themselves.

Wife-battering was common in nineteenth-century India. Indeed, there is some evidence which suggests it was becoming more prevalent within certain communities.[82] If domestic violence was on the increase, the reasons may be located in changing notions of identity and power relations in late-nineteenth-century India. Tarabai Shinde correctly tracks the change to social processes in operation. Wife-beating, she seems to suggest, occurred because women were becoming more rebellious and found the concept of stridharma an already impossible and abstract ideal, even more difficult to follow because Indian men aligned with the Raj and forged new forms of domination over women whilst excluding women from enjoying the benefits of foreign rule. Redefined norms of behaviour among caste groups undergoing processes of change could affect women harshly. In Satara district, for example, it was reported that wife-beating and branding were increasing at an alarming rate, so much so that among the *kunbis* (agricultural castes) it was actually considered an 'act of manliness' to do so.

Individual cases help bring home the degree of cruelty which some women experienced. Yamaji Tulsiram had caused grievous hurt to his wife with a hot iron. During the proceedings of his case it transpired that 'the accused had tied up his wife to a beam and branded her in six places, her breasts, between her buttocks and the calves of her legs'.[83] In another case, Balabhai Rajubhai had chopped off his wife's arm and leg and his rationale was that 'he was only trying to correct her'.[84] At the trial, the townspeople testified that his wife was a chaste woman and that Rajubhai used to beat her savagely,

[82] Especially amongst the Maratha communities of the hinterland: see Anagol, *Emergence of Feminism*, particularly chs 1, 2 and 5.

[83] Proceedings of the case are in 'Return of Cases in which Sentences have been Enhanced by the High Court on review, reference or appeal from 1 January 1878 to 10 September 1885', hereafter Return of Cases, JD, 1885, vol. 99, Comp. no. 532, MSA.

[84] Eighty per cent of the cases that came up for enhancement of penal sentences were about violence towards women, in Return of Cases, JD, 1885.

causing her to run away to her father's house. Jim Masselos's study of patterns of behaviour in Bombay households also enumerates a number of punishments inflicted on adulterous wives by their spouses.[85] Disfiguring wives by mutilating them through cutting off noses and branding were the common methods of discipline and chastisement carried out by Maharashtrian men and sanctioned by society.

In a rare case that came up in the colonial courts, we notice that the custom of polygamy amongst Hindus was cited as a reason for resistance through a crime of 'passion'. One such offender, Kashi, who appealed against the High Court judgment thus, highlights that the institution of polygamy often led to tragic consequences:

> I am scarcely advanced in years or experience, being only twenty-five years of age. My caste is polygamous and I had the misfortune to have had the complainant as a rival wife of my husband. Would that the system of polygamy never have existed in India or that I was never born in a polygamous society; I have now to leave not only my native land and my dearest relations but I have now to leave behind two infant sons to the mercy of any wife that my husband fancies to take . . .[86]

In Kashi's case, she was convicted of attempting to poison her co-wife Baji and her daughter. This was in spite of the fact that the evidence was far from conclusive. The entire case rested on the statement of Baji, whose daughter died after consuming some food. Both the assessors in her case ruled that the evidence was contradictory and that either Baji, the mother herself, or Purshotram (the father) could have caused the death. However, such cases were common enough for the judge to view any statement by co-wives as highly suspect. Women often found themselves in a position where they were forced to fight for the attention of their husbands when they happened to be second or third wives. Squabbles and intrigue were common in polygamous households. Poisoning a co-wife and her child, as in this case, as a result of 'polygamy', must have been a far more generalized picture in nineteenth-century India than the records reveal. Here, we

[85] See Jim Masselos, 'Sexual Property/Sexual Violence: Wives in Nineteenth Century Bombay', *South Asia Research*, vol. 12, no. 2, 1992, pp. 81–99.

[86] See the proceedings in the case of Kashi, JD, 1885, vol. 35, Comp. no. 378, MSA.

have a testimony of a woman confessing that it was marital dishar-mony, as a result of the institution of taking second and third wives, which had caused her to take an extreme route of resistance.

The judiciary often identified poisoning of husbands by wives with unchastity even when husband brutality was most often the reason. Nor did they take into account the social context in which such acts took place. In the case of uxoricide, however, the same cri-minal justice system was quick to recognize the rights of a husband when it accepted murder of a wife even on the inconclusive evidence of adultery by the wife. Judicial records in cases of uxoricide reveal that male offenders were given shorter terms of imprisonment on the grounds that the man had murdered his wife 'in a fit of passion', defined as 'extenuating circumstances'.[87] It is clear that the colonial state not only recognized but also upheld the deeply entrenched no-tions of patriarchal society.

Female crime was often a violent form of resistance, part of a limited range of strategies for survival available to subordinated groups, whether battered wives or unhappy widows in oppressive situations. In cases where extra-marital liaisons existed or the widow wished to remarry, the tightening restrictions of colonial law regarding remarriage as well as the erosion of a customary right to remarriage had resulted in a situation of 'no choice' for the widow, but in such cases it is interesting to see that homicide (against the husband) was interpreted as a 'choice' although it was a crime born of resistance. In the cases studied here, very few considered themselves 'helpless' housewives; rather, they saw their acts as arising from a deeply felt sense of grave injustice. Coming to the contentious issue of autonomy it is difficult to see them in any light other than as agents of their own lives. Their crimes of passion did not directly impact on wider gen-der relations, but they were noted with anxiety by the emerging wo-men's movement in Maharashtra and prominent feminists addressed them appropriately in their measure to combat the iniquity.

[87] See judgment passed by the Sessions Judge on Bhola, 22 June 1879, JD, 1880, vol. 45, Comp. no. 632, MSA; see the case of Bhikia bin Dharma, who had murdered his wife and her lover yet had his sentence reduced from capital pun-ishment to transportation for life when he petitioned, 19 August 1881, BJP, 1881, vol. P/1796, no. 2010, OIOC.

Structures of Women's Resistance:
Concluding Note

I would like to conclude with observations on the three modes of resistance outlined above. Commenting on the first mode of resistance—symbolic resistance—it is well known that certain literary genres allowed for the symbolic expression of utopian worlds constructed by women—of a just and equitable world in which both sexes respected each other's rights and lived in a symbiotic relationship. Further, this genre had the added advantage of accessing a larger number of literate women who formed their audience and helped considerably in the consciousness-raising agendas of early Indian feminists. Certain literary genres, which allowed the symbolic inversion of the world within a plot, had the potential of bringing a transformation in attitudes and behaviour by forcing audiences to think and debate the issues of women's rights and the roles and duties of both men and women. Girijabai Kelkar's play by the sheer act of being performed all over Maharashtra, guaranteed such a response from the theatre-loving public of Maharashtra.

Reflections on the second mode of resistance, namely assertion in the form of seeking the courts and petitioning the government, reveal this as a more benign form of resistance allowing the woman to function within constitutional forms of agitation. Such resistance empowered her to seek help without aggression. Because it had the blessings of the state, petitioning as a mode of resistance held the promise of a satisfactory redressal of grievances. Negotiation, through petitions and appeals, allowed for some bargaining and hence a better chance of successful resolution.

Coming to the third mode of resistance, namely crimes of passion arising within conjugal relations defined here as open resistance, we observe that the wife who killed the husband through premeditated acts did so with the full knowledge of the facts that, firstly, she was flouting the rules of patriarchy; and secondly, that her act would most certainly be discovered and she would face the consequences of her rebellion. What is different here from the previous two modes of resistance is that no solution is being sought to the problem of the total domination of women by patriarchal structures. The objective is an annihilation or obliteration of male authority.

One significant aspect of the resistance to power and domination outlined in this essay is that the forms of women's resistance are shaped almost completely by their location in the custom-bound, caste–class nexus of relations in colonial India. They also arise from male-regulated, if not male-dominated, webs of social relations. Whilst patriarchy was not an invention of the Raj, the erosion of customary laws and the grip of the newly defined colonial version of Hindu law laid obstacles in the way of women asserting their right to remarriage. What is common to all three modes of resistance is that women resorted to either violent or non-violent *resistance*, and their actions arose from their negotiation and engagement with everyday power relations, whether at home or in the larger public sphere.

What links these various modes of resistance by women, whether they are confrontational or non-confrontational, dramatic or otherwise, are factors that I term intention, impact, and target of resistance. The first factor—the 'intention' of the resisters—is evident in the deliberately and carefully chosen decision of Girijabai Kelkar to write a prose play instead of a treatise; in the propertied class of women appealing to the state and courts when resisting unjust acts of deprivation of property and livelihood; in the miserable housewife seeking her own form of justice in the murder of a cruel husband. All these are born out of 'intention'. Consciousness is thus part and parcel of women's resistance, and the purposefulness of their actions is expected to have an impact. In the first mode, Girijabai hoped to influence Maharashtrian society to rethink gender relations, and to some extent she was successful in this hope. In the second mode, women petitioning the courts and the government hoped to resolve and right some of the material and moral wrongs, and they were to a large degree successful in their efforts. In the third mode, the housewife who felt thwarted or rejected within marital structures of feeling—love, affection, and warmth in her domestic and conjugal life—had imbibed a strong sense that what was 'just' and 'fair' play was not hers, and so took measures to address it.

Finally, women's resistance is not born in a vacuum: it arises within the social, economic, political, and legal relations of the society women inhabit. It would not be an unfair generalization that the nineteenth-century Indian woman lived in deeply entrenched structures of patriarchy, and hence the target of her resistance was often a gendered response to the system of thought created by Indian men and their activities. Women's resistance is targeted against perceived male oppressors and male forms of authority, and the political extension of these, the state, which in the end upheld and protected indigenous male structures of power. Even in the second mode of resistance, although the state appears to be the oppressor, eventually the state is used as a humanitarian 'resource' in times of hardship.[88]

It seems imperative that we seek new frameworks to understand women's resistance. Departing somewhat from previous historiography on resistance within Asian societies, I have found it less useful to distinguish women's resistance as purely dramatic or purely non-confrontational: these two forms of protest can run in tandem. I have tried to show that women were almost always conscious agents of resistance—intention and deliberation are constant, and they serve the express purpose of either subverting immediate authority figures or furthering the larger feminist agendas of consciousness-raising. The preoccupation with the question of 'agency', and the state of its 'purity'—is the woman acting autonomously or not—is more of a dead-end quest that obscures rather than uncovers the structures of women's protest behaviour. And finally, the way forward for theorizing and seeking new models of resistance does not lie in mimicking, nor in looking for models that have been set up to understand power relations between a male landlord and a male peasant. It lies I think in observing and learning from models of women's resistance in other societies of the world—both developed and developing.

[88] Aptly termed by Sumit Sarkar, 'Orientalism Revisited: Saidian Frameworks in the Writing of Modern Indian History', *Oxford Literary Review*, vol. 16, 1994, pp. 204–24.

3

SMALL ACTS OF REBELLION: WOMEN TELL THEIR PHOTOGRAPHS

GERALDINE FORBES

Then do one thing. Dress your daughter in up-to-date fashion and take her to a photographer's. They will make her all right in appearance. My younger sister, she had nearly no nose and only dots for eyes, but thanks to Boron Shepad Sahib, she looked in the picture like a fairy with wings off. He will make your daughter's high forehead and sunken cheeks charming.[1]

Spoken in a crowded train headed for Calcutta, this fictional piece of advice was directed at the mother of a too-old, too-dark daughter. The apprehensive mother listened carefully. In the big city, she changed her daughter's name (following her instructor's advice to drop Kalidasi for a more stylish name like Swarnalata or Binodini), had the girl's hair styled, bought fashionable clothes, and headed for a studio. The retouched photo netted an interview and, following her mentor's counsel, the mother applied a great deal of powder to her daughter's face and arranged an evening meeting in a dimly lit room. The groom's side, fooled by the photograph, makeup, and poor lighting, agreed to the match. It was only after the

---

[1] 'The Ugly Bride', by Sita Devi and Santa Devi, in *Tales of Bengal* (Calcutta: Writers Workshop, 1979).

wedding that the groom's mother, the original advice giver, discovered her son had married the ugly girl from the train.[2]

As this short story and other accounts from the turn of the century illustrate, photographs had entered the domestic sphere and had the potential to subvert the established order, although there has been far more emphasis on the camera's role in disciplining subjects. Photography reached the cities of Calcutta and Bombay only a few months after the daguerreotype was launched in Paris and found a market, first with the colonial authorities, and very soon with the new professional class. Imperialists recognized the camera's potential for their designs and employed photographers to document landmarks and people. To Indians, photography was emblematic of all that was modern and scientific; it attracted rich amateurs who bought expensive equipment and set up their own studios, hobbyists who joined photographic societies where they discussed new developments and exhibited their work, and elites who visited expensive studios. While photographs were often used to support the established order, they took on different meanings depending on the transaction. For example, 'showing photographs'[3] reinforced patriarchal norms

[2] The mother's anxiety and preparations were part of her effort to arrange a marriage for her daughter. Throughout India, and in most patriarchal societies, the parents played a major role in deciding whom their children would marry. Relatives, friends, and professional matchmakers would suggest suitable partners, followed by a selection process. Suitability depended on a number of factors, which differed between castes, regions, and religions. Hindus preferred child brides, although consummation generally waited until after puberty, for religious reasons and because they were considered malleable. At the time this story was written, there was no minimum age of marriage but the Age of Consent (the age at which a female could have sexual relations) was 12, well-off urban families had begun to use 'showing photos', and it was common for the relatives to view the bride.

[3] 'Showing photographs', primarily of females, was ordered by the prospective bride's family to be shown to families with eligible grooms. I am not sure how early Indian families began taking their marriageable daughters to studios to be photographed, but the earliest photo of this kind I have found was in the studio of Bourne and Shepherd, taken in the early twentieth century. These images provided clues about the family's status and gender ideology, as well as

by requiring young women to pose for photos that were evaluated by prospective in-laws. At the same time, 'showing photographs' sometimes facilitated the exchange of daughters between like-minded families, offered young people a choice, and provided an opportunity for defiance.

By the last quarter of the nineteenth century, photographs were placed in frames on walls and tables in Indian homes, and elite families developed elaborate albums while the middle-class collected photos, sometimes in simpler albums, but more often in boxes. In urban middle-class families, photographs became an important tool in constructing the family. At first glance this process seems mimetic, a family version of the imperial project to document and control native subjects where the subjects are women. But these images have multiple meanings and my interest is in their meaning for women's history. Using women's statements about specific images in family collections, I argue that photographs are not fixed items in terms of historical identity but rather objects of negotiation between the subject (also the object of the photograph) and the viewer. In this essay, I discuss photographs from three family collections that elicited stories of resistance against patriarchal authority and consider their relevance as documents for studying resistance.

Photographs and History

My interest in photographs stems from my search for sources for women's history. Because women's private papers were so seldom archived, I contacted women who had been active in social reform and political organizations to ask if they had personal collections. This strategy paid off. In addition to documents, I was shown family photographs, which my informants insisted were compelling sources of historical information. When people presented pictures, they pointed

---

choices they made about shoes or no shoes, the tying of the sari, hairstyle, blouse type, jewellery, and decorative items such as books or embroidery. With the proliferation of studios in the 1920s, showing photographs became very popular. These photos are still taken today.

out and talked in detail about individuals, remembered minute facets of events, and told stories about how they felt at the time. Ironically, they often showed me blurred images that I was unable to decipher but which sparked their memories. To the narrators, these pictures spoke volumes and explaining them to me, they generated a new archive. My subjects were deemed 'new women' in the 1920s and 1930s, differing from their grandmothers in education as well as engagement in political and social reform activities. These 'new women,' an artifact of colonialism, have attracted the attention of a number of historians.

Partha Chatterjee's essays on the nation and its women tell us how nationalism resolved the woman question by fashioning a 'new woman' controlled by 'new patriarchy'. These new women differed from both Western women, who were bold and frivolous, and lower-class Indian women, who were loud, quarrelsome, and oppressed. Educated about homemaking and issues in the larger world, they went 'outside' the home but remained subordinate.[4]

Tanika Sarkar has also written extensively about the dynamics of new domesticity in the late nineteenth and early twentieth century. The Hindu home had to imagine/define itself as truly different from the outside world ruled by foreigners. Instead of the overt exercise of political power, love and affection were the organizing principles and relationships were ideally based on self-surrender and self-fulfilment. However, this was a difficult ideal to achieve and Sarkar painted this period as fraught with problems.[5]

Chatterjee and Sarkar have treated the question of women's resistance to the hegemony of the 'new patriarchy' differently. Chatterjee finds no obvious evidence of women's autonomous struggle and suggests that looking for such in archives is futile. The search, he argues, must begin with the home since this was 'the principal site

[4] Partha Chatterjee, *The Nation and Its Fragments: Colonial and Postcolonial Histories* (Princeton, NJ: Princeton University Press, 1993), p. 130.

[5] Tanika Sarkar, 'The Hindu Wife and the Hindu Nation: Domesticity and Nationalism in Nineteenth Century Bengal', *Studies in History*, vol. 8, no. 2, new series, 1992, pp. 214–35.

of the struggle through which the hegemonic structure of the new nationalist patriarchy had to be normalized.'[6] 'Risky moments' of resistance would only be located in family documents.[7]

Sarkar sees more opposition and dissension and claims the archives contain evidence of such. The harmonious development and success of the new patriarchy was problematized, she writes, by a folk tradition which presented women as unhappy with domestic circumstances, nineteenth-century prose that echoed this folk literature, women's own writings published in the new journals, and publications by reformers who exposed coercion within the domestic sphere.[8]

While I agree with Sarkar that women were less docile than imagined and projected, I am also interested in Chatterjee's focus on the family and domestic institutions as a site for resistance. When I turned to family collections, I found far more than pictures; these domestic archives preserved 'memories, document[ed] important moments, and confirm[ed] social relationships and the fact of belonging.'[9] In contrast to photographs in conventional archives, often three or four times removed from the actual event, cropped, and reframed, family photographs are usually in their original form, more easily identified in terms of date and technology, and trigger memories and stories.[10]

---

[6] Chatterjee, p. 133.

[7] Ibid., p. 156.

[8] Sarkar, 'The Hindu Wife and the Hindu Nation', p. 229. See also Tanika Sarkar, 'Conjugality and Hindu Nationalism,' in Tanika Sarkar, *Hindu Wife, Hindu Nation* (London: Hurst and Company, 2001), pp. 191–225. Tanika Sarkar, *Words to Win: The Making of Amar Jiban: A Modern Autobiography* (New Delhi: Kali for Women, 1999), and Sambuddha Chakrabarti, 'Changing Notions of Conjugal Relations in Nineteenth Century Bengal, in *Mind, Body and Society: Life and Mentality in Colonial Bengal*, ed. Rajat Kanta Ray (Calcutta: Oxford University Press, 1995), pp. 297–330.

[9] Anna Helene Tobiassen, 'Private Photographic Collections as an Ethnological Source', *Ethnologia Europaea*, vol. 20, no. 1, 1990, pp. 86–7.

[10] For an interesting discussion of archival photographs, see Patricia Hayes, Jeremy Silvester, and Wolfram Hartmann, 'photography, history and memory', *The Colonising Camera: Photographs in the Making of Namibian History*, ed. Wolfram Hartmann, Jeremy Silvester, and Patricia Hayes (Athens, OH: Ohio

As I began to work with photographs and family stories, I found myself agreeing with James Ryan that photos do not speak for themselves. They are, he tells us, 'invested with meanings framed by and produced within specific cultural conditions and historical circumstances.'[11] Our task is to reconstruct the circumstances under which the photograph was taken, and, wherever possible, the meaning given to it by the subject. In this essay, I include photographs that elicited stories of women's resistance to family patriarchy, both before and after marriage, and to community conservatism that disapproved of women's changing roles. My concern is to use photographs as historical documents and to begin to shift the general trend of history where 'visuality . . . [is always] subordinated to textuality.'[12]

Resisting the Extended Family

1. Family photo Lakshman Rau, with Krishnabai on his lap and his wife Kamalabai standing to his right. Standing to his left is Ramchandran, seated from left: Yamunabai, Indirabai. Studio. *Circa* 1911.

University Press, 1999; first published University of Cape Town Press, 1998), pp. 2–9.

[11] James R. Ryan, *Picturing Empire: Photography and the Visualization of the British Empire* (Chicago: University of Chicago Press, 1997), p. 19.

[12] Quoted from W.J.T. Mitchell's *Picture Theory: Essays on Verbal and Visual Representation* (1994), by Wolfram Hartmann, Jeremy Silvester, and Patricia Hayes, eds, in *The Colonising Camera*, p. 2.

Photo 1 is the family of Krishnabai Rau Nimbkar (b. 1906).[13] Her family lived in Madras where they were part of a tightly knit Maharashtrian community involved in government service. Krishnabai's father, an employee of the Revenue Department, was a Theosophist, while her mother was a reformist Hindu. They welcomed foreigner visitors to their home and encouraged debate on current social and political issues.

2. Kamalabai Rau. *Circa* 1895. Studio Wiele and Klein.

Krishnabai's mother, Kamalabai (photo 2) was married at age 10 but not sent to live with her husband until she was 15 years of age. Kamalabai's parents sent her to a missionary school, and employed tutors for English and Sanskrit. By the 1920s, she was a young mother living in Madras and a member of a number of progressive women's organizations including the Tamil Madar Sangam and the Women's

[13] The material on Krishnabai Rau Nimbkar is based on extensive interviews with her in 1981, 1983, 1989, and 1992 at her home in Pune, her taped interviews in the Nehru Memorial Museum and Library, her mother's published memoir, *Smrutika: The Story of My Mother As Told By Herself,* translated into English by Indirabai Rau, and published by Krishnabai Nimbkar (Pune, 1988), published and unpublished articles written by her, and a series of letters she wrote to me in the United States. All the photographs used are copies of photographs in the Krishnabai Nimbkar Collection.

Indian Association. Krishnabai remembered intense arguments between her mother and father about theology and politics.

3. Indirabai's marriage to R. Madhava Rau.
1913. Studio.

Despite Lakshman and Kamalabai's interest in social reform, the extended family was conservative when it came to marriage. Indirabai, the eldest daughter, was married at age 12 because the family received a proposal from an ideal suitor (photo 3). The second daughter was also married young, but by this time Lakshman Rau had had a stroke and the family's standard of living was in decline.

When Krishnabai came of age, her mother was openly opposed to child marriage and believed girls should be well educated. In an interview for the Nehru Library, Krishnabai recalled '[My mother] wanted me to grow up and get an education. I had also come to form firm views and opinions on whether I wanted to marry early. I wanted to study more and become something big.'[14]

[14] 'Krishnabai Nimbkar', Oral History Project, Nehru Memorial Museum and Library, p. 10.

Her father's stroke in 1918 would have put the topic to rest were it not for relatives. When Krishnabai was visiting Bombay, they took her to a studio and ordered a showing photograph. Then in the ninth standard at school, Krishnabai wanted to continue with her studies, not get married. However, she had no choice but to comply with her relatives' wishes and assume a fashionable pose (photo 4).

4.   Showing photo of Krishnabai Rau, *c.* 1918. Bombay, taken by Mr Samad.

When Krishnabai's father died in 1922, his widow Kamalabai was already taking care of her ailing and widowed mother. With the additional burden of two children to educate, Kamalabai sold their house and found a job as matron in a Home for Women.

Krishnabai won a scholarship to attend Queen Mary's College and would have happily continued with her studies, but family members wanted her married. They insisted she pose for this second showing photograph (photo 5). Krishnabai resisted this time, and said about the experience: 'I looked as mean as possible so that no one would want to marry me.' While 'the look' may not be obvious to the casual viewer,[15] Krishnabai believed it would deter prospective mothers-in-law. It may have worked for there is no evidence of proposals and Krishnabai was able to attend Madras University and

[15] Padma Anagol thinks the look is obvious; she wrote: 'I compared the two photos and . . . thought in the earlier one she looks unhappy but downright grumpy and unhappy in the second one—note the lips are put not in a "pout"

5. Showing photo of Krishnabai Rau, taken
c. 1923. Madras. Das Brothers Studio.

complete a BA in Zoology, join the Gandhian movement, and marry
the man of her choice, Dr V.D. Nimbkar, in 1932.

Resisting In-laws

Kalyani Mukherjee Mallik (b. 1903)[16] (photo 6) was the granddaughter of Swarnakumari Ghosal, Bengal's first woman novelist, and the great granddaughter of the famous Brahmo Samaj leader Maharshi Debendranath Tagore. Kalyani's mother, Hiranmoyee, married to Mr P. Mukherjee of the Indian Educational Service (IES), was overshadowed by her famous sister, Saraladevi Chaudhurani, an early advocate

6. Kalyani Mukherjee, baby photo, *c.* 1903.
Bourne and Shepherd.

but literally brought down like a snarl. She looks really ungracious in the second.' Email communication, 18 August 2005.

[16] Material for this section comes from interviews with Kalyani Mallik, in

of militant nationalism and one of India's first feminists. Kalyani was extremely proud of this lineage and in her conversations with me frequently pointed out her resemblance to her famous uncle Rabindranath Tagore.

7. Kalyani Mukherjee, *c.* 1912. Studio.

Like other girls from the progressive Jorasanko Tagore family, Kalyani attended an English-medium school. Her formal education began at 7 when she was sent to Diocesan Girls' School in Calcutta (photo 7). In 1916, her father, then retired from the IES, became the Director of Public Instruction in the princely state of Indore. Here, Kalyani attended a Hindi-medium school and was tutored in music: sitar, violin, and singing, and sports: tennis, badminton, cycling, horseback riding, and shooting. Although allowed to participate in a number of unusual activities, for example, riding and shooting, her

----

Calcutta, in 1983 and 1989, and copies of her writings. The images are from copies of photos in the Kalyani Mallik Collection.

mother remained watchful and protective. Kalyani recalled that all her private lessons were supervised by family members.

Although only 13 years of age, Kalyani attracted suitors. She recalled one suitor, a Punjabi she described as 'tall, handsome, and fair' and a 'wonderful man'. Her father was not opposed to the idea, but her mother refused: Kalyani was too young and he was from a different community. She recalled that her family also rejected the proposal made by a Kashmiri professor.

8. Kalyani Mukherjee, *c.* 1917. Photo taken by Pratap Rao Jadav of Indore.

This posed photograph (photo 8), showing a very mature young woman, was taken at this time. Showing it to me, Kalyani said, 'Look at that face! What a bold face for a young woman— no mother-in-law would want her son to marry that girl!' She did not claim she had aimed for that look (as had Krishnabai) but implied, with this comment and others, that she had a strong sense of self even at a young age. Unmarried, she continued with her studies.

Returning to Calcutta, Kalyani entered Diocesan College where she studied mathematics and in 1922 completed the intermediate exam. In 1923, her father arranged her marriage to Ajit Nath Mallik, a 'Cambridge Man' and his colleague's son. Kalyani wanted to continue with her studies after marriage and her father had hoped she would, but her mother-in-law objected. The fact Kalyani did not know how to cook became an issue and, one month after her marriage, Kalyani left her father-in-law's house and moved, with her husband, into a house her parents had given her as a wedding present.

Kalyani's first child was born in 1924; six others followed in 1925, 1926, 1927, 1928, 1931, and 1935. In between, she learned to cook and keep house, vacationed in northeast India, wrote stories, and studied for both her BA and BT. These two snapshots (photos 9 and 10) capture Kalyani's remembrance of those years.

9. Kalyani Mallik with baby,
1928.

10. Kalyani Mallik, 'on the
way to Sikkim', 1929.

Kalyani had always wanted children, loved having her own, and was frequently photographed with her growing brood. Despite her frequent pregnancies, she often took her children for holidays at their grandmother's house in Darjeeling. When she showed me the photograph of her driving a car (photo 10), Kalyani proudly announced: 'I was among the first women to cycle in Calcutta and to drive a car.' She went on to connect these skills (and daring) to her experience in Indore, where she had first learned to cycle and ride.

Despite her elite family background, Kalyani was not protected from economic hardship. Her husband had a position in the Eastern Railways, but lost his job when she was pregnant with her third child. After her sixth child was born, she studied privately, completed her BA, and then enrolled in a BT (Bachelors in Teaching) programme (photo 11). Although she studied secretly, her mother-in-law was furious when she found out.

11. Kalyani attends the 1934 Diocesan College Reunion; at this time she was studying for the BT.

After her BT, Kalyani completed her MA degree (photo 12) and decided to study for her Ph.D.[17] These were difficult years—she had seven children, a demanding research project, and an unsympathetic mother-in-law. Her life was made even more difficult by sexual harassment—including love letters from fellow students and overtures from professors. In the end, she chose Gopinath Kobiraj to guide her thesis, partly because of his vast learning, but also because of his reputation as an ascetic. Ironically, he urged her to work on Natha Yogis, a

12. Kalyani Mallik, MA degree, 1936. Calcutta. Edna Lorenz.

[17] She received her PhD from Calcutta University in 1946. In 1982, she was awarded the title Mahamahopadhyaya for India and Nepal in recognition of her scholarship.

Saivite Tantric sect important for the history of medieval Hindu mysticism.[18]

In the course of our talks, Kalyani repeatedly referred to her time in Indore as 'the happiest' time of her life—she clearly enjoyed breaking the rules for proper female behaviour by cycling, riding, and hunting, friendships with other young women, and the encouragement of teachers. However, this experience, and others that contributed to the development of a strong and determined self, placed her in conflict with her mother and later her mother-in-law.

In Kalyani's telling of her life through photographs, it was women, not men, who tried to clip her wings. In Indore, her father wanted her to be daring, while her mother tried to restrict her movements. Back in Calcutta, her mother was keener to arrange her marriage than her father was, and after marriage, her father urged her to complete her BA. Her mother-in-law, not her husband, objected to her studying. When she completed her MA, her father-in-law was very proud and attended her convocation. It was only at this point that her mother-in-law expressed pride in her accomplishments but Kalyani decided she would no longer go to her mother-in-law's home.

Resisting Conservative Norms

13. Latika Ghosh, n.d. Studio unknown.

[18] Smt Kalyani Mallik, *Siddha-Siddhanta Paddhati and Other Works of Nath Yogis* (Poona: Poona Oriental Book House, 1954). In this book, Mallik argues the Nath Yogis were not Tantric.

Latika Ghosh (b. 1902)[19] (photo 13) was the daughter of Manmohan Ghosh, a translator and poet, and niece of Aurobindo Ghosh (better known as Sri Aurobindo), famous first as a revolutionary and later as a philosophical mystic. Educated first at Loreto College, where she completed her BA, Latika was the third generation in her family to be sent to England for higher studies. In England, she married an older cousin in 1924 and took the name Bose.[20] Before she returned to India in 1926, with a BLitt from Oxford University and a diploma in Education, she was encouraged to join the Indian Educational Service. However, back in Bengal, she clashed with the Bethune College Principal, Miss Wright, who decided Latika was too radical for the Educational Service. Nevertheless, the Director of Public Instruction, Mr E.F. Oaten, remained impressed with her credentials and named her school inspectress for the 24 Parganas. Her first report of the schools she visited detailed their failings and recommended a number of changes. This did not please her superiors and Latika was soon without a job.

In 1927, Latika became the organizing secretary of the Saroj Nalini Dutt Association, a village-based women's welfare organization begun by Guru Saday Dutt in memory of his wife. Although successful in organizing women, Latika's political views, aired in newspaper articles and speeches, brought her to the attention of the government and they pressed for her dismissal. Latika was then recruited by C.R. Das to work with the Chittaranjan Seva Sadan where she was to recruit women to complete a training programme in nursing, teach them about politics, and help prepare them to staff rural health centres. She found it difficult to recruit young women and was disappointed that those who completed their training preferred to work in urban hospitals rather than return to rural areas. Meanwhile, Latika began to organize informal social clubs for women where they

[19] The material in the section is drawn from interviews with Latika Ghosh in 1976, letters she wrote to me in 1976 and 1977, and some of her writings in *Banglar Katha*, the daily newspaper of the Swarajja Party.

[20] This marriage was highly unusual. Latika made it clear she did not wish to marry her cousin but did not explain the circumstances that led to their marriage in England. The couple separated in Calcutta; the marriage was annulled in 1935.

would be taught the basics about health and childcare, and about the political situation.

On the eve of the Simon Commission's visit to Calcutta, Bengal Congress leaders Dr B.C. Roy and Sarat Chandra Bose asked Latika to mobilize women for an anti-British demonstration. Her success came to the notice of Subhas Chandra Bose who asked her to form a new political organization for women—the Mahila Rashtriya Sangha. In addition to setting up the MRS, Latika organized clubs where girls and young women could practice dagger and lathi play, and perform cultural programmes (photo 14).

14. Basanti Sakti Mandir (a girls' club), celebrating
Saraswati Puja, Calcutta, 1933.

Latika proved an effective organizer. Deeply committed to freedom for the nation, her writing was forceful and passionate and especially appealing to traditional women. She told women the gods and goddesses were on their side and convinced them that joining the nationalist struggle was the responsibility of a dutiful wife.

For the 1928 Congress session in Calcutta, Subhas Bose decided volunteers would march in military uniforms. He made Latika a colonel and put her in charge of recruiting and training a women's regiment. She was able to recruit Bethune and Victoria College students and Calcutta corporation teachers. Although she was willing to train them to march, she baulked at Subhas' plan to put them into military trousers and boots. Instead, Latika decided on dark green saris with red borders worn over white blouses.

15. Flag-raising ceremony, 1928 Indian National Congress session, Calcutta. The photographer may have been D. Rattan.

Photo 15 reminded Latika of events that have not found their way into the history of this event. On the eve of the meetings, Sarat Bose, backed by C.R. Das' wife Basanti Devi, wanted to abandon the plan least they offend conservative Congressmen. Latika was angry. She had taken great care to avoid scandal—the women did not stay in camp at night, and wore saris instead of the trousers Subhas wanted, and were carefully supervised. She threatened to withdraw her volunteers from all duties, including ticket-taking, ushering people to their seats, and manning the tea stalls, unless they were allowed to march. In the end, Sarat relented and 300 young women marched in the Congress parade.

Instead of this story of struggle, Subhas' decision to have young women march is seen as a forerunner of his later Rani of Jhansi Regiment of the Indian National Army. Those who watched the girls expressed their awe at this visible symbol of equality and solidarity.

But, Latika Ghosh recalled gender discrimination and resistance. However, more than her story of protest against patriarchal respectability has been lost—the photos most reproduced from this event show the leaders without Latika or any of the young women (photo 16).

16. 1928 Congress parade—the more common, cropped version.

Conclusions

When historians first turned their attention to protest and resistance in the third world, they looked for peasant rebellions. However, India did not fit the model. Finding little evidence of peasant uprisings, they characterized South Asian peasants as passive, submissive, and self-repressive,[21] and looked for explanations as to why. One answer was caste (Dumont), considered a unique feature of Indian society. Others (the Cambridge School) argued that horizontal factionalism worked against vertical challenges, while a third group (the Subaltern Collective) maintained that history itself was to blame for leaving them out of the narrative. There is now more attention to everyday and avoidance protests, but none of these approaches has been sensitive to gender and/or women.

[21] Michael Adas, 'South Asian Resistance in Comparative Perspective', *Contesting Power: Resistance and Everyday Social Relations in South Asia*, eds Douglas Haynes and Gyan Prakash (Delhi: Oxford University Press, 1991), pp. 290–306. Here Adas is quoting Barrington Moore, p. 293.

Western historians have generally characterized Indian women as downtrodden and passive and hence not worthy of serious attention. 'No feminist works emerged from behind the Hindu purdah or out of the Moslem harems; centuries of slavery do not provide a fertile soil for intellectual development or expression,' wrote Miriam Schneir in her introduction to a book entitled *Feminism: The Essential Historical Writings*.[22] More recently, historians Mary Morris and Larry O'Connor decided to include only European women in their book about women travellers because they assumed women from colonized regions were totally oppressed by patriarchy and neither travelled nor left behind accounts of their lives.[23] Chandra Mohanty blames hegemonic Western feminism for making 'third world women' a monolithic subject,[24] but Rashmi Luthra finds contemporary Indian feminists guilty of the same mistake. After analysing the feminist case against sex-selective abortion, Luthra concluded that feminist activists portrayed 'ordinary women' as victims without agency in the face of patriarchy and tradition.[25]

This does not mean there are no accounts of women's resistance. Stree Shakti Sanghatana, in *'We were Making History . . .' Life Stories of Women in the Telangana People's Struggle* (1989), and Peter Custers and Kabita Punjabi, in their work on Tebhaga, have detailed the role of women in peasant movements. Radha Kumar has valorized

[22] Miriam Schneir, *Feminism: The Essential Historical Writings* (New York: Vintage, 1972), p. xiv. In the second volume on this theme, *Feminism in Our Time: The Essential Writings, World War II to the Present* (New York: Vintage Books, 1994), Schneir includes only European and American women authors.

[23] Mary Morris and Larry O'Connor, eds, *The Virago Book of Women Travelers* (1994). Quoted by Farish A. Noor, 'Innocents Abroad? The Erasure of the Question of Race and Power in Contemporary Feminist and "Nostalgic" Travelogues', *South East Asia Research*, 5:1 (1997), p. 87.

[24] Chandra Talpade Mohanty, 'Under Western Eyes: Feminist Scholarship and Colonial Discourses', in *Third World Women and the Politics of Feminism* (eds), Chandra Talpade Mohanty, Ann Russo, and Lourdes Torres (Bloomington: Indiana University Press. 1991), pp. 51–80.

[25] Rashmi Luthra, 'The Women's Movement and the Press in India: The Construction of Female Foeticide as a Social Issue', *Women's Studies in Communication*, vol. 22, no. 1, Spring 1999, p. 10.

women's struggle for rights in *The History of Doing: An Illustrated Account of the Movement for Women's Rights and Feminism in India, 1800–1990* (1993), while Ishanee Mukherjee and Tirtha Mandal have written about Bengal's women revolutionaries. There are numerous biographies of individual women who fought the social system, Gandhi's lieutenants in the struggle for freedom, and brave women like Captain Lakshmi who commanded a women's regiment in the Indian National Army. Anthropologists have supplied accounts of day-to-day resistance. To cite only one example, Neema Caughran has analysed women's fasting, feeding others, secret feasting, and discourse about food as 'resistance to the norms of socially sanctioned behaviour for women and to the often cruel and abusive treatment women receive from husbands and their families.'[26] Scholars such as Mandakranta Bose and Nabaneeta Deb-Sen have unearthed and published women's versions of sacred texts.

Can all of these examples be considered resistance? Most of the work on resistance is based on the assumption that Indian gender ideology is derived from the laws of Manu that make all women subordinate. If so, can we regard all women's actions in violation of or opposition to the patriarchal system: songs, spirit possession, withdrawal of sex, return to the father's home, burned food, etc., as resistance? There is some support for this broad concept of resistance. For example, Luthra suggests that feminists opposing sex-selective abortion could include Sunil Khanna's three examples of women's 'resistance' to this practice. One woman avoided abortion by leaving for her natal home, another refused to have sex with her husband after he forced her to abort, and the third asked forgiveness of her unborn the night before the abortion.[27]

There is, however, a danger that the broad use of the term resistance will obfuscate the meaning of women's actions. In a paper that revisits Max Gluckman's classic article on 'rituals of rebellion' (1954),

---

[26] Neema Caughran, 'Fasts, Feasts, and the Slovenly Woman: Strategies of Resistance among North Indian Potter Women', *Asian Folklore Studies*, vol. 57, no. 2, June 1999, pp. 3–4.

[27] In Luthra, p. 10, from S. K. Khanna, 'Prenatal Sex Determination: A New Family Building Strategy', *Manushi*, no. 86, January–February 1995, pp. 23–9.

Todd Sanders offers thoughtful comments about an overdetermined search for resistance. Gluckman concluded that Zulu women's rain-making rituals—where the women stripped naked, sang lewd songs, and insulted and attacked men who got in their way—were instances of rebellion against the established gender hierarchy in which men were dominant and women submissive. Women's performance temporarily subverted the dominant paradigm, and when it was over, they returned to their traditional roles. Revisiting the same region, Sanders found Gluckman's rigid notion of patriarchal control untenable. Although conventional discourse made men superior, Sanders found women dominant in some situations, and equal to men in others. He established that women performed the rainmaking ritual because they were considered 'wetter' by nature, and thus more likely to attract rain. Moreover, their nakedness/'fertile femininity' and aggression/'masculinity' echoed a shared belief that the rains came 'when the cultural categories "male" and "female" conjoin[ed] as equals.'[28] Sanders urges scholars to look for: the 'distinction between representations of gender and gender behaviour,' and the ways 'ideas and ideals about gender in everyday and ritual realms are multiple and multifaceted.'[29]

Following Sanders' advice, I suggest we reject a Manu-centric view of Indian culture, and refine/redefine what qualifies as resistance. The two types of resistance mentioned earlier—everyday resistance and avoidance resistance—capture the examples given by Neema Caughran and other anthropologists but do not shed light on the rebellion of other women. The historical record includes women such as Pandita Ramabai, who denounced high-caste rules for Brahmin widows and became a Christian; Rukhmabai, who refused to cohabit with her husband; Bina Das, who shot a pistol at the governor of Bengal; and Renuka Ray, who spoke in favour of divorce at a women's meeting. Who, or what, were these women rebelling against? We cannot characterize them as fighting a unitary system of patriarchy

[28] Todd Sanders, 'Rains Gone Bad, Women Gone Mad: Rethinking Gender Rituals of Rebellion and Patriarchy', *Royal Anthropological Institute*, vol. 6, 2000, pp. 469–86.

[29] Sanders, p. 471.

and male dominance. We can, however, analyse them using the terms suggested by Padma Anagol in her article in this volume: intentionality, target of resistance, and impact.[30] All the women mentioned were absolutely clear about what they were doing and enacted their resistance in the public sphere. They opposed different ideologies and institutions: Pandita Ramabai opposed Brahmanic rules, Rukhmabai British law, Bina Das colonialism, and Renuka Ray conservatism within the women's movement. These are not examples of day-to-day resistance or avoidance, these women were thoughtful and deliberate in their efforts to disrupt power.

Let me now return to photographs. I have focused on women's stories, told when viewing photographs, of small rebellions. On the one hand, one could argue that the rebellious behaviour of two of these women was ultimately contained, that of the third muted. Krishnabai married a man of her choice and dropped out of politics to study medicine, while Kalyani continued to take care of her family and later became a teacher in Loreto School. Latika's skill at hardball politics, embodied in her threat to withdraw the female volunteers from all activities unless they were allowed to march, had greater impact. A number of young women, including Lakshmi Swaminathan who became Captain Lakshmi of the Indian National Army, were thrilled and inspired by this march. However, Latika's reputation was attacked when she separated from her husband and she finally left Calcutta, and politics, to teach in a hill station.

Using Anagol's terms: intentionality, target of intention, and impact, we are led to a different conclusion. The examples that emerged from 'telling photographs' speak to the ongoing nature of women's resistance to customs that deny their autonomy, rigid definitions of female duty, and forces that deny political rights. All three women claimed that even as children they were aware of gender inequality and efforts to limit their activities. Krishnabai opposed the extended family's right to decide when and who she should marry, Kalyani her mother-in-law's right to control her life, and Latika politicians who would sacrifice women's rights to gain conservative support. Krishnabai and Kalyani remembered resistance in the domestic realm but

---

[30] Padma Anagol, 'From the Symbolic to the Open: Women's Resistance in Colonial Maharashtra', in this volume.

their ultimate target was a system that would prevent them from playing meaningful public roles. By the time Latika became involved with nationalist politics, she was fully cognizant of a bankrupt domesticity. Her defiance of Congress leaders took place after she had fought domestic battles equivalent to those of Krishnabai and Kalyani. That all three women were successful in their resistance meant their lives were different than had they failed and the impact of their small acts can be seen in their life histories. Krishnabai became a medical doctor and had one daughter, but never gave up politics. To mention just a sample of her activities, she was arrested as an individual satygrahi in 1942, created an underground newssheet during Mrs Gandhi's Emergency, and in the 1980s focused attention on environmental issues. Kalyani became a teacher to help support the family and continued her research into a topic many thought un-suitable for a respectable woman. Latika's impact, as mentioned above, was immeasurable since the marching women inspired a generation who became leaders in the 1930s and 1940s. The scandal of her separation and later divorce ended her political career, but she continued to teach, support herself, and thumb her nose at respect-ability. All three women were independent-minded, opinionated, and resourceful. While it is clear they did not draft new laws or hold important political positions, they refused to conform to the norms for women. Michael Adas wrote that we should see 'resistance and protest as ongoing, constantly reworked, predominantly non-violent, and preferably non-confrontational components of evolving social systems.'[31] Their 'ongoing, constantly reworked' resistance provided models for those around them to see.

Do these examples suggest that gender offers a valuable lens to view resistance in colonial India? All women were subject to male authority and patriarchal customs, but for the three individuals in this essay, it was not that simple. Krishnabai's problem was not her father, but the extended family that were conservative about marriage. When Kalyani wanted to study, she had to fight her mother-in-law, not her father, husband, or father-in-law. Latika had a great deal of personal autonomy and received support from politicians like J.M. Sengupta in her confrontation with Sarat Bose. These examples

[31] Adas, p. 301.

make it clear that, in addition to gender, we must consider class, caste, wealth, education, region, family culture, and politics to understand women's acts of resistance.

Finally, what is the value of photographs and this methodology for Indian history and history? Photographs clearly have value beyond illustrating and supplementing text documents. They are especially interesting as historical documents, not because the images can be read for stories of rebellion, but because they invite 'telling', a process that allows for continual renewal of the act of rebellion. In the ninth volume of *Subaltern Studies* (1996), Kamala Visweswaran, in 'Small Speeches, Subaltern Gender: Nationalist Ideology and Historiography', argues in favour of 'rescuing' stories of women's activism for history, recognizing that a record of small rebellions can accelerate social change.[32] The examples in this essay are of small rebellions, rescued from erasure by serendipity and the chemistry of personal interactions. These fragments can open doors to new interpretations only if we learn to analyse them in terms of context and function, as well as rhetoric and recollection,[33] and only if we can shape them into meaningful history.

[32] Kamala Visweswaran, 'Small Speeches, Subaltern Gender: Nationalist Ideology and Historiography', *Subaltern Studies IX*, eds Shahid Amin and Dipesh Chakrabarty (Delhi: Oxford University Press, 1996), p. 8.

[33] Peter Burke, *Eyewitnessing: The Uses of Images as Historical Evidence* (Ithaca: Cornell University Press, 2001), pp. 14–15.

4

WICKED WIDOWS: LAW AND FAITH IN NINETEENTH-CENTURY PUBLIC SPHERE DEBATES

TANIKA SARKAR

A law was enacted in 1856 abrogating an earlier legal and prescriptive prohibition against the remarriage of Hindu widows. This law also underwrote the inheritance rights of sons born of remarriage.[1] Even though a colonial legislature had enacted the law—a legislature where Indians were not represented—the idea of remarriage had originated among a small group of Bengali reformers who had approached and persuaded some members of the Legislative Council. Remarriage was then furiously debated as an issue in the public sphere in most parts of India for the rest of the century. I will underline some of the significant features of the discipline of Hindu widowhood, and then relate these to the debates on remarriage, in order to explore the implications of the reform for a normative system of social power.

A second marriage for widowed women was a scandalous proposition in the eyes of most nineteenth-century Bengali Hindus. It

---

[1] Act No XV, July 1856: An Act to Remove All Legal Obstacles to Marriage of Hindoo Widows; Record Office, India Acts, 1854–7.

was especially so for upper-caste widows, who were specifically prohibited from it by sacred texts and custom, and who were deemed
exemplars of female virtue within a wide sprawl of upwardly mobile
'low' castes.[2] As I have argued elsewhere, it was largely upper-caste
norms of female virtue that pulled together a highly stratified and
diverse caste spectrum into the semblance of a single community.[3]
Spurning the notion of widow remarriage was, perhaps, the most
potent of such norms. This idea not only unified many Hindu
castes—at least at the level of an ethical consensus—it also laid down
the boundary line between Hindus and Muslims. A pre-colonial
verse narrative of the eighteenth century contains a passage within
which a Hindu and a Muslim argue about the respective superiority
of their faiths. While the Muslim avers that the Hindu practice of
celibate widowhood is against the laws of nature, 'since the female
flowers blossom every month to bear fruit and these must not be
wasted', the Hindu protests that widow remarriage is an unnatural
act for humans since only cows run after more than one bull.[4] Clearly, the narrator picked on this issue as the single-most significant
marker of difference between the two communities.

Reformers who urged the legalization of remarriage on colonial
lawmakers therefore challenged a brahmanical mandate—textual as
well as customary—of critical importance. Their proposal was, not
surprisingly, received with incredulous outrage and horror. While
supporters of the bill could mobilize 5191 signatures on their petition
to the legislature, their opponents gathered more than 55,746.[5]
Obviously, the idea was repugnant to most Hindu opinion-makers.
Even after it went through the Legislative Council, it was strenuously
fought in the public and domestic spheres. We have a wide range of

[2] H.H. Risley, *The Tribes and Castes of Bengal* (Calcutta: 1891, rpnt. 1981).

[3] Tanika Sarkar, *Hindu Wife, Hindu Nation: Community, Religion, and Cultural
Nationalism* (Delhi: 2000), pp. 43–4.

[4] Bharatchandra Raygunakar, *Annadamangal, circa* 1752; Brajendranath
Bandyopadhyaya and Sajanikanta Das, eds, *Bharatchandra Granthabali* (Calcutta: 1943), pp. 340–4.

[5] Out of a total of 51 petitions sent to the Legislative Council on the issue,
23 were in favour of the bill and 28 were opposed to it. Legislative Department,
Papers Relating to Act XV of 1856, Part 2.

nineteenth-century biographies and autobiographies which provide a vivid sense of the social turbulence of the time. Widows, their second husbands, and their supporters faced violent intimidation, social ostracism, disinheritance, and savage and obscene lampooning in the press. Weddings in the colonial metropolis of Calcutta had to be performed under elaborate police protection, which was notoriously lacking in villages. Peasants who supported remarriage were evicted, beaten up, and expelled from their villages by upper-caste landlords and their low-caste musclemen. Reformist appeals for help in such cases were ignored by Hindu deputy magistrates and police officers.[6]

Ishwarchandra Vidyasagar, who masterminded the reformist campaign, was threatened with death, which he managed to avert only with prodigious, strategic gifts to local brahmans.[7] The chief of the great Krishnagore estate, a reformer, was booed by children on the streets of his kingdom.[8] More difficult was opposition within the family: a reformer who helped his brother and cousin marry widows never got to speak to his mother again; another had to postpone his own marriage to a widow till his mother died, for she threatened to commit suicide if he married within her lifetime.[9]

Widows who desired remarriage were sometimes abducted to distant places and kept there under extreme vigilance by their outraged families. Their lovers and reformist friends had to arrange counter-abductions. Quite a few such marriages eventually broke up because the man faced disinheritance. Vidyasagar funded most such weddings himself and also set up households for brides and grooms whose families had cut off all connection with them.[10] A fairly wealthy

[6] Sambhuchandra Vidyaratna, *Vidyasagar Jivancarit* (Calcutta: 1891, rpnt. 1992), pp. 42–3.

[7] Ibid. See also Chandicharan Bandyopadhyaya, *Vidyasagar* (Calcutta: 1893, rpnt. 1969).

[8] Rajnarain Bose, in Baridbaran Ghose, ed., *Rajnarain Bose: Nirbachita Bangla Rachana Samgraha* (Calcutta: 1908, rpnt. 1995, pp. 50–1.

[9] Ibid. See also, Shibnath Shastri, *Ramtanu Lahiri O Tatkalin Bangasamaj* (Calcutta: 1903), p. 126.

[10] See Shambhucharan Vidyaratna and Chandicharan Bandyopadhyaya, op. cit. Kalyani Datta recalled the life of her aunt, a widow at ten, who was left on

upper-caste man who eloped with a widow was forced to work as a domestic servant for a few years to make both ends meet.[11]

The state, too, had to pay. A year after the bill passed into law, British rule faced a massive insurrection all over North India. Taking stock of this traumatic event later, colonial rulers strongly felt that the widow remarriage law had been one of the precipitating factors of rebellion, and they needed to be far more cautious when supporting reform in future. Queen Victoria hastened to assure her Indian subjects that there would be no further interference with their religious practices and beliefs. In any case, it soon became evident that the movement was losing momentum. By the early 1860s the spate of widow remarriages had tapered off. Till then, the total of such remarriages in Bengal had been about sixty—not, however, as insignificant a number as it may seem. What is more significant is that most such remarriages happened in upper-caste families, in which the prohibition was absolute.[12] A new and radical marriage regulation was introduced in 1872, providing for widow remarriage—inter-caste, consensual, and adult, monogamous marriages among partners who had to declare themselves as not belonging to any particular religious denomination. It is quite possible that, after its enactment, a number of widows married under this Special Act rather than under the 1856 Act, especially if they contracted inter-caste marriages.

On balance, the 1856 Act did not enable renewed conjugal-sexual life for the vast majority of Hindu widows in Bengal. Nor was it different elsewhere. In Bombay and in the South, widow remarriage was the central plank of reformism, but the returns to these intense campaigns were uniformly disappointing. In North India, Swami Dayanand tried to propagate an authoritarian, non-consensual form of remarriage between childless widows and widowers who would meet at appointed times just to breed and who would have to forgo all mutual connection after they had produced several children. The

---

Vidyasagar's doorstep by well-wishers. Vidyasagar kept her at his home till a willing groom could be found, and he set up the household himself. Datta, *Pinjare Basiya* (Calcutta: 1996), p. 2.

[11] Gurucharan Mahalanobis, *Atmacharit* (Calcutta: n.d.).

[12] Shambhucharan Vidyaratna, op. cit.

Swami's Arya Samaj was somewhat embarrassed by such a proposal and did not try to push forward remarriage in either this or any other form.[13]

All this goes to show that there was an exceptionally stable and secure normative common sense about widowhood regulations; norms which lost the legal battle but won the social one. At the same time—and this is my main argument—in multiple, insidious, and subterranean ways the campaign and the law fractured the older ethical convictions. At least they made them uncertain, somewhat apologetic, and in need of justification. There was also an accretion to the new questioning, for it came to exceed the specific limits of the remarriage issue and embraced the larger domain of gender power, social inequality, and the ideological basis of scriptural prescription as customary practice.

I feel it is important to retrieve a sense of the movement in its own time, to reinstate it as a scandal in the mid-nineteenth century. It is important to do this because of a historiographical shift in reading nineteenth-century liberal reform. In Sangari and Vaid's enormously influential interpretation, reform appears as a pale imitation of the Victorian master narrative of companionate domesticity that an emergent and compradore Indian bourgeoisie embraced. It recast patriarchy on Western lines. This, I think, suggests a double negative teleology: i.e. the change was not a serious transformation but a re-iteration of patriarchy in different words. And that it was, moreover, a patriarchy not even our own.[14] This negative teleology makes Indian modernity synonymous with colonial capitalism. If modernity is stripped of all possibilities except state-driven modernization of social and economic relations, which necessarily flow in the same direction and express identical processes (although the very concept of a smooth transplantation of capitalist relations in India is a highly contested and problematic notion), then modern times are rendered bleak, a time of near-absolute loss and regress. Was it really so bad?

[13] Madhu Kishwar, 'Daughters of Aryavarta', in J. Krishnamurty, ed., *Women in Colonial India: Essyas on Survival, Work and the State* (Delhi: 1989).

[14] Kumkum Sangari and Sudesh Vaid, eds, *Recasting Women: Essays in Colonial History* (Delhi: 1989).

Despite its theoretical sophistication and the power of its critique, I find elements of a somewhat decontextualized critique in the suspicion and deep scepticism towards liberal reform. The perspective seems to undermine or dilute the far more powerful politics of Hindu orthodoxy, chauvinism, and status-quoism that continued to pervade the colonial era. The origins of reformism are traced back to a Western middle-class order of gender and domesticity that masked vast asymmetries in gender roles. The meanings of a political concept such as this, however, need not be fixed by its original functions and intentions. Liberalism, which developed in an imperial West, nonetheless played a revolutionary role in slave insurrections elsewhere.[15] Likewise, companionate marriage was as an idea probably more a daring political intervention in Hindu sexual-emotional lives than a patriarchal ploy to sweeten and mask the subjection of women. I think that it eventually enabled a new female self-fashioning.

Liberal middle-class politics was neither hegemonic nor triumphant in colonial India. By the end of the century it was overshadowed by a cultural nationalism that decried all reform as a surrender to colonial meanings, the loss of 'authentic' Hindu selfhood. The same middle class, moreover, threw up the orthodoxy, the revivalists, and the Hindu chauvinists along with the reformers. So, class origins explain little. The critique of liberal reform short circuits precisely that which I find to be the key question: what did Hindu common sense find so offensive about widow remarriage? At the same time, it is somewhat limiting just to ask how many widows remarried The real implications of the campaign lay, perhaps, in what it allowed to become sayable, thinkable, arguable—and against what odds.

My ensuing reading of reforms may run a different kind of risk. It may veer close to an older, overly laudatory appraisal of reformism that charted a teleology of progress—from emancipatory reform to emancipated nationhood. I will not annex nineteenth-century liberal reform to that trajectory, but will read it for traces of another reference. This is in part because a new normative imperative was born during the widow remarriage debates. Quite a few times, the word

[15] Paul Gilroy, *The Black Atlantic: Modernity and Double Consciousness* (Cambridge: 1993).

'equality' was spoken with revulsion and fear by the orthodoxy, and with defiance by at least some of the reformers. A number of petitioners supporting remarriage wrote to the Legislative Council saying God intended men and women to be equals in society since he made their natural capacities equal.[16] Opponents, on the other hand, were alarmed that remarriage might roll on to gender equality, this notion in their lexicon being opposed to the laws of nature as well as to the laws of Hindus, who were bound by the theory of *anupatbad*: that is, returns according to capabilities which are inherently unequal between men and women.[17] This does not mean that the legitimization of remarriage led inexorably to equality, to a new gender regime. But a word—new, disturbing, destabilizing—had been spoken, a word which would generate historical resonances beyond its immediate context. What is more interesting is how it got to be spoken, since the context for its utterance was, then, so very resistant to any such articulation. A number of discrete and tentative modes emerged for thinking about the possibility—all of these riddled with contradictions and internal divisions, all of them touching the nebulous idea with caution, uncertainty, and excitement. Around this inchoate counter-norm a social criticism—about gender relations, about consent and coercion, about the ideological basis of an ethic of hierarchy—came to cohere in and through the sex public debates. Eventually, a few women entered this arena of arguments and controversies.

II

The fact that projects of gender reform emerged under colonialism and were occasionally enabled by colonial laws does not indicate that the idea of reform was a gift from the colonial masters: in fact, some feminist scholars argue that colonialism was, if anything, complicit

---

[16] Among many others like this, a petition from 'the inhabitants of Barasat' stated: 'Women are naturally the equal of men.' Papers Relating to Act XV of 1856.

[17] Prasannakumar Sharma, *Bidhababibaha Shastrabirudhha* (Mymensingh: 1886), p. 47.

with upper-caste patriarchy.[18] Since the late eighteenth century, colonial law had enclosed an entire realm of social practices and prescriptions—of caste, inheritance, adoption, succession, dower, marriage, divorce, religious belief and practice—which was to be governed by Hindu and Muslim scripture and custom as interpreted by the authorized religious leaders of their communities.[19] The legal guidelines were meant for courts and the judiciary and, in theory, the Legislative Council did not need to abide by the constraints. In practice, however, the legislature too, observed the strictures as a self-imposed limitation upon its powers.[20] This, then, was an arena where the colonial state abrogated its sovereignty. It would intervene in this field only when community leaders could prove that an existing law contravened more authentic religious prescription.[21] This made religion, family, and community norms among the very rare spaces left for self-fashioning by the colonized. The field of gender was, consequently, marked by numerous openings, many possibilities, rather than by closures and fixities. At the same time, the colonial enclosure of 'personal laws' as a religious domain renewed and refurbished religious prescription as the source of all social regulations. Some of the petitioners to the Council complained that the state bound itself unnecessarily to religious commands over matters that ought to be the domain of civil law. The debate over the bill, in fact,

[18] See Mrinalini Sinha, 'Potent Protest: The Age of Consent Controversy in 1891', in *Colonial Masculinity: The 'Manly' Englishman and the 'Effeminate Bengali' in the Late Nineteenth Century* (Manchester: 1995). Also Tanika Sarkar, 'Conjugality and Hindu Nationalism', in *Hindu Wife*, op. cit.

[19] M.K. Jain, *Outline of Indian Legal History* (Bombay: 1969), pp. 554–710.

[20] Archana Parashar, *Women and Family Law Reform in India* (Delhi: 1992), p. 67.

[21] Lata Mani ignores this crucial point in her excellent study of widow immolation debates when she says that since reformers relied so overwhelmingly on religious arguments, their primary concern was Hindu tradition: gender was merely a site on which tradition was reconstituted. She overlooks the constraint that faced reformers when they wanted a new law which could only be made on the basis of scriptural citations. *Contentious Traditions: The Debates on Sati in Colonial India* (Berkeley: 1995).

was something of a playground for radical social imaginaries. Some even suggested its extension to a system of civil, inter-caste, and adult, consensual, monogamous marriages. If the discipline of chaste widowhood could be breached, a whole new world of intimate human relations could also be imagined for the near future.[22]

When the Second Law Commission met in 1837, the state briefly considered widow remarriage. In order to stamp out infanticide, Sir John Shore proposed the criminalizing of concealed pregnancies, and the Sudder Diwani Adawlut of the North Western Provinces added that the concealment of dead infants or their secret disposal should be classified as a 'misdemeanour'. The Law Commission rejected the idea since it would make a suspected offence of possible infanticide into a 'positive offence' without definite proof. In its place, it suggested that since most cases of infanticide emanated from illicit pregnancies among widows, it would be more kind and effective if a new law enabled widows to remarry: 'The Commissioners think that much of this crime may be owing to the cruel law which prevents Hindoo widows from remarrying.' The provincial courts, however, strongly advised against any such law. The Sudder Court of Madras said that since the upper castes believed brides must be virgins, they would accuse the law of dragging them down to the level of low castes. R. Macan, Officiating Registrar, Sudder Court, Calcutta, wrote that in the 'unqualified opinion of the Court', the law would be 'an open violation of the pledged faith of the government' and that it would not alter religious practice. For Hindus, widow remarriage 'involves guilt and disgrace on earth and exclusion from heaven'; it would flout 'the usage and obligation of Caste and Custom.' Moreover, 'the whole framework of the Hindoo Law of Inheritance would be shaken and subverted.' The Registrar of the Allahabad Sudder Court reiterated this view, saying that the widow's 'life of chastity and privation' was 'both a religious and a moral obligation.'[23]

[22] Petition from the Inhabitants of Calcutta, 1 February 1856; Bhugwan Chunder Bose wrote from Mymensingh on 1 May 1856, that he would have supported the bill even if it had flown in the face of scripture. Papers Relating to Act XV, op. cit.

[23] Abstract of the Letter from J.P. Grant, Officiating Secretary, Indian Law

A great sensitivity is undoubtedly evident in the tone of several such comments on the discipline of Hindu widowhood. It surpasses the fear of provoking orthodoxy or of reneging upon a pledge to respect scripture and custom: it indicates a more positive commitment. Yet overall, if in colonial times, a few Indians felt enabled to imagine a radical restructuring of domestic inequalities by detaching marriage from scriptural injunctions, and by hoping to use a state agency that was not organically tied to them, the colonial rulers in their turn seemed to be content to consolidate a patriarchy in India that was more extreme and uncompromising about female chastity than even the standards of Victorian morality. India, to them, was probably a playground for a different social imagination, one that would enforce here what Western men had lost in their own homes.[24]

If this was so, what induced the change of attitude in 1856? It is significant that while official hesitation over abolishing widow immolation lasted sixty years, widow remarriage was decided upon fairly quickly. Though the idea was rejected in 1837, it was revived in official circles again in 1855 when Vidyasagar approached Grant and Colville with a plea and a scriptural citation in favour of widow remarriage. A bill was quickly prepared and brought to the Council on 10 November 1855. Its first reading began on 17 November.[25] By July 1856 the act was in place. It is true, of course, that the sati debates were initiated in the Orientalist phase, whereas widow remarriage was discussed by state officials in an intellectual climate within which Utilitarian impatience with traditional institutions had for the moment the upper hand; it would subside markedly after the panic of 1857. Yet the Utilitarian moment chronologically also included the time of the Second Law Commission, when the idea had been thrown out summarily. Moreover, even when the bill was

-----

Commission, to W.H. MacNaughten, Secretary, Government of India, 4 July 1837: see Papers Relating to Act XV, op. cit.

[24] Pompa Bannerjee points out that till the seventeenth century widow remarriage was looked down upon in Britain. She interestingly derives the plot of Shakespeare's *Hamlet* from this disapproval. *Burning Women: Widows, Witches and Early Modern Travellers in India* (London: 2003), p. 3.

[25] Legislative Council Proceedings: The Hindoo Widows' Remarriage Bill, November 1855.

moving quite rapidly through three readings, we find that the legislators built the case for the bill not on arguments for social intervention and Utilitarian transformative designs, but on scriptural arguments offered by Vidyasagar, a brahman of legendary Sanskrit scholarship and orthodox habits. Legislators claimed that the scope of the bill was modest; unlike the Sati Act, it would not impose a decision on any Hindu who did not agree with the terms of the act. It would merely enable those Hindus who believed that scripture allowed remarriage to live by this interpretation of their faith. The law-makers abjured even a refereeing function for the state in relation to religious matters; that is, state officials would not be able to pronounce on whether or not a particular interpretation was valid; the field was, by this legislation, being left open for all practitioners of religion to abide by their belief via removing the earlier legal disability against remarriage. It was a 'permissive law', they said, again and again. Vidyasagar's importance to the state lay not in his liberal reformism, but in his stature as a traditional brahman pandit.[26] This was, therefore, a rather modest sort of Utilitarianism which expressed itself in its greater readiness to accept a liberal version of dogma—but only because it came from an authorized interpreter of faith. Interestingly, the disinclination in 1837 to allow widow remarriage may be analogously attributed to the absence of scriptural citation, and partly to the espousal of the liberal cause by a group of radical, iconoclast, defiant bohemians of Hindu origin, namely, the Young Bengal group, who were equally feared by Hindus and state officials.[27] In 1855, in reassuring contrast, reformers and liberal colonials had a learned brahman quoting Sanskrit scripture to plead the cause.

Interestingly, Protestant missionaries who had been at the forefront of the anti-immolation agitation in the 1820s, reinterpreting Hindu scripture to delegitimize sati, played a fairly marginal role in 1855–6. They certainly supported the bill,[28] but they feared it would be a

---

[26] Legislative Council Proceedings, op. cit., November 1855, July 1856.

[27] See Sumit Sarkar. 'The Complexities of Young Bengal', in *A Critique of Colonial India* (Calcutta: 1985).

[28] Letter from J. Wenger on behalf of the Calcutta Missionary Council, 22 December 1855. Papers Relating to Act XV, 1855, op. cit.

dead letter.[29] This was a time when the focus of missionary activism had shifted away from recalcitrant Hindu upper-caste, middle-class circles to the more amenable lower orders, who seemed riper plums for conversion. Missionaries were also far more engrossed with tenancy reforms for peasants, and with agitations against European indigo planters in Bengal.[30] So, unlike the anti-immolation agitation, the campaign for remarriage was rather entirely an Indian initiative.

Shortly before the act was passed, the Council decided to print, for public circulation, all its internal proceedings. The press reported widely on the nature of Council discussions and on the different stages of the bill's progress.[31] There was, thus, a circularity to the flow of information about social and legislative opinion. Just as Indians read about discussions in the Council, legislators came to know how the matter was viewed in the Indian press. Even though Indians were not yet admitted into the Council's ranks, there was a reciprocal transparency of opinion. Shortly before this, moreover, there had been a parliamentary enquiry about whether or not there should be nominated Indian representatives on the Council in a consultative capacity, members who might advise the legislature about Indian opinion. Widow remarriage was cited as one of the possible issues on which such a group would be of value. Officialdom, however, decided to consult representative Indian opinion informally, outside the Council, for to nominate some Hindus on delicate and controversial matters would be to lay itself open to charges of partiality and discrimination.[32] The circular flow of information thus provided circuits of informal consultation between Indians and law-makers, over and above the more usual channels of private connection.

[29] *Friend of India*, 29 November 1855.

[30] G.A. Oddie, *Missionaries, Rebellions and Proto Nationalism: James Long of Bengal, 1814–87* (London: 1999).

[31] *Hindoo Patriot*, 11 November 1855.

[32] Petition on Notes on the Evidence on Indian Affairs by Peareychand Mitter, 1853, commenting on the Parliamentary Committee Report of 1852, on Admission of Natives in Legislative Council, British India Association Papers, 1855–6.

III

Let us turn to what authorized interpreters of the scripture had to say about the fundamental and foundational norms of Hindu domestic practice. These views were built up from the late eighteenth century and were well authenticated by scriptural citations from the ancient Dharmashastras, later glosses, and medieval and early modern regional legal treatises. At the outset, it is important to establish a distinction between prescription and transgressive practice. In all societies, legitimate norms are violated or defied secretly but the defiance does not necessarily invalidate the normativeness of prescriptive laws, nor does it set up counter-norms. People driven to defiance of social prescription who came to constitute a minority of social outcastes rarely articulated a systematic alternative of just norms or developed a movement explicitly claiming their terms for transgression. Dakshinaranjan Mukhopadhyay, for example, a radical, eloped with a queen of the Burdwan estate and later married her under the Special Marriage Act. They moved to far-off Awadh where nobody knew them; here he lived a life of conspicuously blameless orthodoxy to woo social acceptance.[33] Second, even when norms were stratified according to social location—lower castes not being obliged to observe the rigours of upper-caste domestic practice, for instance— the more chaste disciplinary model still enjoyed a reputation for higher virtue and goodness and the alternatives continued to be regarded as markers of lowliness. Upper-caste gender rules therefore continuously encouraged the lower castes to move 'up' towards them, if possible.[34]

[33] Shibnath Shastri, op. cit.

[34] Sekhar Bandyopadhyaya observes correctly that through these means the respectable classes, the bhadralok, in Bengal remained an open category. Even when they practised remarriage, lower castes expressed contempt for the form of 'senga' or 'sanga' which lacked the full ceremonial features of marriage, and therefore the full status as well. Even the women's magazine of an upwardly mobile Shudra group, the Mahishyamahila, in 1911 'approved of the self abnegation of chaste widows.' 'Caste, Widow Remarriage and the Reform of Popular Culture', in Bharati Ray, ed., *From the Seams of History: Essays on Indian*

The gender regime prescribed by ancient scripture had laid down that marriage was sacramental. The girl needed to be married off—gifted away—in her infancy. Wifehood swallowed up the possibility of any enjoyment of female childhood or girlhood. When that vital procreative state came to an end, the widow was condemned to a life of total abstinence, even though the widower was obliged to remarry in order to conduct the rites of a householder. Wifehood was thus the core state, with a brief prelude before it commenced and a life of nullity after it ended. Disciplined, punitive widowhood was mandatory, even if there had been no actual contact or sexual relationship between husband and wife, and even if the husband happened to have died the instant the marriage rites were over. Hindu marriage did not depend upon consummation for its formalization, it was considered complete and fixed the moment the ritual of the sacrament was performed. The man, however, could remarry any number of times and could desert his wife. The wife had no such option. She remained subordinate at all stages of life: to her father in childhood, to her husband over her youth, to her son through old age. 'On no account is she to enjoy autonomy', prescribed Manu, the eponymous ancient lawgiver, the most venerated among all authorities.[35]

Manu considered the wife to be *ardhangini*—the half-body of her husband. This meant that a husband lived on in his wife even after his death; thereby the marriage tie remained in place, and any subsequent relationship between the widow and a man could only be adulterous. Manu prescribed for her a regime of harsh and continuous self-flagellation and self-deprivation, a renunciation of all pleasures of life—sexual, dietary, sartorial, and ritual.[36] At the same time, he and several other Smriti authorities, like Boudhayana, acknowledged the category of second marriages (Punarbhu). Acknowledgement, however, did not signify acceptance: it merely recorded

---

Women (Delhi: 1995), p. 181. Risley found that the poorer low and untouchable castes took the brahmanical injunction very seriously. Risley, op. cit.

[35] Cited in Prasannakumar Sharma, *Bidhababibaha Shastrabiruddha* (Mymensingh: 1886).

[36] Ibid., p. 23.

a social fact. Manu, in fact, quite explicitly prescribed against such a custom: 'A good woman does not take a second husband', and 'Mantras related to marriage rites apply only to the marriage of a virgin.'[37] Other Smriti texts prohibited marriage with the offspring of a remarried widow. Interestingly, later Smriti authorities mention remarriage as customarily defunct, even though older lawbooks mention their existence.[38]

Vidyasagar used a verse in the Parasharasamhita which recommended remarriage under a set of five conditions: 'If the husband was a ruined man, or dead, or a renunciate, or impotent or an outcaste, under such special circumstances, a woman is allowed to take another husband.' He himself wrote two successive tracts in Bengali to prove that in Kaliyuga—the last and most degenerate of ages in the Hindu cycle of time—Parashara was the greatest of authorities and his opinion must override all others.[39] While we shall see later how his opponents replied to this verse and to Vidyasagar's interpretation, it is pertinent to point out here that older commentators tried vigorously to disprove an interpretation of the verse which might signify legitimate second marriages.[40] Nandapandita (*c.* AD 1550–1630), in his commentary on Parashara, for instance, warned that the five contingencies referred to a state of betrothal and did not apply to married women.[41] During the nineteenth-century debates, the orthodoxy, too, made this point, but they made no reference to Nandapandita; clearly, textual knowledge was as yet quite restricted and selective: print culture consolidated a comprehensive range of texts somewhat later. Similarly, Vidyasagar could have used an alternative commentary of Kamesvara (eighteenth century), who allowed

[37] An excellent discussion of the older Smriti texts is to be found in Krishna Datta, 'A Controversy Over a Verse on the Remarriage of Hindu Women', in Mandakranta Bose, ed., *Faces of the Feminine in Ancient, Medieval and Modern India* (Delhi: 2000).

[38] Ibid., pp. 9–13.

[39] Ishwarchandra Vidyasagar, *Bidhababibaha Prachalita Hoya Uchit Ki Na Etadbishayak Prastab* (5th edition, 1872), in Vidyasagar Smarak Jatiya Samiti, ed., *Vidyasagar Rachana Samgraha*, vol. 2 (Calcutta: 1972), pp. 16–18.

[40] Krishna Datta, op. cit.

[41] Ibid., p. 14.

remarriage in the name of Parashara, but Vidyasagar made no mention of him in his two tracts. In fact, his legendary 'discovery' of Parashara's verse in a moth-eaten manuscript, hidden away in a corner of the Sanskrit College Library, points to the scant and fragmentary archive of texts available at the time.[42]

Vidyasagar tried to demarcate a boundary between what he postulated as a benevolent scriptural regime, and a harsh but less legitimate later legal system and custom. Whether he was right or not about the lack of sanctity of customary practices, he was certainly right about their harshness. Raghunandan, the sixteenth-century authority for Bengali practices under the Dayabhaga school of law (and the major influence on customary practices), had tightened up the discipline of widowhood. The provision for the ritual fortnightly Ekadasi fast, during which not a drop of water could pass the widow's lips, had become mandatory even for infant and dying widows. Not even medicine could be consumed on that day, no matter how fatal the illness.[43] The widow had to ensure a series of rites for the comfort of the soul of her husband and his ancestors. On this condition the Dayabhaga school of inheritance and succession laws that operated in Bengal ensured a modicum of usufruct rights to her husband's share of the property. She could not, however, alienate the property. Raghunandan had also laid down that in all disputes involving relations of domestic power—between father and son, husband and wife, teacher and student, master and servant—the state had no right to adjudicate. Nor would women, children and slaves be allowed to depose against their guardians in courts since, by definition, they were not autonomous beings—they were '*aswatantra*'.[44] From Manu to Raghunandan, the woman was defined as embodying lack—of autonomy, of self-possession.

In the eighteenth century the royal estate of Krishnagore rigorously enforced Smarta orthodoxy over the entire province under the highly conservative social leadership of Maharaja Krishnachandra

[42] Chandicharan Bandyopadhyaya, op. cit.

[43] Kantichandra Rarhi, ed., *Nabadwip Mahima* (Calcutta: 1937), p. 193. Also Sureshchandra Bandyopadhyaya, *Smritishastre Bangali* (Calcutta: 1961), p. 71.

[44] Ibid., p. 141.

Ray. Ray was particularly uncompromising about the discipline of
'*nirjala ekadasi*', the fortnightly fast without water. When a financier
of the Baidya caste, Rajballabh, tried to get a verdict from brahman
authorities in favour of the remarriage of virgin and infant widows,
he was defeated by Krishnachandra. The raja's pandits apparently
retorted that if it was merely customary and not scriptural to forbid
remarriage, people might as well begin to eat beef, since the prohibition against beef too was situated in custom and not scripture.[45]

The Young Bengal activists had, as we saw, agitated for remarriage
in the 1830s and 1840s. Their extreme and open iconoclasm, however,
put a taint on their proposal and the state would not regard them as
representative Hindus who could propose changes in Hindu laws.[46]
In 1845 the issue came up again, as a man of a cleaner Shudra rank
tried to persuade pandits to issue a verdict in favour of the remarriage
of virgin child widows. This category was known as '*akshatayoni*
(literally, woman with unwounded vagina), in contrast to *khsatayoni*
or *dattayoni*' ('woman whose genitals have been wounded or given
away in marriage'). The British India Society of Bengali landlords
corresponded with the orthodox Dharma Sabha on the matter and
the orthodoxy once again firmly countermanded the suggestion.[47]

1V

Child marriage—widespread among all castes—had produced a
very large range of child widows; quite a few who married under the
new act had been widowed at 3 or 4. Almost all of them had been
widowed by 10.[48] According to the 1891 census, widows under the
age of 10 formed 6 per cent of the total population of married
girls.[49] The preponderance of child widows, all destined to mature

<hr>

[45] Diwan Kartikeyachandra Ray, *Kshitish Bangshabali Charit*, in Kanchan
Basu, ed., *Dushprapya Sahitya Sangraha* (Calcutta: 1992).

[46] See, for instance, Maheschandra Deb, *A Sketch of the Condition of the
Hindoo Woman* (Calcutta: 1839).

[47] R.C. Majumdar, *Maharaja Rajballabh* (Calcutta: 1947), p. 91.

[48] See Sureshchandra Bandyopadhyaya, op. cit.

[49] *The Census of India, Lower Provinces of Bengal* (Calcutta: 1891).

within a regime of privation, made it imperative to construct an elaborate mechanism for the repression of their basic physical needs.

Widowhood required brutal dietary, dress, and ritual deprivations. The nineteenth century saw numerous debates on ritual niceties: since a sip of holy Ganga water was deemed compulsory before death, what were widows dying on Ekadasi day supposed to do? A late-nineteenth-century orthodox manual admitted that the lack of water drove many child widows to their death, especially in the hot summer months.[50]

The scant diet was made more restricted by the apparently aphrodisiacal properties of certain kinds of food. The widow was denied a number of pulses and vegetables that might overheat her body and stimulate unseemly desire. Her dress—a stark white and no jewellery, symbolizing her status as non-wife—was obviously aimed to maximize her unattractiveness. She was debarred from ritual ceremonies and all collective female rites that lit up the lives of other women. Most child widows would go back to their parental homes, and here a bitter irony vitiated the natal household. Married mothers would eat fish and other Bengali delicacies, would wear colourful clothes and jewellery, and would share their husbands' beds in the presence of their widowed children—who were strangers to all such pleasures. In fact, on Ekadasi days the wife was ritually commanded to have a meal with fish in order to demarcate her absolute difference from the widow.[51]

This imposed and ceaseless flagellation shows that the prescribed codes did not really expect that bereavement would by itself cause the drying up of the widow's sexual life. At the same time, she was supposed to behave as if her deprivations were voluntary. There was, thus, a constitutive tension or paradox within the widowhood regime: on the one hand an authoritative order that claimed perfect hegemony

---

[50] Ishanchandra Bidyabagish, *Ekadashivyavastha* (Boalia: 1868).

[51] See for instance, an undated nineteenth-century play in which the widowed daughters remark how their orthodox father demands that their mother comes to his bed punctually every single night, whereas he refuses to allow remarriage to the young daughters. See Anon, *Bidhaba Shukher Dasha* (Serampore: second edition, 1862).

by grounding itself in the will of the subaltern—by being interpellated within her self-understanding; on the other hand coercion and a penal regime coexisting with that, belying the hegemonic claim, and clearly revealing that widows were in fact very imperfectly positioned within the dominant ideological discipline.

Widows were, thus, doomed to a suspect existence. They were like the notified or criminal tribes of British India, whose crime lay not in the nature of individual action but in their collective social location. We find early-nineteenth-century Bengali proverbs within which the widow without a son is described as the messenger of death, her Ekadasi fast always suspect for she may sip water as she bathes in the pond. You cannot trust the woman till she is burnt to ashes and her ashes are scattered to the winds, goes another. A desperate widow can make a spouse of her granddaughter's husband, runs yet another.[52] A very large number of widows were inevitably young and nubile, if not infants, and their celibacy was always under scrutiny. For the old widow, it was more a question of enforcing ritual and dietary conformity. A paradox arose out of the domestic policing of her conduct, for her male guardians could sexually exploit the young widow and no real stigma would be attached to such behaviour. In fact, some opponents of remarriage apparently saw nothing grotesque in complaining that homes denuded of young widows would be so unattractive that men would perforce turn to brothels and thus deplete family fortunes.[53]

Male desire for the widow was not, however, always exploitative. Widows provided almost the only possible route to consensual love and self-willed romance, because the wife, married in infancy and crushed under domestic and procreative labour, was rarely a figure of romance, and the wives of other men were less responsive and less available sexually. Some men were, occasionally, more daring, or more committed. The radical young reformist Dakshinaranjan Mukhopadhyay managed to elope with a widowed queen of the Burdwan estate shortly before the law was enacted. Rammohun Roy's father was charged with adultery with another earlier queen of

[52] See Rev. James Long, ed., *Prabadmala* (Calcutta: 1872, rpnt. 1979).

[53] Tarakrishna Haldar, *Chamatkar Swapnadarshan* (Calcutta: 1868).

the same estate.[54] Obviously, these powerful women of royal house-holds enjoyed a certain licence as adult widows. Widows from more humble homes became equally forthcoming, once they had a licit end to the relationship in sight, which happened as the law came to be publicized. A rural upper-caste widow approached a young reformist in the 1860s and persuaded him to marry her even though he was in love with another widow.[55]

In the first Bengali book written by a woman, in 1856, there is a short skit in which two widows discuss the new law with great joy, and one tells the other that now they will have to proposition the men they fancy since their families won't fix up a second marriage for them.[56] Widow remarriages thus not only bestowed legal sanction on romances and initiated love marriages within Hindu conjugality, they also overturned norms of female conduct within the relationship. Desire could now, as we saw in the case cited above, be a female initiative and a female expression.

The widow was the source, by her decreed social existence, of another kind of anxiety. The laws of Manu placed her in a risky liminality: Manu recommended that the woman be dependent, non-autonomous, all her life. The very law prohibiting widow remarriage made her a being at the margins, without a guardian, inhabiting quite literally a no-man's land, especially if she did not have a son to be her guardian in old age. So, more than her sexuality, her possible autonomy made her dangerous to the domestic order. During the re-marriage discussions, advocates and opponents both made interesting use of this liminal location. The orthodoxy insisted—and the 1837 Law Commission was persuaded—that remarriage was no marriage. Marriage required the essential rite of a woman being given away from one lineage or family to another, as a gift in exchange. Her father had once given her away and thus forfeited his possession of her; she had become the property of her husband. He being dead, now there was no one to give her away, for she had no right in her

---

[54] John R. McLane, *Land and Local Kingship in Eighteenth Century Bengal* (Cambridge: 1993).

[55] Gurucharan Mahalanobis, op. cit.

[56] Krishnakamini Dasi, *Chittabilashini* (Calcutta: 1856).

own person and could not perform the ritual of *kanyadan*, or gift of the daughter. Ergo, if the marriage ritual could not be performed in its entirety, it was legally invalid.[57]

On the other hand, there is the instance of the reformer Durga-mohan Das who married off his young stepmother to his friend as they were in love with each other. Under Manu's dictum, the mother was now under his guardianship and he was entitled to give her away. Of course, very few widows were so lucky.[58] An orthodox tract branded remarriage as unnatural because it violated not sexual laws but property laws upon which the world rested—it amounted to the cultivation of a field without the consent of the rightful owner.[59] The harvested crop—the children born of the remarriage—were therefore monstrous births.[60] It was precisely here that the law made a very daring intervention. It laid down that while for infant widows a guardian would perform the marriage rites, for the adult and mature widow, her own consent was enough to legalize the nuptials.[61] The implications of a clause in the new law made over rights to her own person to herself: the woman became legally a self-possessed being. Of course, legal notions were not translated into social understanding, but they did set up cracks and fissures paving some sort of road towards a systemic unravelling of the existing order of gender.

In the 1880s a woman writer found an interesting compromise formula through which she tried to stretch out the boundaries of non-consensual marriage. She claimed that, in a girl's infancy, the father gives away her person to her husband, but he cannot own her body, and hence cannot gift it. Only when she is a desiring adult can she do so herself to the husband to whom she has been married off in infancy. This second step alone completes the marriage. Since the

[57] Petition of a thousand pandits of Bengal, 13 February 1856. Papers Relating to Act XV, op. cit.

[58] Shibnath Shastri, op. cit.

[59] Many such tracts were published. See, for instance, Hemchandra Mukhopadhyay, *Gyan Sudharnaba* (Calcutta: 1863). Or Ramdhan Tarkapanchanan Bhattacharya, *Bidhababedan Nishedhak Pustak* (Boalia: 1863).

[60] See Jogindranath Tarkachuramani, *The Remarriage of Aryan Ladies Confuted* (Calcutta: 1859).

[61] Clause 8, Act XV, op. cit.

body has remained her property, a child widow—a *virgo intacta*—can therefore later gift herself to a second husband, since she has not done so to the first, her first marriage never having been complete.[62] The parameters of non-consensual marriage are preserved in this compromise, and the only valid remarriages are of child widows. Nonetheless, an interesting distinction gets drawn here between the outer fold of the person, which is the property of a male guardian, and the sexual inner body, which the woman alone possesses. So, an area of selfhood manages to be reserved to herself, as her own belonging, this being the space of desire, of sexuality. As a wife she is compelled to direct it only at a given focus; but if that does not happen, she can choose for herself. The widow is thus able to lay claim to a larger autonomy over her life than can a wife.

Widowhood norms also expressed, as we noted earlier, a constitutive contradiction within Hindu domesticity. These norms outlawed desire for and of the widow, yet simultaneously made her a focus of desire, necessarily extra-marital, that might otherwise be directed at prostitutes. In brothels there was no certainty of reciprocity, or of meaningful relationships. Since both widow and prostitute functioned under the same sign of non-prescribed and undomesticated desire, it is no wonder that the same Bengali colloquial term (*ranrh*) denotes both kinds of women. When remarriage was suggested, there was an explosion of obscene writings that lampooned the lustful widow. The dominant trope was that of the natural and the unnatural. If the widow is allowed to fulfil her 'natural' desire, asked a tract, what of the father who may lust after his nubile daughter?[63]

The desiring widow, moreover, offended the economy of hypergamous marriages where girls competed for pure-caste men. She was counterposed in plays and tracts to childlike and innocent wives and virgin unmarried daughters who would not be able to

---

[62] A brahman woman wrote this from Baharampore to *Sanjibani*, 27 Baisakh 1292 (AD 1884). See Kanailal Chattopadhyay, ed., *Samayikpatre Samajchitra: Sanjibani* (Calcutta: 1989), p. 153.

[63] Prasannakumar Sharma, *Bidhababibaha Shastrabiruddha* (Mymensingh: 1887); Koylash Chunder Tarkaratna, *Ritimul* (Hooghly: 1862); Tarakrishna Haldar, *Chamatkar Swapnadarshan* (Calcutta: 1868).

match her wily, adult manipulations and pungent sexuality, and who would lose out in the marriage market.[64] What is more interesting is that even songs and plays that applauded the reform veered very close to the obscene and the ridiculous even as they tried to characterize a widow who wanted to remarry: even as they endorsed her desire, their representation of her legitimated desire still carried a tinge of the salacious, the dubious. There was a gap—a distance between social ideas on the one hand and an adequate vocabulary or expressive codes on the other. The most influential play advocating remarriage shows an inner tension as a widow tries to express her sexual ache and needs in a romantic vein. Her friend, appalled and uncomprehending, insistently translates her words on the register of crude and mindless lust.[65] The powerful radical reformer Shibnath Shastri, a great pillar of strength for the cause, wrote novels that spoke of the painful lives of widows and at the same time applauded her will to celibacy: the widow who remarries is admirable but not the widow who obviously does so out of sexual hunger.[66]

One of the major beneficial effects of the law, and the official legalization of such desire, was the gradual absorption of love and widowhood within the framework of licit romance, their distancing from the register of salacious scandal and pulp satire. Some of the greatest novels of the nineteenth and early-twentieth centuries are about the love of and for widows.[67] In these the seriousness of the love is in fact measured by its explosive and disruptive impact on the normative order.

V

Since the normative order was so fraught with tension between its own discipline and the certainty of transgression, it prescribed very

[64] Jogendrachandra Basu, *Chinibas Charitamrita* (Calcutta: n.d.).

[65] Umeschandra Mitra, *Bidhababibaha Natak* (Calcutta: 1856).

[66] See a discussion in Sunitiranjan Raychoudhury, *Unisher Shatake Nabya Hindu Andoloner Kayekjan Nayak* (Calcutta: 1981), p. 123. See also Ramdulal Basu, *Bankimchandrer Samasamayik Gauna Oupanyasik* (Calcutta: 1981), pp. 54–130.

[67] Bankimchandra Chattopadhyay, *Bishabriksha* (Calcutta: 1873), and Rabindranath Tagore, *Chokher Bali* (Calcutta: 1903), among many others.

severe penalties for defiance. There were ritual penalties, often sanctioned by formal caste councils, that punished the entire family with loss of caste status for such shameful things. This, in turn, made familial policing of the widow's conduct and punishments more stringent. Secret abortions or infanticides were staggeringly numerous among widows. Ranajit Guha has studied the death of a young untouchable widow who died of a botched abortion in 1849. Ironically, this widow belonged to a caste that was not only exempted from the ban but even infamous for its supposed sexual permissiveness.[68] Murders were quite a common penalty. One of the late-nineteenth-century reformers, Dwarkanath Ganguly, became involved in the remarriage movement when his childhood friend, a brahman widow, died under suspicious circumstances and he discovered that her family had punished her illicit pregnancy with poisoning. His investigations in the same village exposed scores of such deaths over the previous ten years.[69] A Calcutta coroner reported in 1886 on the death of a young widow who had been married at 10 and widowed at 13. She had been thrown out of her natal and matrimonial homes and, somewhere during her search for shelter, had become pregnant. She found no one to help her as she went from door to door among relatives and kinsmen, men and women. Eventually, she came to her old and abandoned ancestral home to die alone at night of a miscarriage or a self-induced abortion. Right across the street, at that very moment, her wealthy relatives were living in their new house. The coroner concluded his report: 'The body was on the bare floor, with a bundle of dirty clothes under her head . . . otherwise she was quite nude . . . these clothes were all matted with blood . . . There was no food, water nor an ordinary lamp . . . Although recently decided by the High Court that a Hindu widow has a legal right to share in the property of her . . . husband, even if she be unchaste, this poor woman was literally hunted from house to house.'[70] The

<hr>

[68] Ranajit Guha, 'Chandra's Deatha', in Guha, ed., *Subaltern Studies V* (Delhi: 1987).

[69] Shibnath Shastri, op. cit.

[70] Bidisha Chakravarty, *Sarkari Nathite Unish Shataker Banglar Nari* (Calcutta: 2002).

act, obviously, had not disrupted the penal regime of social ostracism. It is important to underline these secret killings, the terror and the violence that were the consequences of the normative order which colonial law feebly tried to counteract. Far too often, violence in colonial times is located entirely within the state, with tradition and custom taken as signs of resistance, or as subaltern opposition to the politics of the state.

VI

Normative discipline further protected itself by rendering the widow economically vulnerable. Rammohun Roy, who had agitated against widow-burning, had written of her financial helplessness. It is very significant that, in his writing on the issue, the word 'rights' was used in its modern sense, perhaps for the first time by an Indian.[71] Even though the customary law allowed her usufruct rights to the husband's share of property, she was most often cheated of it, and the law gave her no part in her father's property. Her survival depended on grudging charity and the barest maintenance. Until 1855 she could be legally excluded from her matrimonial home if she left it to find a kinder shelter at her father's home.[72] And until 1873, any hint of 'unchastity' after widowhood would ensure an end to her usufruct property entitlement.[73] Since widows with adult sons fared far better, childless younger widows were the most vulnerable. Reformers and officials were embarrassed to find a disproportionately large number of brahman widows in Calcutta brothels.[74] Later, as census

---

[71] Rammohun was obliged to make a case that ancient scripture allowed the widow more secure property rights whereas her present vulnerability was a function of recent custom. *Brief Remarks Regarding Modern Encroachments on the Ancient Rights of Females*, in Kalidas Nag and Debajyoti Burman, eds, *The English Works of Raja Rammohun Roy*, Part 1 (Calcutta: 1945).

[72] The Privy Council granted her the right in a decision in August 1855. *Hindoo Patriot*, 3 August 1855.

[73] This was reversed in the landmark judgment over the Kerry Kolitani Case of 1873. It is remarkable that a notion of the absolute right of private property forced a breach in the order of Hindu norms.

[74] Reformers tried to respond to orthodox charges that remarriage was gross

figures were circulated, the question of enforced widowhood produced anxieties over declining Hindu numbers. The community, it was feared, would lose widows through conversion and elopement with Muslims—who allowed remarriage.[75]

It was not even simply a question of widows' property rights, for the remarriage debates also revolved very largely around orthodox opposition to the inheritance rights of sons born of remarriage—which the law underwrote. The orthodox argued that such sons were of polluted origin and could not be allowed to override the superior claims of pure born even if more distant male heirs. Moreover, property rights allowed such impure sons full incorporation within the joint family which, however, considered itself polluted even if one person within the family had different views or had married a widow. In short, Hindu marriage, succession, and inheritance were collective, lineage decisions, they argued, whereas the state had operated on a narrowly individualistic basis in thinking the law affected only two partners.[76]

The only category of sons who could inherit their father's property, said the orthodox, were either *dattak*—adopted—or *auras*, born of the legal father. A *pounarbhaba*—the son of a second relationship by his mother—was excluded from that right. Interestingly, the literal sense of the Sanskrit word *auras* is 'one born of his father's seed'. But so entrenched was the notion of the illegitimacy of the natural father who produced a male heir via marriage to a widow that the term could not be used to describe the pounarbhaba, even though he was born of his father's seed.[77] Vidyasagar unearthed a passage in an ancient law code that mentioned only dattak and auras as categories of

---

immorality by a counter-charge that precisely its absence stimulated immorality and sinfulness: prostitution and infanticide were directly related to enforced and unnatural celibacy. See petitions on both sides in Papers Related to Act XV, op. cit.

[75] Pradip K. Datta, *Carving Blocs: Communal Ideology in Early Twentieth Century Bengal* (Delhi: 1999).

[76] Petition of a thousand pandits, 13 February 1856, op. cit.

[77] Ibid. See also Prasannakumar Sharma, op. cit.

sons known in Kaliyuga: it did not mention the category of pounar-bhaba. He stretched this to argue that this meant, in present times, that the category of pounarbhaba had been engrossed within the category of auras—the legal heir. The new law should therefore entitle the sons born of remarriage to their fathers' property.[78] The colonial government accepted Vidyasagar's interpretation. The law, however, tried to disarm orthodox opposition by laying down that the remarried widow would forfeit all rights to the first husband's property on remarriage, even though many low castes allowed widows to remarry and hold on to the first husband's property. Legally, they now lost that right, and later many widows went on to lodge lawsuits claiming inheritance on the basis of caste custom. Different high courts had different responses to this situation, but sometimes they did argue that the law should be 'most enabling', only conferring new rights and not abolishing existing ones.[79]

The law was far less favourable in another respect. The remarried widow lost all custodial rights to the children by her first marriage.[80] Strangely, there was no opposition to this provision. There may even have been an unspoken acceptance in reformist minds that widows with children should additionally forfeit sexual desire, alongside property rights and custody of their children by the first marriage—so powerful was the hegemony of orthodoxy at the time in relation to widows.

VII

The trope of 'littleness' was very much in evidence within reformist discourse. To argue their case for remarriage, they evoked the image

[78] Vidyasagar, *Bidhababibaha Prachalita Hoya Uchit Ki Na*, op. cit. For a refutation, see Pitambar Sen, *Bidhababibahanishedh* (Calcutta: 1875).

[79] Lucy Carroll, 'Law, Custom and Statutory Reform: The Hindu Widows' Remarriage Act of 1856', in J. Krishnamurty, ed., *Women in Colonial India: Essays on Survival, Work and the State* (Delhi: 1989). In this pathbreaking essay, however, Carroll takes it for granted that actually existing customary rights were being withheld. It could also be the case that such rights were being invented or dormant ones reactivated by widows in the law courts.

[80] Act XV, op. cit.

of a frail, tiny girl who does not know she has lost the world because it is lost even before she knows what the world is. When he introduced the bill to the Legislative Council, Grant eloquently described 'a little prattling girl of five years old, taken from her dolls and her toys . . . into widowhood'.[81] To mobilize support for widow remarriage, and to disarm opposition via shame and guilt about cruelty to innocents, Vidyasagar persistently used this pathetic figure of a little innocent girl. In fact, there was a strong chance that, had he restricted his campaign to the marriage of virgin widows, he would have mustered a wide consensus, for quite a few orthodox pandits were prepared to concede him that much.[82] But Vidyasagar did not use that loophole and resolutely refused to impose any ceiling on either age or sexual experience. He personally conducted the marriage of several post-pubertal widows, and when his son Narayan decided to marry one he was overjoyed.[83] The support he obtained for the remarriage of adult and sexually experienced widows meant that he sank an icepick into the foundational norm of absolute female monogamy, ruining the orthodox view of woman's entitlement to only a single sexual relationship in one lifetime. Depriving women of both the right to divorce and the right to remarry, the Hindu marriage system had decreed a condition of the most perfect female subordination. Vidyasagar's recommendation of remarriage even after one or more sexual connections in previous marriages threatened that cornerstone of an entire system of power. This was the wider and far more radical collateral damage caused to orthodoxy even by a limited legislation. With this breach, the unravelling of an entire system of gender oppression became possible.

[81] Legislative Assembly Proceedings, op. cit., 17 November 1855.

[82] Rajballabh in the eighteenth century, and Shyamacharan Das Karmakar in 1845 had pleaded for the remarriage of *akshatayoni* child widows. They had both mobilized a considerable number of pandits on their side. Some of the petitioners who opposed the bill, granted that remarriage for child widows was a valid possibility. A number of tracts and newspapers made the same point, while being totally opposed to the idea of remarriage for widows who had enjoyed a sexual relationship with their husbands. See Papers Related to Act XV, op. cit. Also Kantichandra Rarhi, op. cit. Also *Sambad Prabhakar*, 1 Baisakh 1855.

[83] See Shambhucharan Vidyaratna, op. cit.

Vidyasagar's opponents contested his selection of Parashara as the supreme textual authority for their times. They said he had wrongly translated and interpreted the passage, and that Manu was a higher authority than Parashara. But Vidyasagar had mastered the skills of Sanskrit scholastic argumentation better than them, and one by one they fell silent. They could not even argue effectively against his sleight of hand: whatever was cited in sacred texts as the sign of a degenerate age, including sexual laxity, he translated as an ideal behavioural code for the times. Dystopia was transposed into a kind of utopia. Vidyasagar also used a loophole in the Bengal legal-judicial model. Although the colonial state had decreed that both sacred texts and custom would be seen as sources of personal law, Bengali judges and legislators respected written texts more than custom. In this sense, they were different from their counterparts in the Bombay Presidency and Punjab. Vidyasagar repeatedly told them that ancient texts allowed remarriage, and that later custom had countermanded the practice.

Moreover, he had mastered the skills of conduct in the public sphere. As founder of a serviceable, polished Bengali prose, he wrote his tracts in Bengali, saying he wrote for mass education 'in a language that is accessible to the people at large'.[84] In contrast, the language of orthodox tracts was clumsy, stilted, burdensomely Sanskritized, full of untranslated Sanskrit passages. Orthodox petitions were often written in Sanskrit, and those in Bengali would now and then use Sanskrit signs. Obviously, their vernacular was awkward, not yet a tool for persuasion: it was unequal to the democratic potential of reformist writings. Before the wave of reformist enthusiasm in villages could be stamped out, a number of low- and artisanal-caste people from district towns and villages signed petitions in favour of the bill, whereas most of the orthodox petitioners were brahmans or upper castes.

Vidyasagar was also skilled in the art of lobbying. He had met Colville and when he persuaded Grant to introduce the bill he already had a massive petition to hand over in November 1855. In contrast, the orthodox mobilization started late. The first petition arrived only on 13 February 1856. By that time a flood of reformist petitions

---

[84] Vidyasagar, op. cit., p. 21.

and newspaper articles had been organized, so that the government was fully convinced that the reformers represented a very substantial body of Hindu opinion. Finally, the orthodoxy reactivated the Dharma Sabha which had become defunct after the sati debates, and managed to get together a signature campaign that outnumbered reformists by a huge margin. But the legislative will in favour of the law was already in place.

VIII

Vidyasagar sought to persuade the state that remarriage was scriptural and that it merely violated false custom. He tried to disarm orthodoxy by pointing out the harm that prohibition did to orthodox morality: secret liaison, foeticide, infanticide. But that was not all. He stepped beyond his strict brief often and passionately: 'The sages wanted the same laws for men and women', he argued. In the name of such sages he posited legal equality, which pandits refuted by referring to the theory of *anupatabad*—entitlements according to merit whereby women are fated to receive less than men. Vidyasagar also put a question mark against a cardinal rule of Hindu conjugality: namely, that women are expected to lose desire when the legitimate source of desire is gone. He said: 'You think their bodies turn to stone as soon as they are widowed . . . that they become immune to desire . . . alas, in this land men have no compassion, no virtue, they do not know what is right and what is wrong . . . they only know what is custom. Let no woman be born in such a land any more. Alas our women! For what sin in your past births are you sent to be born in Bharatbarsha?'[85]

The query seemed innocent, indeed, naïve, but it was nonetheless deeply mischievous in relation to the orthodox. Putting them on the back foot it compelled them to admit what needed to be kept implicit: that the rules were different for men and women, and for no obvious reason. His question, in a sense, castrated the existing sexual double standards and exposed orthodox piety as ideology.

[85] Ibid.

Where did this passion come from? Vidyasagar's was a life that left a massive pile of biographies and popular anecdotes in its wake.[86] A number of them derive his reformist concern from either his mother's command, as she melted with pity at the sight of a child widow, or from his own copious weeping as he came across one.[87] Obviously, a direct, immediate, personal experience was preferred as the authentic source of compassion and reformist conviction rather than commitment to an intellectual notion of rights and justice. The reformer had to be both a suffering subject and compassionate saviour figure, the latter conjugated from the former.[88] There was, however, yet another step, one that went unnoticed or unexplained in Bengali commemorations: the element of anger, of enraged activism, of guilt at male privilege. It was guilt and anger that saved Vidyasagar's words from a bland, protectionist paternalism.

But it was not only the commemorations that personalized his reformist impulse and made his politics a matter of somewhat narrow experiential imperative. Vidyasagar himself came close to representing himself thus, on occasion. He came to see the reform so much as his own handiwork that, at least once, he demanded that he decide when and to whom it could be granted. When the parents of a widow came to him in huge distress in his native village and asked him to prevent her remarriage, which was planned by his son and brother, he was seized with pity and promised them it would not happen. Vidyasagar's relatives, however, defied his order and secretly married her off. Discovering this, he flew into a rage, and left the village, vowing never to return to a place where his pledge had been dishonoured.[89] To remarry or not to remarry seemed to him, in this case, a matter within his personal dispensation, a decision entailing two kinds of pity— for the parents and for the girl—that had to be weighed against each other by him. These involved a trade-off between his reformism and

[86] Sumit Sarkar, 'Vidyasagar and Brahmanical Society', op. cit.

[87] Chandicharan Bandyaoadhyaya and Shambhucharan Vidyaratna, op. cit.

[88] On this, also see Dipesh Chakrabarty, *Provincialising Europe* (Delhi, 2000).

[89] Shambhucharan Vidyaratna, op. cit.

his word of honour—and both belonged to him. Remarriage, then, was grounded in his decision, and was not something that belonged irrevocably to man and woman.

IX

When women begin to publish their writings, they used much of the basic reformist vocabulary. Often, however, accusation of men broadened into an explicit accusation of custom, religion, families. Bamasundari Dasi, in 1861, railed against the want of basic compassion among Hindus,[90] and Kailashbashini Debi in 1863 talked about Ekadasi cruelties.[91] In 1905, a Muslim woman spoke of the 'heartless, ruthless treatment of widows' among Hindus.[92] In 1875, a woman wrote a poem: 'I will dance a wild dance and I will cry out / Custom, go meet your death / Hindus, you are worse than animals / Since you call cruelty your religion / Do you have no morality, nor a bit of shame / How dare you call Muslims butchers?'[93]

On the other side of the divide, Hindu orthodoxy employed savage satire to poke fun at widows' desires. The most cited argument against remarriage was that it would encourage women to murder unattractive and elderly husbands. They would be led astray by their innate depravity, for they had no education to understand the baseness of such instincts.[94] It is interesting that these orthodox arguments are based on a clear-sighted understanding of the faultlines in the prescriptive discipline: the prevention of education among women and asymmetrical marriages.

[90] Bamasundari Dasi, 'What Are the Superstitions that Must Be Removed from the Betterment of Our Country?' Reproduced in Malini Bhattacharya and Abhijit Sen, eds, *Talking of Power: Early Writings of Women in Bengal* (Calcutta: Stree, 2004).

[91] *Hindu Mahilaganer Heenabastha* (Calcutta, 1863).

[92] Begum Rokeya Sakhawat Hossein, 'Naripuja', in Malini Bhattacharya, op. cit.

[93] Brajabala Debi, 'Ami Ki Unmadini?' in *Bangamahila*, cited in Ghulam Murshid, *Samaj Sanskar Andolan O Bangla Natak* (Dacca, 1997).

[94] See papers Related to Act XV, op. cit. Also *Jagacchandra Guha*, Ranrher Biye Dismiss, Calcutta, 1867. Or Umeshchandra Mukhopadhyay, *Puna Punah, Arthat Bidhababibahe Sheshphal* (Dacca, 1869).

But the arguments began to change over time. Conservatives, too, came to build on the notion of female love spontaneously given. Celibate widowhood was now removed from the register of custom, law, routine, and transvalued as aching pain for a beloved husband, as the self-chosen abdication of all pleasure for a life that could find no pleasure in anything any more.[95] Widowhood was translated as *viraha*, the trope of classical literature which lyricizes the longing for an absent lover. Ritual was rewritten as love. It was also reinvented as a national icon, an indigenous aesthetic principle. The dramatist Amritalal Basu wrote a poem about his dying mother who refused medicine and water on Ekadasi day;

> The Bengali widow surpasses all goddesses in her sacred aura
> Never demolish this precious image, never wipe out this wondrous
>   painting
> The poet entreats you.[96]

The plea is meant for reformers, about to turn the beauty of chaste widowhood into dross.

Once widowhood was relocated on the register of love for the dead husband, as an icon of grave beauty, remarriage as an idea lost some of its emotional edge. To want to remarry in this new rhetorical environment would be tantamount to a declaration that the first marriage had been empty of love. At the same time, it is most interesting that custom and scripture survived and outwitted law by attaching themselves to the notion of freely willed love.

Reformers and orthodoxy were now unified in the sovereignty of love.

---

[95] Anon, *Bidhaba Bangabala* (Calcutta, n.d.) The frontispiece says 'Where do you get a more precious woman than the widow of Bengal'.

[96] Cited in Kalyani Datta, op. cit., p. 2.

5

SUBTLE SUBVERSIONS AND PRESUMPTUOUS INTERVENTIONS: REFORMING WOMEN'S HEALTH IN BHOPAL STATE IN THE EARLY TWENTIETH CENTURY

Siobhan Lambert-Hurley

Historians of colonial India have taken up the theme of women's health only recently, after previously focusing on education, work, political organization and nationalism as these related to women and gender. In Geraldine Forbes' otherwise excellent *Women in Modern India*, for instance, women's health issues are discussed only fleetingly, primarily in the context of the opening of medical careers to Indian women from the late nineteenth century.[1] Contributors to Kumkum Sangari and Sudesh Vaid's groundbreaking work, *Recasting Women*, also failed to draw out this issue in any detail, even as they sought to relate gender difference to

---

This essay is a revised version of ch. 5 in my book, *Muslim Women, Reform and Princely Patronage: Nawab Sultan Jahan Begam of Bhopal* (London: Routledge, 2007).

[1] Geraldine Forbes, *Women in Modern India* (Cambridge: Cambridge University Press, 1996), pp. 161–7.

a wider set of social relations.[2] This omission may perhaps be linked to the association of women's health with reproduction and motherhood, a topic not deemed worthy of discussion by the Western feminists who were at the forefront of developing women's history as a genre from the 1970s. That said, there has been a conscious, if belated, effort in the last few years to make up for that earlier neglect of the historical experiences of women as mothers through a burgeoning of writing on maternity, childbirth, and child welfare in a variety of colonial and postcolonial settings.[3] Yet, as in relation to other themes, Muslim women in India remain largely invisible to this discourse, with only preliminary efforts being made to examine their engagement with Western or indigenous systems of medicine, despite what it might tell us about women's 'everyday resistance' to gendered colonial discourses and contemporary patriarchal structures.[4]

[2] Kumkum Sangari and Sudesh Vaid (eds), *Recasting Women: Essays in Colonial India* (New Delhi: Kali for Women, 1989).

[3] See, for instance, Kalpana Ram and Margaret Jolly (eds), *Maternities and Modernities: Colonial and Postcolonial Experiences in Asia and the Pacific* (Cambridge: Cambridge University Press, 1998). On the Indian context, see P. Jeffrey, R. Jeffrey, and A. Lyon, *Labour Pains and Labour Power: Women and Childbearing in India* (London: Zed Books, 1989); Geraldine Forbes, 'Managing Midwifery in India', in Dagmar Engels and Shula Marks (eds), *Contesting Colonial Hegemony: State and Society in Africa and India* (London: British Academic Press, 1994), pp. 152–72; Dagmar Engels, *Beyond Purdah? Women in Bengal, 1890–1939* (New Delhi: Oxford University Press, 1996), ch. 4; Supriya Guha, 'A History of the Medicalization of Childbirth in Bengal in the Late Nineteenth and Early Twentieth Century' (unpublished PhD thesis, University of Calcutta, 1996); and Cecilia Van Hollen, *Birth on the Threshold: Childbirth and Modernity in South India* (Berkeley: University of California Press, 2003). Also see Barbara Ramusack's forthcoming publications on the topic.

[4] For what has been done, see ch. 3 of Azra Asghar Ali's *The Emergence of Feminism Among Indian Muslim Women 1920–1947* (Karachi: Oxford University Press, 2000) on 'Opening a Public Space for Women: The Role of Health Care Arrangements'; and ch. 5 of Guy Attewell's 'Authority, Knowledge and Practice in Unani Tibb in India, *c.* 1890–1930' (Unpublished PhD thesis, University of London, 2004) on 'Treating Women: Women's Engagement with Unani Tibb and its Engagement with Women in Early Twentieth-Century India'.

This essay aims to further this process by focusing on women's health reforms in the princely state of Bhopal in Central India in the early twentieth century. This historical setting provides a unique location in which to explore this volume's aims, as they relate to gender and power relations in South Asian history and society, in that, as a princely state, Bhopal's position within the imperial hierarchy was defined by the system of paramountcy. What this meant, in simple terms, was that it—along with nearly 600 other principalities—retained its own rulers, system of law, and even rudimentary military force, but sacrificed control of its foreign affairs to the British government and accepted the appointment of a resident British adviser as a result of a 'treaty of friendship and co-operation' that was signed with the East India Company in the early nineteenth century.[5] Perhaps even more pertinent to this historiographical context is that, thanks to a lack of male heirs and a seeming female penchant for administration within the ruling family, Bhopal was ruled by a succession of Muslim women throughout the nineteenth and early twentieth centuries. The last of these Nawab Begams, Sultan Jahan (1858–1930; ruled 1901–26), was renowned throughout India and beyond for her efforts to improve the status of women, particularly in the sphere of education, though also in relation to other spheres. To that end, she not only wrote extensively on female education, veiling and women's rights in the form of reformist tracts, advice manuals, and allegorical stories, but she also established and patronized myriad girls' schools, women's organizations, and other public institutions in Bhopal and beyond.[6]

[5] For a more detailed discussion of Bhopal and paramountcy, see my 'Princes, Paramountcy and the Politics of Muslim Identity: The Begam of Bhopal on the Indian National Stage, 1901–1926', *South Asia: Journal of South Asian Studies* 26: 2 (2003), pp. 169–95. A broader overview of paramountcy may be found in Ian Copland, *The Princes of India in the Endgame of Empire 1917–1947* (Cambridge: Cambridge University Press, 1997), ch. 2.

[6] For more on these activities, see my *Muslim Women, Reform and Princely Patronage: Nawab Sultan Jahan Begam of Bhopal* (London: Routledge, 2007), as well as my 'Fostering Sisterhood: Muslim Women and the All-India Ladies' Association', *Journal of Women's History* 16:2 (summer 2004), pp. 40–65; and

Also attracting the last Begam's interest was the cause of reforming women's health. An analysis of her writings and activities on this topic draws attention to three interrelated layers of hegemonic power and what may just be called 'resistance'—or, perhaps better, 'subversion'. I make this point on the basis that the delicate manner in which it was parleyed means that, more often than not, the struggle was, in the language of this volume's Introduction, 'hardly visible'. The first layer and, hence, section of this essay addresses Sultan Jahan Begam's creative adaptation of the colonial discourse on health, specifically as it was associated with professionalization and the medicalization of obstetrics. To illustrate this point, I concentrate on the revival of unani medicine in Bhopal state, as well as the ruling Begam's rejection of the 'dangerous *dai*' mantra, as it was omnipresent in British India. The next section then looks at Bhopali women's manipulation of indigenous patriarchal structures, as they were inherent in Islam and the reformist agenda, through the assertion of women's agency and autonomy. In other words, I focus on the idea that these women were taking charge of their own health and, in turn, their own bodies by learning basic medicine, becoming practitioners, and even teaching others. In fulfilment of this latter point, the third section discusses elite Muslim women's attempts to dominate each other and poorer women in Bhopal, while also seeking to recover any resistance to this process—for example, by gauging responses to the ruling Begam's programme to educate mothers. In positing women as perpetrators, as well as dissenters, and breaking down the category of 'woman' along lines of wealth and status, this case thus points to the complexity of female negotiations with existing power structures, particularly within the distinct colonial context of a princely state.

Echoing the Memsahib's Mantra?

By the late nineteenth century, the process of rationalizing women's health care was well under way in Britain with midwives and other

---

'Out of India: The Journeys of the Begam of Bhopal, 1901–1930', *Women's Studies' International Forum* 21:3 (June 1998), pp. 263–76.

female healers having been discredited through centuries of vilification, nurses receiving professional training in the Florence Nightingale image, and women doctors even beginning to graduate from the London School of Medicine for Women.[7] The need for this process was tied to concerns about depopulation, as high rates of infant mortality were understood to be shrinking the labour pool—and particularly the *male* labour pool—on which the British industrial economy relied. These anxieties in the metropole were transferred to India and other colonial settings where government officials, missionaries, and other colonial sympathizers spread the message of improving women's health, particularly through the medicalization of obstetrics. Yet, as Foucault and others have argued, this interest in maternity and child welfare cannot be reduced to depopulation alone, given concerns about the extension of government power and control, particularly into the 'dark' reaches of the zenana, acting as an underlying factor.[8] The primary agent of this colonial project in Bhopal was the Agency Surgeon, who managed an allopathic hospital at the British cantonment at Sehore and toured a circuit of dispensaries, promoting vaccination and other forms of Western medicine. Also involved through their programme of 'zenana visiting' in the state were representatives of the Friends' Foreign Mission Association—though, as I have argued elsewhere, their efforts should not be implicated in the imperial agenda to the degree of other missionaries on account of their Quaker ideology of egalitarianism as it applied to gender, class, and racial hierarchies.[9]

[7] Antoinette Burton, 'Contesting the Zenana: The Mission to Make "Lady Doctors for India", 1874–1885', *Journal of British Studies* 35:3 (July 1996), 368–97; Rosemary Fitzgerald, ' "Making and Moulding the Nursing of the Indian Empire": Recasting Nurses in Colonial India', in Avril A. Powell and Siobhan Lambert-Hurley (eds), *Rhetoric and Reality: Gender and the Colonial Experience in South Asia* (New Delhi: Oxford University Press, 2006), pp. 185–222; and van Hollen, *Birth on the Threshold*, p. 40.

[8] Michel Foucault, *Discipline and Punish: The Birth of the Prison*, trans. A. Sheridan (New York: Vintage Books, 1979). In the Indian context, see David Arnold, *Colonizing the Body: State Medicine and Epidemic Disease in Nineteenth-Century India* (Berkeley: University of California Press, 1993).

[9] See my 'An Embassy of Equality? Quaker Missionaries in Bhopal State, 1890–1930', in Powell and Lambert-Hurley, *Rhetoric and Reality*, pp. 247–81.

At the national level in India, this focus on maternal health led to the establishment of two government-supported, though not fully funded, institutions intended to bring Western biomedicine to Indian women, namely, the National Association for Supplying Female Medical Aid to the Women of India (known as the Dufferin Fund after the Countess of Dufferin who acted as its patron) and the Victoria Memorial Scholarship Fund. The first was established in 1885 with the aim of providing medical women who could attend to India's female population, believed to be unwilling to visit male doctors due to the constraints of purdah. The second was a spin-off focused on training indigenous midwives (or *dais*) in Western medical methods and sanitary procedures, largely as a 'stopgap' measure until they could be replaced with women doctors and nurses who would oversee births in hospitals.[10] As Geraldine Forbes has noted, these projects received the effusive support of 'famous and titled Indians', including reformers, nationalists, and princely rulers, who shared the colonial government's views on modern science as a means of 'civilizing'—India—or perhaps simply sought the titles and imperial favours that could be awarded for supporting the vicereine's scheme.[11] This reality has led Cecilia Van Hollen to argue, in line with Lata Mani's position on sati, that women's health was the 'grounds', rather than the 'subject', of colonial and nationalist discourses on childbirth.[12]

Yet some women, notably the Begam of Bhopal, did seek to resist or at least reclaim this discourse through selective accommodation and creative adaptation of Western medical ideas. Perhaps the best example of this process involves her establishment of a medical school in her state, known as the Asfia School, intended to train indigenous medical practitioners, or *hakims*, in unani tibb. This indigenous system of medicine, originating in a Greco-Arabic tradition but enriched in the Indian environment through contact with

[10] Van Hollen, *Birth on the Threshold*, p. 53. Also see Maneesha Lal, 'The Politics of Gender and Medicine in Colonial India: The Countess of Dufferin's Fund, 1885–8', *Bulletin of the History of Medicine* 68: 1, pp. 29–66.

[11] Forbes, 'Managing Midwifery', p. 159.

[12] Van Hollen, *Birth on the Threshold*, pp. 37, 55. On sati, see Lata Mani, *Contentious Traditions: The Debate on Sati in Colonial India* (Berkeley: University of California Press, 1998).

ayurvedic specialists, had, as has been documented by David Arnold, been unscrupulously discredited by the colonial power in the nineteenth century.[13] But the ruling Begam recognized its continuing popularity with the majority of her subjects, asserting in her autobiography that it had endured for two reasons: 'The first is the fact of the people having been using it successfully for centuries, and the second is the comparative cheapness of the Unani drugs which is a great consideration with the poor classes.'[14] At the same time, she realized that there were problems with it as it stood, largely due to the lack of assured standards of practice and the neglect of surgery, this activity usually being left in Bhopal to 'clever barbers.'[15] The response of the Central India Agency's Medical Officer to this poor standard of unani treatment was, typical of colonial officers, to recommend that 'native' physicians be retired and replaced with allopathic doctors.[16] The Begam's reaction, on the other hand, was to make a diploma from the Bhopal institution, including a course in surgery, a requirement for state medical employees, thus reconciling a traditional style of treatment with modern methods.[17]

Efforts were also made to cultivate other unani facilities in the state. Realizing that unani medicines sold in the Bhopal bazaar were of poor quality, Sultan Jahan Begam established a state shop under the direct supervision of the chief physician, Hakim Noor-ul-Hasan, to sell goods that were not 'inferior or adulterated'.[18] Over thirty unani dispensaries were also maintained by the state, most of which were in the *mofussil*, where they were accessible to the bulk of the

[13] Arnold, *Colonizing the Body*, pp. 43–58.

[14] Sultan Jahan Begam, *An Account of My Life*, vol. II, trans. Abdus Samad Khan (Bombay: The Times Press, 1922), p. 142.

[15] Ibid., p. 143. For comparison with the efforts of Hakim Ajmal Khan, see Barbara Metcalf, 'Nationalist Muslims in British India: The Case of Hakim Ajmal Khan', *Modern Asian Studies* 19:1 (1985), pp. 1–28.

[16] 'Copy of remarks made by the Administrative Medical Officer in Central India [V. Harrington]', National Archives of India (New Delhi), hereafter NAI(ND), Government of India, hereafter GOI, Bhopal Political Agency, hereafter BPA, no. 12, 1905.

[17] Sultan Jahan, *Account*, vol. II, pp. 141–6.

[18] Ibid., p. 147.

population, including rural women. Indeed, the unani system of medicine grew in popularity throughout the reign of the Begam to such a degree that, on average, another dispensary was opened in the state each year. By the 1920s, it had become so prevalent that as many as seven new dispensaries were opened in 1921, replacing nine allopathic dispensaries that had previously existed. The Agency Surgeon assigned to the state complained bitterly about this change, suggesting that the Begam may wish to reconsider her decision and reopen them. But Bhopal's Political Secretary defended her actions on the basis that the unani system was highly favoured by the state's subjects.[19] The legitimacy of his claim is apparent from the records of attendance at various medical institutions: over twice as many patients visited unani dispensaries as did European-style hospitals and dispensaries.[20] It was also noted in the administrative report of 1920, in a patent case of 'everyday resistance', that 'most of the people in the district simply refuse to be treated by the allopathic system'.[21] Clearly, the ruling Begam had been able to rejuvenate a long-standing medical tradition in her state despite colonial opposition, placing Bhopal at the centre of a reformist Muslim and later nationalist project to revive unani tibb.[22]

Another example of subversion of colonial medical discourse that relates more explicitly to this volume's focus on women involved Sultan Jahan Begam's plan, realized in 1909, to begin a class in Bhopal city to train women that belonged to the hereditary dai caste. This scheme, projected as being in line with the aims of the Victoria Memorial Scholarship Fund, was initiated when all of the traditional

[19] C.B. McConaghy, Agency Surgeon, to Haidar Abbasi, Political Secretary, 24 October 1921; and Abbasi to McConaghy, 25 October 1921, National Archives of India (Bhopal), hereafter NAI(B), Bhopal State Records, hereafter BSR, no. 11 (B. 72), 1921.

[20] See, for example, *Administration Report of Bhopal State, 1912–1913* (Bhopal: Qudsia Press, 1916), p. 19. In that year, over 300,000 patients were treated in unani dispensaries, as compared to just over 100,000 patients in European-style hospitals.

[21] 'Administration Report of 1920', in NAI(ND), GOI, BPA no. 289, 1920.

[22] For the significance of unani tibb to these wider debates, see Metcalf, 'Nationalist Muslims in British India', pp. 1–28.

birthing attendants in Bhopal city were called, along with their daughters, to attend classes at the Lady Lansdowne Hospital, a purdah women's hospital established in the state in 1891. Classes were given by the superintendent, a Mrs F.D. Barnes MD, or a member of her medical team, women's attendance being assured through the provision of a monthly stipend. Once they were 'properly trained' and examined by an officer of the Indian Medical Service, they were granted a certificate without which they could not practise their profession legally in the state. This compulsory instruction and registration process, intended to prevent those unnecessary injuries or even deaths attributed to untrained dais, was more rigorous than anything to be found at the time in larger princely states, like Hyderabad or Gwalior, or even British India.[23] The effect was that it took only until 1914 before the last and most elderly of the indigenous dais in Bhopal city completed their training.[24] This success in the capital meant that several European and Anglo-Indian midwives were then hired by the state in subsequent years to provide instruction to dais in regional centres, including Ashta, Raisen, and Ichhawar. In a reversal of the perhaps expected course of medical knowledge from colonial state to colonial subject, the agents of the British crown in Bhopal, namely, the Political Agent and the Agency Surgeon, also followed the Begam's lead by starting a class in Sehore in 1917 to provide instruction to Indian midwives of both the cantonment and the *qasba*.[25]

The popularity of this dai training scheme in Bhopal may be contrasted with efforts in British India, where the dropout rate was nearly 100 per cent. According to Geraldine Forbes, this lack of success on the part of the colonial state may be attributed to the fact that 'none of the schemes developed was really designed to train the *dai*, but rather to replace her entirely.' For instance, training classes were

[23] Sultan Jahan Begam, *An Account of My Life*, vol. III, trans. C.H. Payne (Bombay: The Times Press, 1927), pp. 23–5.

[24] *Thirtieth Annual Report of the National Association for Supplying Female Medical Aid to the Women of India for the year 1914* (Delhi: Superintendent Government Printing, 1915), pp. 109–10.

[25] See correspondence in NAI(B), BSR no. 2 (B. 34), 1917.

taught in English in a 'regular classroom format', rather than in Urdu on a part-time basis in a way that made it possible for practising midwives to attend, as they were in Bhopal.[26] The annual reports of the Dufferin Fund also point to the 'keen personal interest' of the ruling Begam as being a major contributing factor, a judgement that corresponds with Dagmar Engels' findings in Bengal that initiatives by local women to reform the practice of childbirth were far more successful than those promoted by European practitioners.[27] Fittingly, inspectors of the Victoria Memorial Scholarship Fund commended these efforts by the Begam, but they also expressed their concern that pupils in Bhopal were not receiving sufficient practical training along European lines or enough chances to view European methods.[28] Their criticisms reflect the tendency among British activists, as highlighted by Forbes, to favour the replacement of traditional birthing attendants with midwives trained in Western medicine, even though the former often provided a higher and more personal standard of care to their clients. The Begam of Bhopal clearly refused to conform to their expectations. When Dr Dagmar Curjel, a representative of the Victoria Memorial Scholarship Fund, visited the state in 1919—ten years after the establishment of the scheme—she noted that, though a percentage of students in midwifery classes were tribals and Muslims, by far the largest numbers were still members of the traditional dai caste.[29]

Sultan Jahan Begam's distinctive approach to the dai issue as it represents a case for resistance to gendered regimes of power may also be seen in a speech given at the Maternity and Child Welfare Exhibition held in Delhi in February 1920. On that occasion, she argued

[26] Forbes, 'Managing Midwifery', p. 171. The methods employed in training classes in Bhopal are discussed most comprehensively in A. Lankaster, Agency Surgeon, to Abdul Raoof, Political Secretary, 16 February 1917; 'Qasba Dais'; and 'Scheme for the Control of Maternity Nurses, Sehore Cantt', in NAI(B), BSR no. 2 (B. 34), 1917.

[27] *Thirtieth Annual Report*, pp. 109–10; and Engels, *Beyond Purdah*, p. 148.

[28] See, for example, *Thirty Third Annual Report of the National Association for Supplying Female Medical Aid to the Women of India for the year 1917* (Delhi: Superintendent Government Printing, 1918), p. 74.

[29] 'Report of Dr Dagmar Curjel', in NAI(B), BSR no. 24 (B. 82), 1922.

that it was a grave error to blame indigenous dais for all of the problems associated with childbirth on the basis that they had treated maternity cases and other female ailments 'in olden days' with 'remarkable success'. What was needed instead, she maintained, was 'proper organisation' to stop this 'class of midwives' from 'fast disappearing under the new order of things'.[30] No mention was made of the 'dangerous' or 'demon' dai that was to become the staple of colonial and nationalist discourses on women's health.[31] That is not to say that this maligned figure did not ever appear in Bhopal. In a speech given on the occasion of Sultan Jahan Begam's twentieth accession anniversary in 1921, to take just one example, the state's leading female unani practitioner, Bismillah Khanam, spoke of the 'great dangers' of handing over a pregnant woman to an 'ignorant, incapable, dirty and uneducated midwife with filthy fingernails.'[32] Yet her very position as a unani practitioner and her express conviction, as articulated in the same speech, that it was acceptable for pregnant Bhopali women to seek medical treatment from a lady doctor, *hakima*, Western-style midwife or dai, as long as they were 'qualified' and 'certified', demonstrates that her stance, like that of her esteemed employer, involved taking control of colonial medical discourses, rather than just echoing the mantras of the memsahibs. The autonomy that Indian women were to gain through this process was also evident in that she encouraged her audience to learn about women's health issues so that they may 'look after themselves.'[33] This implicit resistance to indigenous patriarchal structures, particularly through the manipulation of a discourse on sanitation, will be explored in the following section.

[30] *Speech of H.H. Nawab Sultan Jahan Begam of Bhopal at the Maternity & Child Welfare Exhibition held at Delhi on the 23rd February 1920* (Bhopal: Sultani Press, 1920), p. 6.

[31] Forbes, 'Managing Midwifery', pp. 163–8. Also see Sean Lang, 'Drop the Demon Dai: Maternal Mortality and the State in Colonial Madras, 1840–1875', *Social History of Medicine* 18:3, pp. 357–78.

[32] Bismillah Khanam's speech on the precautions to be observed in houses, both rich and poor, before and after a childbirth, in Abru Begam (ed.), *Rehbar-i-sehat* (Bhopal: Hamidia Art Press, 1922), p. 53.

[33] Ibid., pp. 54, 59–60.

Treating Women as Heavenly Ornaments?

While vicereines limited their attention to maternity and child welfare, it was sanitation as it related to public health that was at the centre of the colonial state's medical policy in India from the nineteenth century. This focus may be attributed to contemporary medical theories in Europe in which the spread of disease was attributed to miasmatic factors such as the 'poisonous emissions' and 'pestiferous exhalations' of decaying vegetable and human waste matter, particularly in a crowded setting.[34] This understanding dovetailed nicely with unani conceptions of the spread of disease and the maintenance of health in that it also emphasized the need to achieve a balance between certain essential qualities, like air and water, although, notably, in terms of the individual's body, rather than the physical environment. This overlap stimulated unani practitioners to engage with the colonial discourse on health and sanitation, leading to a proliferation of reformist works in the early twentieth century on what was referred to as *hifz-i-sehat*. As Guy Attewell has noted, this phrase, as it was derived from Arabic, translated literally as 'the preservation of health', but was equated with sanitation in its 'western medical connotations'.[35] A key example of this process that is especially relevant to this context was book nine of Maulana Ashraf Ali Thanawi's renowned advice manual, *Bihishti Zewar* (Heavenly Ornaments), first published in 1905, in which the basic principles of unani medicine were presented to women in an accessible and appropriate manner.[36] Indeed, the association of sanitation with cleanliness in the home meant that, more often than not, it was women, those most closely identified with this domain, who were charged with promoting it.

Sultan Jahan Begam also recognized this special responsibility, asserting in a speech given at the Princess of Wales Ladies' Club that had been founded in Bhopal in 1909: 'It is specially incumbent on womenfolk, to whom has been entrusted the high duty of the

[34] David Arnold, *Science, Technology and Medicine in Colonial India* (Cambridge: Cambridge University Press, 2000), p. 81.

[35] Attewell, 'Authority, Knowledge and Practice', ch. 5.

[36] See Barbara Daly Metcalf, *Perfecting Women: Maulana Ashraf 'Ali Thanawi's Bihishti Zewar* (Berkeley: University of California Press, 1990), ch. 2.

preservation of the race, that they should pay special regard towards the observance of these life giving and life-preserving rules.'[37] Unlike many of her male predecessors and contemporaries, however, she resisted an indigenous patriarchal framework at least in part by emphasizing women's agency and autonomy in the process. Specifically, she encouraged her female employees and dependants to give speeches on this theme at the ladies' club, a key example being the two-part lecture on hygiene presented by her youngest daughter-in-law, Maimoona Sultan, around 1912. Though only 11 or 12 years old at the time, she demonstrated her familiarity with 'modern medical research' by attributing the spread of disease to miasmatic factors, like 'impure air'. She sounded very much like a British medical officer when she advised, above all, 'not to keep rubbish things lying inside the house or in the neighbourhood and to have your dwelling well ventilated.'[38] Yet she also revealed a debt to unani medicine in that she spoke of the need to regulate the 'animal temperature' in the body through controlled breathing.[39] Her speeches also invite favourable comparison with Thanawi's *Bihishti Zewar* in that Islamic injunctions—'Verily God loves the penitent and the clean and pure', among others—were employed to motivate Muslim women in their pursuit of personal cleanliness.[40]

This capacity to operate within an Islamic framework while still referencing a colonial discourse may also be seen in the writings of Sultan Jahan Begam herself. In 1916, she published a manual on health and sanitation for women, revealingly titled *Hifz-i-sehat*, in which she encouraged women not only to maintain physical fitness through exercise and a balanced diet, but also to improve sanitary conditions within the home in order to reduce the causes of sickness.[41]

---

[37] 'English translation of a short speech delivered by Her Highness in the Ladies' Club, Bhopal', in *A Brief Decennial Report of 'The Princess of Wales Ladies' Club', Bhopal* (Calcutta: Thacker, Spink & Co., 1922), p. 88.

[38] 'Maimoona Sultan's Second Lecture on Hygiene', in *Decennial Report*, pp. 63, 65.

[39] Ibid., pp. 62–4.

[40] 'Maimoona Sultan's First Lecture on Hygiene', in *Decennial Report*, pp. 57, 60.

[41] Sultan Jahan Begam, *Hifz-i-sehat* (Bhopal: Sultania Press, 1916).

This holistic approach to women's health reflected her acceptance of the basic principles of unani tibb with its emphasis on preventive measures, as well as her engagement with Western scientific theories on the spread of disease. To be sure, her tendency to blend indigenous and colonial systems of medicine may be seen in that, as Attewell has noted, she defined hygiene in terms reminiscent of British officials as cleanliness of 'air, water, food, the body, clothing and place,' yet, at the same time, drew on unani principles to express a 'teleological conception of the functioning of the body' in which weakness in one organ was understood to spread to others.[42] Her debt to European and Indian medical practitioners alike was also made explicit in the preface to her work when she thanked representatives of both systems for their helpful comments on her draft.[43] In recognizing women's potential to take responsibility for their own health by giving them access to selective medical knowledge, the Begam's text resembled Thanawi's earlier work. Yet she also went a step further than the Deobandi *alim* in asserting women's autonomy in that she identified health and sanitation as a cause that could justify women's independent actions not only in their own homes, but also outside of them.

A useful example of this trend was Sultan Jahan Begam's establishment of unani dispensaries throughout her state that served women exclusively and operated under the care of female health practitioners who were said to have 'taken proper Tibbi training and received certificates.'[44] The Asfia Zenana Dispensary in Bhopal city, for instance, was operated in the 1920s by the trained hakima mentioned in the previous section, Bismillah Khanam, who, along with two male health practitioners, had the status of 'Sub-Assistant Surgeon' in the Bhopal state service.[45] Other related specialists included 'tibbiya health visitors', who attended to the medical needs of purdah-bound women and their children in their homes free of

[42] Attewell, 'Authority, Knowledge and Practice', ch. 5.

[43] Sultan Jahan, *Hifz-i-sehat*, p. 1.

[44] See Abru Begam's introductory article on welfare work for women and children in Bhopal in *Rehbar-i-sehat*, p. 3.

[45] Liakat Husain, 'Administration Report of 1923', in NAI(ND), GOI, BPA no. 206, 1923.

charge in imitation of the Willingdon Health Scheme in Bombay, but employing the principles of unani tibb in which they had received comprehensive instruction.[46] This concentration of female unani practitioners is somewhat remarkable if one considers, as Guy Attewell has done, that the largest Muslim princely state, Hyderabad, had only one in government service up to the late 1930s. It may, however, be seen to parallel developments in Delhi where a new department was added to the Sharifi family's Madrasa-i-tibbiya in 1908 with the express purpose of offering unani instruction to women. Together, these developments in Delhi and Bhopal set a precedent for the establishment of a number of unani schools for women in other Indian cities, including Allahabad and Mysore, leading to the erosion of male dominance in this profession from the 1940s. As Attewell has noted, some of these 'unani lady doctors' even advertised their services in women's journals, like *Tehzib un-Niswan*, emphasizing their ability to offer a confidential, authoritative and sympathetic service to their fellow women.[47]

Also worth noting in this connection is that female health visitors not only offered unani medical care in the home, but also gave lectures on sanitation and hygiene in deprived districts and at the Princess of Wales Ladies' Club. A key example was a talk presented by a health visitor called Mehrunnisa on the occasion of the well-attended celebrations to mark the ruling Begam's twentieth accession anniversary in which she addressed sanitary methods to be followed in 'poor Hindustani homes.'[48] Sultan Jahan Begam also encouraged members of the ladies' club to spread the 'wholesome knowledge of right living' by visiting those dwellings where 'the rules of hygiene [were] not fully observed' to give advice on this matter. To highlight her support for this scheme, she offered a pecuniary allowance and

---

[46] 'Report of Dr. Dagmar Curjel on Work of Victoria Memorial Scholarship Fund in Bhopal, 31 October, 1919', in NAI(B), BSR no. 24 (B. 82), 1922; and Abru Begam, *Rehbar-i-sehat*, pp. 2–3.

[47] Attewell, 'Authority, Knowledge and Practice', ch. 5.

[48] Mehrunnisa's speech on the question of what kinds of principles should be followed for the protection of health in poor Hindustani houses, in Abru Begam, *Rehbar-i-sehat*, pp. 60–9.

the use of a conveyance to those women willing to take it up. This charitable act, while recognized as being 'very painful', was portrayed as allowing elite women the opportunity to offer 'practical sympathy' to their poor sisters by helping them to 'remove their self-inflicted miseries'.[49] This reference to Victorian notions of personal responsibility suggests that these activities may have been stimulated by the example of upper-class British women who were actively involved in social welfare work of a similar kind, both in India and in Britain. Like them, elite Bhopali women were being encouraged to affirm their own sense of agency and autonomy in connection with reformist discourses, while, at the same time, asserting their authority over poorer women by bringing them their own notion of 'right living.' This point will be explored further, specifically with reference to the ruling Begam's project to educate mothers, in the following section.

Spreading the Knowledge of Right Living?

The colonial concern with maternity and child welfare led not only to dai training schemes as seen in the first section, but also to a coordinated attempt to educate mothers. As van Hollen has noted, 'the Indian woman' was constructed in colonial discourse as a figure of ignorance with regard to her own health and that of her children, but one that was 'eminently malleable': a childlike figure who could be moulded into a 'good mother' if she was introduced to European methods of childbirth and childcare.[50] Margaret Jolly has noted the 'resonances' between this discourse and the 'strategies of intervention in the lives of working-class mothers in Britain.'[51] In that context, policy-makers were motivated by the women's suffrage movement and the poor physical performance of troops during the First World War, among other factors, to pass a Maternity and Child Welfare Act in 1918, after which women's hospitals, infant welfare centres, and

[49] *Decennial Report*, pp. 88–91.

[50] Van Hollen, *Birth on the Threshold*, pp. 49–51.

[51] Margaret Jolly, 'Introduction: Colonial and Postcolonial Plots in Histories of Maternities and Modernities', in Ram and Jolly, *Maternities and Modernities*, p. 9.

'baby shows' were organized across the country.[52] When transferred to the Indian colony, this interest led to the formation of the All-India League for Maternity and Child Welfare by Lady Chelmsford in 1919 and the 'Baby Week' movement by Lady Reading in 1924. Both of these initiatives intended to educate Indian women, especially of the poorer classes, in methods of bearing and raising children in the British model through pamphlets and travelling exhibits. This programme, thus, provides an example of the way in which the colonial state used medicine to reach into the Indian home and assert its hegemony, although Geraldine Forbes has noted how middle-class Indian women also manipulated this process, particularly as it related to midwifery, by using it to assert their own autonomy—a notable act of resistance.[53]

Sultan Jahan Begam's own assumption of a hegemonic role in relation to educating mothers, even as she sought to rework colonial constructs, may be seen in her establishment of what she called a 'School for Mothers' in 1919 as part of the Princess of Wales Ladies' Club. This project aimed to professionalize the tasks that women already performed by transforming them into a taught programme of home economics that included childcare and training, cookery, sewing, needlework, elementary hygiene, home nursing, and housekeeping, very similar to those on offer in England and the United States. Yet attempts were also made to adapt this scheme to the specific requirements of women in Bhopal, as the Begam understood them. Instruction, for instance, was to be provided in the form of lectures and practical demonstrations in Urdu by female health officers of the state, rather than by the English lectures and book learning that were to make similar undertakings so unsuccessful in the provinces of British India. Home visits were also deemed necessary so that teaching could be adapted to individual needs and its application 'rationally enforced', while women's customary obligations were recognized through the provision of covered conveyances to

[52] Anna Davin, 'Imperialism and Motherhood,' *History Workshop Journal* 5 (1978), p. 43.

[53] Forbes, 'Managing Midwifery', esp. p. 172. Also see David Arnold, 'Public Health and Public Power: Medicine and Hegemony in Colonial India', in Engels and Marks, *Contesting Colonial Hegemony*, pp. 131–51.

take women to and from the club and childcare while it was in session. Similarly, the project was justified on the basis of providing mothers of childbearing age with adequate preparation for the 'responsible vocation' of bringing up healthy children who would ultimately become 'useful citizens of the State', however ironic this language of citizenship might have been in the colonial or princely context.[54]

In an effort to fulfil this purpose, the ruling Begam introduced her scheme to Bhopali women themselves at a grand meeting attended by members of the ladies' club and recent graduates of local girls' schools on the occasion of the anniversary of her accession to the throne in January 1919. Shortly after, classes in first aid, hygiene and home nursing were actually begun for eleven Muslim women, all of whom were wives of the Bhopal gentry or high officers of the state, thus emphasizing the elite nature of this venture in its early stages.[55] The syllabus was based on that devised by the Indian Council of the St John's Ambulance Association, a branch of which had been opened in Bhopal in 1911–12 and which had actually extended first aid classes to women of the ladies' club as early as 1914.[56] But, as planned, these new classes were taught by female health practitioners in Bhopal, primarily the superintendent of the Lady Lansdowne Hospital, Miss A.E. Paul, and the superintendent of the Asfia Zenana Dispensary, Bismillah Khanam. Continued colonial influence was also evident in that a member of the Indian Medical Service, usually the Agency Surgeon posted to Bhopal, was called in every six months to hold examinations and reward successful candidates with medals. Yet the format was negotiated to fit the Islamic environment in Bhopal; as nearly all of the club's members were in purdah, the male examiner would sit on one side of a curtain and the women on the

[54] 'School for Mothers', attached to a letter from Sultan Jahan Begam to Lady Reading, 6 October 1921, NAI(B), BSR no. 5 (B. 72), 1921. For comparison with projects in the West, see Van Hollen, *Birth on the Threshold*, p. 51.

[55] 'A Brief Decennial Report of "The Princess of Wales Ladies' Club", Bhopal', in *Decennial Report*, pp. 13–14.

[56] See *Regulations for the Formation of Male or Female Classes in Connection with Centres: With the Syllabus of the Various Courses of Instruction* (Simla: Indian Headquarters of the St John's Ambulance Association, 1917).

other, while a young boy moved back and forth between the two groups, checking that the right woman was answering the questions and acting as a patient for the students to treat.[57]

The dynamic way in which women in Bhopal engaged with their ruler's programme may be seen in the accounts of European visitors to the state. When Dr Dagmar Curjel of the Victoria Memorial Scholarship Fund visited the ladies' club late in 1919, for instance, she highlighted that, since classes had commenced, attendance at the bi-weekly meetings had increased and become more regular. She also noted that the women were 'very keen' about what they were learning—in fact, so 'eager' that it was 'quite difficult' for her to get away.[58] Ruth Frances Woodsmall, a guest to the club in the late 1920s, reiterated this point, giving the example of 'one very colourful old Begam,' who, despite being 'very aristocratic' and spending her whole life in 'orthodox purdah', showed utter 'delight and joy' in her scholastic achievements. These women's acceptance of the domestic purpose of their health training was also evident in that the same elderly Begam was reported to have told her, 'Not that we expect to do nursing . . . but now we know how to take care of our own families and make better homes.'[59] Yet, at the same time, Bhopali women were clearly selective in what they deemed to be useful knowledge, in this way demonstrating that barely perceptible, though still significant negotiation with power that is a feature of this volume. The School for Mothers was intended to have six classes—gestation, art and games, and nursing, as well as the three mentioned above— yet various reports in the early 1920s suggest that women only attended regularly and got satisfactory grades in first aid. In 1924, to take just one example, the Agency Surgeon noted that 31 ladies had passed the first aid examination, while only 4 or 5 had completed courses in home nursing and hygiene.[60]

---

[57] Ruth Frances Woodsmall, *Moslem Women Enter a New World* (London: George Allen & Unwin, 1936), p. 307.

[58] 'Report of Dr Dagmar Curjel', in NAI(B), BSR no. 24 (B. 82), 1922.

[59] Woodsmall, *Moslem Women*, pp. 306–7.

[60] McConaghy to Sultan Jahan Begam, 29 October 1924, NAI(B), BSR no. 53 (B. 100), 1924–5.

The status of Sultan Jahan Begam and other elite Bhopali women as perpetrators, as well as resisters, of gendered power structures may also be seen in the events organized to honour the ruler's twentieth accession anniversary in 1921. This gala celebration was staged over two days with the first taking the form of an exhibition on children's health and the second being dedicated to a series of health lectures by female practitioners in the state, many of which were on the theme of bearing and raising children, though not necessarily in the European model. Mrs Bashirullah Khan, a midwife and health visitor, for instance, addressed her audience on the precautions to be taken when a mother was breastfeeding, highlighting the importance of keeping milk pots and bottles clean, while Mehmooda Begam, a tibbiya health visitor, discussed the reasons for children's diseases and the methods to stop them using the principle of unani tibb.[61] As noted above, Bismillah Khanam also spoke on this occasion on the precautions to be taken before and after childbirth with the emphasis being on the utilization of trained medical practitioners, whether they were allopathic doctors, unani physicians *or* indigenous midwives. That this message was well received—or at least widely heard—in the Bhopali context is evident from reports that this event was attended in 'huge numbers beyond expectation' by 'ladies of all classes', as were a series of 'baby shows' organized in the state in 1924.[62] This situation differed again from that in colonial Bengal where similar events were deemed exceedingly unsuccessful due to fears of the 'evil eye'.[63]

Elite Bhopali women's interest in educating as many women as possible in the principles of maternity and child welfare as they understood them was also confirmed by the themes of some of the

[61] Mrs Bashirullah Khan's speech on the precautions to be taken when a mother is breastfeeding and Mehmooda Begam's speech on the reasons for children's diseases, in Abru Begam, *Rehbar-i-sehat*, pp. 70–97.

[62] 'Decennial Report', pp. 169–72; 'Report on the Baby Week in Bhopal State held during the month of January, 1924', in NAI(B), BSR no. 149 (B. 93), 1923–4.

[63] Shudha Mazumdar, *A Pattern of Life: The Memoirs of an Indian Woman*, trans. and ed. Geraldine Forbes (New Delhi: Manohar Book Service, 1979), p. 175.

lectures at the celebrations in 1921. Bismillah Khanam, for instance, directed her discussion on childbirth to those living in houses, 'both rich and poor'.[64] A closer analysis of her lecture, however, reveals a lack of understanding of women unlike herself. Evidence of this trend may be seen in that she considered the 'funny' habits of village women for the 'pleasure' of her audience, describing with apparent glee how they bore their children while working in the forests or the field, cut the umbilical cord with a sharp stone, washed their newborn baby with leaves, then walked home with it under their arm, seemingly unaware that they may not have had the luxury not to. Though she admired these women for their 'natural' quality, comparing them to 'wild trees' that did not need the care of a gardener, she dismissed their method of childbirth as invalid, claiming that children born in this way did not undergo proper mental development, nor prove able to resist disease. She then turned her full attention to the case of rich women living in purdah in the cities.[65] This elite bias suggested a convergence in terms of class interests on the part of Muslim female reformers in Bhopal and their British counterparts who, as suggested above, were making equally presumptuous 'interventions' into the lives of working-class women in their own country.[66]

Conclusion

By the time Sultan Jahan Begam abdicated to her son in 1926, Bhopal state had a fairly comprehensive programme for treating women's health. There were allopathic hospitals, unani dispensaries and health visiting programmes in the capital and the mofussil to serve women living in and out of purdah, as well as accredited schemes to train unani practitioners and indigenous dais. In light of women's identification with the home, they had also been targeted to spread the principles of sanitation and hygiene, both in their own neighbourhoods and those of less fortunate women, primarily through manuals and speeches. Women's perceived function as mothers meant that

[64] Bismillah Khanam's speech in Abru Begam, *Rehbar-i-sehat*, p. 60.

[65] Ibid., pp. 51–2.

[66] See, for instance, J. Lewis, *The Politics of Motherhood: Child and Maternal Welfare in England, 1900–1939* (London: Croom Helm, 1980).

there were also schemes to educate them in the basics of first aid, childbirth, and nursing, whether in the form of regular classes, special exhibitions or 'baby shows'.[67] In recognition of her pioneering efforts, the Begam of Bhopal was hailed by visitors to the state in the late 1920s, including Ruth Frances Woodsmall and Sir Harcourt Butler, who remarked that she had engaged with women's health issues long before other princely rulers.[68] Yet it was not just timing that distinguished her initiatives. What was also important was her selective and, indeed, creative approach to reforming women's health, as it drew on a number of different medical traditions—from Western systems of scientific knowledge to the indigenous methods of unani tibb. Following the example of Gyan Prakash, then, this analysis highlights the process of 'hybridization' that went on in terms of knowledge in the colonial setting, whereby Western ideas were combined with 'local cultural and religious understanding'—though I would also emphasize the multiple and interlocking ways in which this was achieved, rather than postulating a simple dichotomous distinction between 'Western' and 'Indian' modernity.[69]

Indeed, the disruptive effect of gender when it comes to defining modernities may be seen in that Sultan Jahan Begam and other women in Bhopal were not limited by colonial or Muslim patriarchal models of reform, but instead in a subtle act of subversion manipulated them to address the specific circumstances and concerns of Indian Muslim women. Bhopal's status as a princely state may also be seen as relevant to this process in that, in this semi-autonomous context, there was at least some space to resist colonial hegemony as it was asserted through medicine, whether that be through reviving unani tibb to the detriment of allopathic dispensaries or favouring

---

[67] There has not been space to expand on all of these initiatives here, but an extended discussion is available in ch. 5 of my book, *Muslim Women, Reform and Princely Patronage*.

[68] Woodsmall, *Moslem Women*, p. 305; and diary of Sir Harcourt Butler while on tour with the Indian States' Commission, Bhopal, 26 March 1926, India Office Library, Butler Collection, MSS. Eur. F. 116/108.

[69] See Gyan Prakash, *Another Reason: Science and the Imagination of Modern India* (Princeton: Princeton University Press, 1999).

indigenous dais over Western-trained midwives. The patronizing approach of many Muslim male reformers by which—as Gail Minault has argued with reference to the Delhi novelist, journalist, and educationalist, Rashid ul-Khairi[70]—women were treated as objects to be reformed, rather than active participants in their own regeneration was also rejected through the provision of medical knowledge and employment to women. In terms of their participation in socio-religious reform movements, Bhopali Muslim women should also be distinguished from their male counterparts in that most of the latter displayed their lack of interest in women outside the *ashraf* class by reducing them, as Ayesha Jalal has noted, to 'prostitutes' and 'demons'.[71] What this matter also highlights, however, is the way in which the Begam of Bhopal, her female medical staff, and women of the ladies' club were, like their co-elites in Britain, involved in a hegemonic enterprise by which they sought to inculcate each other and less privileged women with their own reformist ideas about childbirth, childcare, and sanitation—though even that process was not uncontested. To simply valorize women's resistance or even attempt to theorize about it thus proves to be a problematic task.

[70] Gail Minault, *Secluded Scholars: Women's Education and Muslim Social Reform in Colonial India* (New Delhi: Oxford University Press, 1998), p. 145.

[71] Ayesha Jalal, *Self and Sovereignty: Individual and Community in South Asian Islam since 1850* (London: Routledge, 2000), p. 70.

6

GENDER, SUBALTERNITY, AND
SILENCE: RECOVERING CONVICT
WOMEN'S EXPERIENCES FROM
HISTORIES OF TRANSPORTATION,
c. 1780–1857[1]

CLARE ANDERSON

Ann Laura Stoler and Frederick Cooper have provided another reminder that one cannot simply 'do' colonial history. What constitutes the archive—what is included and what is excluded from it—reflects the cultural politics of colonialism itself.[2] Nicholas B. Dirks has made a similar observation, describing the archive as a

[1] This research has been generously supported by the British Academy, British Academy Committee for South East Asian Studies, Carnegie Trust for the Universities of Scotland, Economic and Social Research Council, and Faculty of the Social Sciences, University of Leicester. I would also like to thank Indrani Chatterjee, Anindita Ghosh, Durba Ghosh, and Anoma Pieris for constructive suggestions on the ideas presented here.

[2] Ann Laura Stoler and Frederick Cooper, 'Between Metropole and Colony: Rethinking a Research Agenda', in Ann Laura Stoler and Frederick Cooper, eds, *Tensions of Empire: Colonial Cultures in a Bourgeois World* (Berkeley: 1997), p. 18.

discursive formation that reflects the categories and operations of the colonial state.[3] Few postcolonial historians or anthropologists would find these claims controversial now, but the question remains: if we accept them, how can historical research proceed, particularly the recovery of non-elite histories and experiences like those of subaltern women? Since the 1980s, scholars in the Subaltern Studies collective have been providing imaginative readings of colonial sources to trace the emergence of subaltern consciousness and experiences. The problem is, of course, that subalterns are far from autonomous social actors, but emerge from traces in the archives that define them in relation to elites.[4] Perhaps for this reason, some post-colonial theorists, notably Gayatri Chakravorty Spivak, question whether subaltern consciousness can be recovered at all. For Spivak, the best historians can do is to point to the silences in the archives, and trace the production of what she terms 'the subaltern subject-effect', for the subaltern is never produced in and through him or herself, but through the knotting together of particular, and contingent, historical strands.[5]

The complexities of this endeavour are further complicated by scholars' own agency in the production of history. We slot historical remnants (or subject-effects) into neat historical categories—yet if we did not do so, we would be unable to write about the past at all.[6] The retrieval of women's experiences is particularly difficult in this respect. As Kamala Visweswaran has shown persuasively, one of the problems of the theorization of gender by the Subaltern Studies project has been the production of gender as a separate social category,

[3] Nicholas B. Dirks, 'The Crimes of Colonialism: Anthropology and the Textualization of India', in Peter Pels and Oscar Salemink, eds, *Colonial Subjects: Essays on the Practical History of Anthropology* (Ann Arbor, 2000), p. 175.

[4] Rosalind O'Hanlon, 'Recovering the Subject: *Subaltern Studies* and Histories of Resistance in Colonial South Asia', *Modern Asian Studies*, vol. 22 (1), 1988, pp. 189–224.

[5] Gayatri Chakravorty Spivak, 'Introduction; Subaltern Studies: Deconstructing Historiography', in Ranajit Guha and Gayatri Chakravorty Spivak, eds, *Selected Subaltern Studies* (Oxford: 1998), pp. 12–13.

[6] Rosalind O'Hanlon and David Washbrook, 'After Orientalism: Culture, Criticism, and Politics in the Third World', *Comparative Studies in Society and History*, vol. 34 (1), 1992, pp. 141–67.

marginal to caste and class. For Visweswaran, the concept of 'woman' was central to class formation, and so 'subaltern women' and 'women as subaltern' must be conceptualized differently.[7] We could add the colonial category of race here; race, gender and class are what Anne McClintock calls 'articulated categories', formed *in and through* relation to each other'.[8]

I would like to explore some of the theoretical complexities around the retrieval of women's experiences in considering the transportation of Indian convict women to penal settlements in Mauritius (1815–53) and South East Asia—Bencoolen (1787–1825), Penang (1790–1860), Malacca and Singapore (1825–60), and the Burmese provinces of Arakan and Tenasserim (1828–62). I will argue that, during this period, colonial administrations gendered the criminal body in their organization of both convict labour and the penal hierarchy. Such gendering was inflected with colonial categories of hierarchy, racial difference, and criminality.[9] This essay explores three broad themes. First, I look at the relationship between the body, space, and punishment. Second, I consider the construction of colonial discourses of convict sexuality that transformed convict women into embodied sites of criminal reproduction. Third, I make some suggestions about the meaning of female convicts' 'silences' and 'voices' in the colonial archive. Comparative literature has shown how the purpose of colonial sources can be both interrogated and inflected to reveal how historical agents subvert the official meaning of the documents in which they appear.[10] Women's agency thus begins to emerge from cracks in the colonial archaeology of knowledge.[11]

[7] Kamala Visweswaran, 'Small Speeches, Subaltern Gender: Nationalist Ideology and Its Historiography', in Shahid Amin and Dipesh Chakrabarty, eds, *Subaltern Studies IX* (Delhi: 1996), p. 88.

[8] Anne McClintock, *Imperial Leather: Race, Gender and Sexuality in the Colonial Contest* (London: 1995), p. 5 (author's emphasis).

[9] O'Hanlon and Washbrook, 'After Orientalism', p. 149.

[10] Ian Duffield, '"Stated This Offence": High-density Convict Micro-narratives', in Lucy Frost and Hamish Maxwell-Stewart, eds, *Chain Letters: Narrating Convict Lives* (Melbourne: 2001), pp. 119–35.

[11] Gyan Prakash, 'Subaltern Studies as Postcolonial Criticism', *American Historical Review*, vol. 99 (5), 1994, p. 1486.

Gendered Bodies and Convict Responses

This essay argues that gendered interventions were central to colonization and the production of colonial boundaries in Indian penal settlements. These boundaries were, however, inherently unstable. On the one hand, colonial practices marked significant departures from pre-colonial social hierarchies. As Radhika Singha has shown, the effect of European rationalism on colonial penology produced sharp differences in the punishment of women. For instance, the East India Company rendered subject women open to punishments previously accorded only to men. Women could be executed for wilful murder, a departure from pre-colonial practice in parts of India.[12] From the late eighteenth century it also made women subject to the practice of penal tattooing on the forehead *(godna)*, until the practice was banned in 1849.[13]

Yet, not entirely consistently, some years earlier in 1825 the Company had banned the flogging of women on the grounds of 'delicacy and humanity'. In 1839 it also exempted female prisoners in Bengal from fettering, the Faujdari Adalat (Criminal Court) noting that it was 'for obvious reasons improper'.[14] Such penal interventions were reflected in changing prison management techniques. As Indian jails were increasingly transformed into productive spaces during the 1840s, women were put to work on indoor labour (notably the hand mill to grind wheat, but also 'domestic' work such as spinning, weaving, and cleaning),[15] as an alternative to those forms of hard labour (outdoor labour such as road building or land clearance) considered

[12] Radhika Singha, *A Despotism of Law: Crime and Justice in Early Colonial India* (Delhi: 1998), p. 139.

[13] Clare Anderson, *Legible Bodies: Race, Criminality and Colonialism in Colonial South Asia* (Oxford: 2004), ch. 3.

[14] India Office Records (IOR) P/141/43 (2 January 1840), Circular of the *Faujdari Adalat*, no number, 11 October 1849.

[15] IOR P/141/53 (30 March 1841): H. Hawkins, Register *Nizamat Adalat*, to F.J. Halliday, Sec. to Gvt Bengal, 19 March 1841, enclosing 'Statement exhibiting the number of female convicts, 31 December 1840, in the jails of the several districts in the Lower Provinces'.

suitable for men. By the time the Prison Discipline Committee published its report in 1838, this was the case in all mainland jails, with just one exception.[16] The gendered division of penal servitude produced a sharp distinction between 'public' and 'private' productive space, reflecting bourgeois metropolitan aspirations about the appropriate sexual division of labour, and the visibility of women in work, rather than *necessarily* replicating pre-existing productive spheres.

There is a good deal of suggestive evidence that, like male prisoners, women resisted aspects of the prison regime, such as the infringements of caste caused by the attempted institution of common messing during the 1840s.[17] Their employment at what was traditionally low-caste labour—sweeping and cleaning—was always a potential flashpoint. Refusal to work, insolence, disobedience, sexual impropriety, and bartering rations for stimulants and other goods were important forms of 'everyday resistance' in which women engaged. Contemporaries often refused to take such resistance seriously. When W.H. Marshall (a former editor of the *Rangoon Chronicle*) visited Moulmein prison in the 1850s, for instance, he described how a local female prisoner had attempted to dodge the prison guards and climb the prison wall. He claimed that it was 'not likely' to have been an escape attempt, and compared her actions to a game of hide and seek.[18] Nevertheless, female prisoners were commonly awarded punishments such as grinding grain or mortar, or, more dramatically, had their hair cut.[19] There is further evidence that in penal settlements where

[16] *Report of the Committee on Prison Discipline, 8 January 1838* (Calcutta: 1838), henceforth *PDC*, para. 25; appendix 4, question 2; Singha, *A Despotism of Law*, pp. 248–9, 255 (n. 123), 265.

[17] David Arnold, 'The Colonial Prison: Power, Knowledge and Penology in Nineteenth-Century India', in David Arnold and David Hardiman, eds, *Subaltern Studies VIII* (Delhi: 1994), pp. 150–2; Anand A. Yang, 'Disciplining "Natives": Prisons and Prisoners in Early Nineteenth Century India', *South Asia*, vol. 10(2), 1987, pp. 29–45.

[18] W.H. Marshall, *Four Years in Burmah, Vol. II* (London: 1860), pp. 169–71.

[19] Tamil Nadu State Archives (TNSA) Judicial Proceedings 326B: S.G. Bonham, Resident Councillor Singapore, to Henry Chamier, Chief Sec. to Gvt, 21 April 1837, enc. a copy of Convict Regulations, Straits Settlements; IOR P/142/

male convicts were commonly hired out as servants to private employers, women were 'always unwilling to take service' and preferred to remain in jail.[20] That women forced the hand of the administration in this respect perhaps explains the latter's concurrent lack of ideological commitment to the construction of a socially (as opposed to productively) distinct penal sphere for the incarceration of female convicts.

During the 1820s penal administrators attempted to implement a variety of disciplinary strategies, including separate accommodation for men and women. I would argue that this was a response to the recognition that it was not the colonial authorities that determined how convicts experienced incarceration but to a large degree convicts themselves. Regulations in Bencoolen first ordered the separation of convict men and women, and these were later extended to the Straits Settlements and Burma.[21] However, in practice convict men and women continued to live together and the authorities were generally unwilling to interfere with their kinship networks. Note the answers given by administrators in the Straits Settlements when the Prison Discipline Committee asked about them:

Malacca: 'The jailer has discretional power in permitting access to the family and friends of persons under sentence.'

Penang: 'Women and other visitors have (with permission) access to the convict lines.'

Singapore: 'Visitors are supposed to be excluded from the Jail, but I have no doubt they could find means of access if inclination or profit

---

37 (17 September 1845): Governor W.J. Butterworth to Turnbull, 26 February 1845, enc. Report A: Present System of Management and Discipline of Convicts at Singapore, Suptd D.A. Stevenson, 9 January 1845: IOR P/142/44 (25 February 1846): Commissioner H.M. Durand to Halliday, 19 December 1845, enc. Rules for the Management of the Convicts in the Tenasserim Provinces.

[20] IOR P/136/31 (26 August 1824): Minute of W.E. Phillips on the mode of treatment of convicts transported to Prince of Wales Island [Penang], 15 April 1824.

[21] IOR P/142/37 (17 September 1845): Butterworth to Turnbull, 26 February 1845, enc. Regulations for Convict Management, 23 June 1825 (revised 1 December 1825).

tempted them to try it . . . I confess I should not, under certain restrictions, object to women visiting the convict lines so long as such visits were not the cause of confusion or riot.'[22]

It is in administrative attempts to gender penal space as well as penal servitude that traces of women's experiences of transportation begin to emerge. H.G. Bonham, the Resident Councillor at Singapore, informed the Prison Discipline Committee that women 'reside as wives to any of the convicts with whom they *choose* to live.'[23] Female convicts shipped to the penal settlement at Mauritius (which the Committee more or less ignored, because it was not Company territory) also lived with male convicts there.[24] It was not until the 1840s—following the recommendations of the Committee that existing rules and regulations be more strictly enforced[25]—that the settlements began to develop separate accommodation for women. However, as late as 1845 the Resident Councillor of Malacca reported that no special notice of convicts' families had ever been taken.[26] Convict men and women were also still living together in the Singapore lines.[27]

It is impossible to say to what extent the imbalanced gender ratio (women made up just five per cent of the total at the very most) gave convict women in Singapore the choice of male partner that Bonham told the Prison Discipline Committee that they had. Satadru Sen certainly argues that this was the case in the Andaman Islands penal

[22] *PDC*, appendix 4. This followed practice amongst prison labour gangs in Bengal: Singha, *A Despotism of Law*, p. 254. On the families of convicts transported to Mauritius, see Clare Anderson, *Convicts in the Indian Ocean: Transportation from South Asia to Mauritius, 1815–53* (Basingstoke: 2000), pp. 86–91.

[23] IOR P/141/1 (13 September 1836): Bonham to J.P. Grant, Sec. Prison Discipline Committee, 5 April 1836; *PDC*, para 118, p. 51 (my emphasis).

[24] Anderson, *Convicts In The Indian Ocean*, p. 90.

[25] *PDC*, p. 12 (recommendation 51).

[26] IOR P/142/37 (17 September 1845): C.H. Lushington, Resident Councillor Malacca, to Butterworth, 23 January 1845.

[27] IOR P/142/37 (17 September 1845): Butterworth to Turnbull, 26 February 1845, enc. Report A: Present System of Management and Discipline of Convicts at Singapore, Suptd. D.A. Stevenson, 9 January 1845.

colony after 1857.[28] Marina Carter too has drawn similar conclusions for female indentured migrants in Mauritius.[29] In these early penal colonies, however, it may be that a male partner was a necessary option for convict women, offering protection and access to additional resources in newly colonized and often harsh environments. When convict women were released, they were issued documents detailing their employment, penal class, secondary punishment, and marriage. It seems that convict women 'chose' men employed as petty officers, positions of authority through which they enjoyed considerable material and other privileges, notably with regard to separate accommodation, enhanced food rations, and/or pay. There were other factors at play; partners frequently came from the same region of India—indicative of shared language and culture, in a broad sense.[30] Yet it is far from clear that the establishment of such partnerships represents the choices of convict women rather than the exercise or extension of power by male convicts in positions of relative authority (notably *jemadars*, the most senior of convict overseers). I would like to shape these emergent archival patterns to ascribe agency to these convict women. However, I fear that this would reflect my own desire to award weapons to the weak, rather than the opacity of the historical problem.

I have written elsewhere about the Eurasian convict Maria Davis, shipped to Mauritius in 1828. The Calcutta Supreme Court had convicted her of murder and sentenced her to death, later commuting the sentence to life transportation. Davis had beaten her female slave—Nuseebun *alias* Nancy Burn—to death at her house in Cossitollah, whilst in a drunken stupor. Shortly afterwards, she was transported to Mauritius with her eleven-year-old daughter Emma. Their arrival caused considerable annoyance to the British colonial authorities. At first they tried to back out of their agreement to receive convicts from the Bengal Presidency, arguing that as Davis had been sentenced to transportation to Mauritius specifically, rather

[28] Satadru Sen, 'Rationing Sex: Female Convicts in the Andamans', *South Asia*, vol. 30 (1), 1999, pp. 35–6.

[29] Marina Carter, *Lakshmi's Legacy: The Testimonies of Indian Women in 19th-Century Mauritius* (Rose-Hill, Mauritius: 1994).

[30] Survey of release documents found in TNSA Judicial Proceedings.

than transportation generally, her sentence was unlawful. The Calcutta Supreme Court disagreed, and confirmed the legality of the sentence. The Mauritian government therefore agreed to keep the women, but lodged them entirely separately from the other Indian convicts, male and female. They were placed in separate accommodation and given a quite extraordinary quantity of goods, including a bed and mattress, two chairs and a table, six pairs of shoes, cloth for *chemises* (blouses), sixty yards of 'gown stuff', a dozen cotton stockings, and a piece of sheeting. The problem was solved for the Mauritian government at least when Davis and her daughter fell ill with tuberculosis soon afterwards. They died in 1830, Davis having repeatedly refused to go to hospital.[31]

Another female convict, Victoria Adelaide Hassey, was transported from Calcutta to Singapore in 1855. The ship indent records the following: her father was named Daniel Hassey; she was convicted of being an accomplice in the murder of Jugeroop and the theft of property valued at 115 Rupees; she was tried in Benares on 19 November 1853, and sentenced life transportation 'with labor suited to her sex'; and, she was a Christian. Her Eurasian status is further hinted at in the roll—'wheat color'—the usual description for convicts with fair skin.[32] Victoria Hassey's transportation to the Straits provoked a similar response to Maria Davis' arrival in Mauritius some twenty-five years earlier. According to Governor W.J. Butterworth, there was 'much sympathy and compassion here especially among the ladies of the community—This person is young, educated, and a Christian, yet she is mixed with heathen females, and no instructions have been sent to me to treat her otherwise than an ordinary native female criminal.'[33]

The contingency and instability of colonial categories of race, class, criminality, and gender—and most significantly the multiple articulations between them—emerge through a consideration of the

[31] On Maria Davis, see also Anderson, *Convicts in the Indian Ocean*, pp. 20–1; IOR SM46: *The Government Gazette* (and *Supplement*), 7 August 1828.

[32] IOR P/145/10 (3 May 1855): List of 38 female convicts for Singapore *per Soobrow Salam*, 26 April 1855.

[33] IOR P/145/22 (8 November 1855): Extract from a letter from W.J. Butterworth, 12 July 1855.

transportation of Maria Davis and Victoria Hassey. They were treated quite differently to those women—from Britain and across the empire—shipped to the penal settlements in Australia at about the same time.[34] This was largely due to differences in the articulation of racial categories. Up until the 1830s, Eurasians were increasingly marginalized from 'white' society in India.[35] Yet they were in a loose sense still connected to the colonial elite. In Mauritius and Singapore, evidence of Eurasian criminality, especially by female Christians, potentially brought the authority of the governing classes into disrepute. Europeans therefore chose to ignore these women's class and criminality, and to forge alliances with them on the basis of race. This seems extraordinary, particularly for Davis who was found guilty of a capital offence. In the Antipodean settler societies, the picture was entirely different. Free settlers self-consciously distanced themselves from convicts (most of whom were convicted for crimes against property), and the 'stain' they brought with them.

At the same time, the cases of Maria Davis and Victoria Hassey further underline the need to make a distinction between 'convict women as subaltern' and 'subaltern convict women'. Till now, I have been referring to 'female convicts' or 'convict women', for it is in that collective and anonymous form that they usually appear in colonial reports. However, female convicts were neither ascribed nor took on an undifferentiated identity. It would be misguided indeed to claim that all convicts came from marginalized communities and embodied or expressed a distinct convict identity. Of course, at one level the process of transportation transformed all convicts into a subaltern community. At another, convicts produced distinctions amongst themselves through forms of self-categorization and negation.[36] In

[34] Joy Damousi, *Depraved and Disorderly: Female Convicts, Sexuality and Gender in Colonial Australia* (Cambridge: 1997); Kay Daniels, *Convict Women* (St Leonard's: 1998); Frost and Maxwell-Stewart, eds, *Chain Letters*. On convict women shipped from British colonies to Australia, see Duffield, '"Stated This Offence"', pp. 127–32 (on the slave Maria, shipped from Honduras to Van Diemen's Land in 1828).

[35] C.J. Hawes, *Poor Relations: The Making of a Eurasian Community in British India, 1773–1833* (Richmond: 1996).

[36] For an overview of *Subaltern Studies* explorations of negation ('the violation

this sense, women's experiences and identities were not necessarily predicated on colonial (or local communities') definitions of them, and sometimes revealed their ambiguities, perhaps—as we have seen—in alliances of kinship.

Other forms of self-categorization may have related to social background in a more general sense. The ship indents that accompanied every convict into transportation show that women came from a wide range of religious and caste backgrounds.[37] Ship indents also reveal the diversity of crimes for which women were transported. There is growing evidence to suggest that radical shifts in landholding and patterns of taxation stimulated crime during the early nineteenth century.[38] Whilst some women were sentenced for such crimes, others were convicted of infanticide, murder, and other violent offences against the person.[39] Transportation to an overseas penal settlement provided a space in which convicts could reproduce or reformulate social identities. In the South East Asian settlements, some low-caste women converted to Islam,[40] a not unusual strategy for social betterment amongst all transportation convicts. Later on, the potential fluidity of identity was seen as good reason to transport female offenders who had broken community strictures as well as the law. As one judge wrote of one Nale Lingi, convicted of infanticide in 1884:

---

of signs, precisely as a process of identification'), see O'Hanlon, 'Recovering the Subject', pp. 204–6.

[37] From analysis of the 82 ship indents noted below.

[38] The best collection to date remains Anand A. Yang, ed., *Crime and Criminality in British India* (Tucson: 1985).

[39] Analysis of records of 82 women transported to the Straits Settlements and the Tenasserim Provinces shows that 24 were transported for infanticide/procuring abortion, 32 for murder, 17 for property offences (including poisoning) and 5 for thuggee (IOR Bengal Judicial Proceedings). Peter Zinoman has similarly noted that 'official and popular attitudes towards crime in Indochina emphasized fundamental differences between male and female criminality', despite suggestive evidence to the contrary: *The Colonial Bastille: A History of Imprisonment in Vietnam, 1862–1940* (Berkeley: 2001), pp. 104–8.

[40] IOR P/144/2 (14 May 1851): A.P. Phayre, Commissioner of Arakan, to J.P. Grant, Sec to Gvt Bengal, 21 April 1851, enclosing A. Fytche, Principal Assistant Commissioner Arakan, to Phayre, 15 March 1851.

'The woman confessed her crime. She was a widow and had committed the offence when suffering heavily from the disgrace consequent on her condition and had been roughly treated by her relations who had refused her shelter. In concluding my judgment [of transportation for life], I made no recommendation on her behalf for I think the truest kindness will be not to do so but to let her go to a new country.'[41]

It is perhaps also worth mentioning another piece of evidence, the Singapore Medical Officer's 1856 report on four blind convict women—Shahiboo, Boreboh, Suddon and Hurro. He wrote, 'it does not task the imagination highly to understand the wretched plight of such poor helpless creatures put on board ship and left to the tender mercies of their sister murdereses [sic], who are far more likely to deprive them of their allowance of food than assist them to any additional comfort, the state I have seen these unfortunates reduced to is but too corroborative of the suspicion.'[42] If he was correct, the report reveals the production of other sorts of social distinctions, formulated by convict women themselves.

Cracks in the Archaeology of Convict Knowledge: The Hidden Transcript

So rarely do we find the words of convict women reproduced in the archives that I would like to cite the petition of Ragoo, a female convict transported to Mauritius in 1834, in full:

> To His Excellency J.M. Higginson Esq. Governor & Commander in Chief in & over the Island of Mauritius and its Dependencies &c. &c.
>
> May it please Your Excellency.
>   The Petition of Ragoo, a Female Convict.
> Most humbly showeth
>   Your petitioner was transported to this Colony for life in the year 1834 & consequently has served 17 years & during that period she has

---

[41] TNSA Judicial Proceedings, 7 November 1884, 2888: L.A. Campbell, Sessions Judge Nellore, to J.A. Davies, Registrar High Court, 24 September 1884.

[42] IOL P/145/60 (19 March 1857): Extract from a Report of the Medical Officer at Singapore, 1 May 1856.

conducted herself with propriety and being now fifty five years old; she respectfully begs of Your Excellency to grant her pardon on the same conditions as was granted some time back to 100 Male Convicts.

And, as in duty bound, Your Petitioner will ever pray.

Ragoo X her mark
Port Louis 13th January 1851[43]

Evidently this petition is a mediated representation of Ragoo's experiences of transportation. In all probability written by a scribe well versed in the art of petition writing, the content, language, and tone reveal very little other than the fact that Ragoo was still alive seventeen years after her transportation to the island—and that she has been able to pay the writer. He (for it was certainly a he) was aware of the rules of this colonial game. Ragoo is humble and in duty bound; her conduct has been proper. The petition reveals little else, other than Ragoo's inability to sign her name. No mention is made of her child, for instance, the existence of whom is recorded elsewhere in the Mauritian archive. I think that this is because, as I have argued elsewhere, while male convicts' efforts to establish kin networks in Mauritius won the support of the colonial authorities, for female convicts it was evidence of sexual activity, which in itself was equated with questionable morality.[44]

Moreover, the very existence of this mediated document is evidence of Ragoo's gendered marginality, for she had been excluded from the general liberation of convicts, which affected only men—the vast majority of convicts.[45] In this sense, its silences speak volumes. To be sure, there are no parallels with the deep texts available to historians of female convicts in Australia, narratives that lend themselves to nuanced considerations of gender, experience, and identity.[46] This is

[43] MA RA1148: Petition of Ragoo, 13 January 1851.

[44] Anderson, *Convicts in the Indian Ocean*, pp. 86–91.

[45] On the liberation of convicts in Mauritius, see Anderson, *Convicts In The Indian Ocean*, ch. 6.

[46] K.M. Reid, '"Contumacious, Ungovernable and Incorrigible": Convict Women and Workplace Resistance; Van Diemen's Land, 1820–1839', in Ian Duffield and James Bradley, eds, *Representing Convicts: New Perspectives on Convict Forced Labour Migration* (London: 1997), pp. 106–23; Duffield, '"Stated

at least partly a problem of sources, and one that brings us back to the problem of the near-invisibility of Indian convict women in the colonial archive.[47] If our subaltern does not speak, how do we set about further untangling the historical context in which particular subject-effects were produced?

As we have seen, there are only fleeting references to convict women during the period to the 1840s, largely when they were described in ship indents, codified in the drawing up of rules, enumerated in annual reports or represented in release documents. By the 1840s and 1850s, however, they began to appear in colonial correspondence for the first time, represented as a disciplinary problem and the cause of socio-sexual disorder. In this section, I would like to trace and explain the genesis of this shift. I will focus on Inspector-General of Prisons F.J. Mouat's 1856 report on transported women in Sandoway Jail, Arakan, and local administrators' responses to it, to argue that discourses of women's sexual immorality were produced by the authorities' recognition of their failure to establish entirely separate convict spheres. I will go on to suggest reasons why this became an issue so long after the Prison Discipline Committee's 1838 call for tighter discipline. At the same time, like Spivak, I want to point to the significance of convict women's silences in my interpretation of gender relations.

In 1846, A. Bogle, Commissioner of Arakan, wrote that he thought that convict women incarcerated at Kyaukpyu (Ramree Island) 'will give rise to very serious trouble, probably to murders', and that another female convict in Sandoway Jail 'occasions a great deal of trouble'. These were veiled references to sexual activity in the jails and, more particularly, to the competition between male convicts for sexual access to these women. Bogle's assistant, D. Williams, wrote that the genesis of the 'jealousies created by them' was the lack of separate accommodation. Bogle proposed a solution to the problem: that the

---

This Offence'", pp. 127–32; Lucy Frost, 'Eliza Churchill . . . tells . . .', in Frost and Maxwell-Stewart, eds, *Chain Letters*, pp. 79–90.

[47] Marina Carter has faced the same dilemma, constructing a picture of labourers' experiences of indenture almost exclusively through letters written by men: *Voices from Indenture*.

women be sent back to Alipur Jail near Calcutta, from where they had been transported. The Bengal authorities disagreed, and wrote that the officer in charge of the jail should 'make the proper arrangements for preventing irregularities'.[48]

Governor W.J. Butterworth's comments on convict women in Penang the following year are worth quoting at length:

> I . . . urge the inexpediency of sending convict women to the Straits. There is the greatest difficulty, without additional overseers and the construction of new buildings, to keep them entirely separate from the men. The details given me by the Sergeant in charge of the Lines on my recent visit to Penang, when remarking on the disgraceful fact of there [*sic*] being 'enciente' [pregnant], are too disgusting to commit to paper. I mention one anecdote. The party of women (22 in number) [were] transported from Bengal per Fire Queen and Phlegethon, in November 1846 and September 1847. They were at first confined in a Room with a window looking on the Road which was well secured with iron bars. This window was kept open, to let light and fresh air in. It was altogether a place apparently well suited to females, but they were obliged to be removed from it, in consequence of being found cohabiting with the townspeople through the grating of the window![49]

In some ways, Butterworth's report simply confirms the picture already painted in Arakan. In others, his allusion to sexual transactions by convict women is more complex, in that it suggests that they were trading sexual services for cash or other goods. In this sense convict women did possess some sort of agency—or at the very least were able to employ what James C. Scott has termed the 'weapons of the weak'.[50] Butterworth repeated his request the following year. Convict

---

[48] IOR P/142/54 (28 October 1846): Bogle to Halliday, 11 September 1846, enc. D. Williams, Principal Asst. Commissioner, to Bogle, 11 September 1846; A.R. Young, Under Sec. to Gvt Bengal, to Bogle, 28 October 1846.

[49] IOR P/143/16 (22 March 1848): Butterworth to Young, 12 November 1847, enc. S. Garling, Resident Councillor Penang, to Butterworth, 11 September 1847.

[50] James C. Scott, *Domination and the Arts of Resistance: Hidden Transcripts* (London: 1990).

women, the Resident Councillor of Penang, S. Garling, reported, were 'a source of great inconvenience and give much occasion for unpleasant remarks by the Grand Jury and the Bench'.[51]

What is most intriguing about these comments is why their anxiety emerged during the second half of the 1840s, fifty years after women were made liable to transportation,[52] and ten years after the Committee on Prison Discipline was set up. I suspect that the answer lies in enhanced administrative efforts at the regulation of sexual access to convict women or, to put it another way, interference in the organization of gender/sexual relations by and between convicts. Yet the question remains: why at this particular moment? The answer seems to lie in emergent fears about hereditary crime, through which convict women's motherhood took on a new meaning. We know little about birth rates amongst convicts. A general census of Fort Marlborough and Bencoolen taken in 1820 shows that 569 convict families had 76 children—compared to 182 for 150 free Bengali families—which seems quite low.[53] During the same period, convicts' children were allowed to attend Penang Free School.[54] Until the middle of the nineteenth century, pregnant Indian women were not exempt from transportation.[55] Women with small children took them into transportation, keeping them with them until they were 4 or 5 years old. The children were then given over to orphanages.[56]

[51] IOR P/143/22 (28 August 1848): Garling to Butterworth, 6 March 1848.

[52] IOR P/128/37 (4 May 1798): J. Duncan, H. Stuart, J. Rivett and W. Page, Bombay Castle, to John Shore, Governor General in Council, 3 April 1798. One of the first women sentenced to transportation was Satoo Bowrin: IOR P/128/ 56 (17 December 1801): J. Stuart, Registrar Fort William, to G. Dowdeswell, Sec to Gvt Bombay, 9 December 1801, enc. extract of a letter from the Acting Magistrate of the Zillah of Beerbhoom, 2 December 1801.

[53] John Bastin, ed., 'The Journal of Thomas Otho Travers 1813–1820: Appendix II Report on the Population, &c., of the Town and Suburbs of Marlborough [W.R. Jennings, Edward Presgrave and James Lumsdaine, 1820]', *Memoirs of the Raffles Museum*, vol. 4, 1957, p. 171.

[54] IOR P/136/31 (26 August 1824): Minute of W.E. Phillips on the mode of treatment of convicts transported to Prince of Wales Island, 15 April 1824.

[55] IOR P/143/36 (29 August 1849): List of 82 convicts to Moulmein *per Tenasserim*, 12 July 1849 (no. 79 Musst Puchooee).

[56] For example: IOR P/144/2 (14 May 1851): Phayre to Grant, 21 April 1851.

Ranajit Guha has famously noted the colonial archive's appropriation of the language of 'infestation' as 'the prose of counter-insurgency'.[57] I would like to suggest that it adopted similar linguistic turns to describe convict women's sexuality. It is no coincidence that such language emerged at the time penal settlements began to receive women convicted of thuggee, an offence that encompassed a broad range of offences (including murder, poisoning, kidnapping). In Arakan and Penang, for instance, Commissioner A. Bogle and Superintendent of Convicts S. Garling used the words 'hatch', 'breed', and 'brood' to describe the conception and birth of their children.[58] The shift from ambivalence to concern about women's sexual activity coincided with a change in thinking about hereditary criminality, particularly the genesis of the idea that criminal tendencies could be passed between parent and child. By the middle of the nineteenth century, convicts' sexual freedom was also seen as the antithesis of discipline. A note pencilled on correspondence received from E.A. Blundell, Governor of the Straits, by T. Pycroft, Chief Secretary to Government Madras, observed that the idea of two convicts living together and having a family 'gives a curious idea of the Straits, as Penal Settlements'.[59] In 1857, F.J. Mouat issued a circular prohibiting women from taking their children into transportation with them at all. Women with young children would be detained in jail until they reached the age of 2; the women would then be transported, and their children treated as foundlings.[60]

I would now like to turn to F.J. Mouat's 1856 inspection of Sandoway Jail, which he conducted during his general tour of the district jails in Arakan. This is an extract from his official report:

> The worst feature in the Jail is the women's department. There are ten female life prisoners, most of them confined for murder, and with them is associated a Mugh woman [i.e. locally convicted] sentenced to a year's

[57] Ranajit Guha, 'The Prose of Counter-Insurgency'.

[58] IOR P/142/54 (28 October 1846): Bogle to Halliday, 11 September 1846; IOR P/143/16 (22 March 1848): Garling to Butterworth, 11 September 1847.

[59] TNSA Judicial Proceedings, 15 July 1859, 31–2: E.A. Blundell, Governor Straits Settlements, to T. Pycroft, Chief Sec. to Gvt Madras, 10 June 1859.

[60] IOR P/145/64 (25 June 1857): H. Fergusson, Supdt Alipur Jail, to C.J. Buckland, Sec. to Gvt Bengal, 6 April 1857.

imprisonment for theft. They occupied the end of one of the male wards, separated by a mat partition, through which they can at any time be overlooked by their neighbours. I found that one of them, named Budnee, had a child at the breast, two years old. She was sentenced in 1849, and has been in the Sandoway Jail more than three years. Another, named Jusseah, who was imprisoned in 1845, has been in the Sandoway Jail for six years. She has a child three years old, and miscarried a year ago. If all that I heard regarding this female ward be true, it is little better than a brothel, and a scandal to the prison.[61]

This report actually tells us little beyond Mouat's outrage at female prisoners engaging in sexual activity, leaving us with a tantalizing 'if all that I heard . . . be true'. His representation of convict women's sexual immorality is, in many ways, predictable. Middle-class observers commonly accused subaltern women of engaging in prostitution at this time—accusations which tell us rather more about the eye of the middle-class beholder than subaltern gender practices.[62] In describing Sandoway as 'little better than a brothel' Mouat's official report simply reproduced earlier administrative discourses. Visitors to penal settlements were equally unremitting in their accounts of convict women. Clementina Benthall (wife of magistrate Edward) wrote that a shipload of female convicts en route to Arakan in 1847 were 'horrid creatures'.[63] The Earl of Elgin (later Viceroy of India) wrote of a visit to Singapore ten years' later: 'I cannot say that their

[61] Mouat, *Reports on Jails*, pp. 188–9.

[62] Michael Sturma, 'Eye of the Beholder: The Stereotype of Women Convicts, 1788–1852', *Labour History*, vol. 34, 1978, pp. 3–10.

[63] Centre of South Asian Studies, University of Cambridge: Benthall Papers: Box XXX, part i: *Diaries kept by Mrs Clementina Benthall,* January 1849–March 1850 (typescript copy at Box XXX, part iii.) The women were travelling from Calcutta *per Enterprize*. There were five women on board. See: IOR P/143/30 (21 February 1849): List of 61 convicts to Moulmein *per Enterprize*, 10 February 1849. Clementina Benthall noted that she thought the women were poisoners. The indent is rather ambiguous on this: one had been convicted of being an accomplice in the murder of her husband, a second of the wilful murder of a servant, two of being accomplices in the murder of a new born child, and another of the infanticide of her one-year-old daughter by throwing her down a well.

appearance made me envy the [male] convicts much.'[64] John Furnivall's uncritical reading of the nineteenth-century colonial archive of the Tenasserim Provinces brings him to the same conclusion, reducing convict women to 'the constant cause of quarrels and insubordination'.[65]

In his report, Mouat hints that he heard rather more about the circumstances of the pregnancies than was published. For further details, we need to delve deeper into the archive, in search of what Scott has termed the 'hidden transcript'. What follows is taken from records of his correspondence with the Henry Hopkinson, Commissioner of Arakan, and James Emerson, the Principal Assistant Commissioner in Sandoway, who served as Magistrate and Superintendent of Sandoway Jail. They questioned the accuracy of many of Mouat's claims. When Mouat arrived at Sandoway, the superintendent had been absent on business for some weeks, so he was received by the jail *darogah*. Mouat's written report hinges on 'all that [he] heard', information imparted by the darogah and most likely some of the convicts—though he doesn't specifically mention what either said. James Emerson quickly intervened to set the record straight:

> There are ten female life prisoners in the jail but only one of the number, Jussia, has been proved guilty of having had intercourse of a criminal nature with any one belonging to or connected with the Jail, who was once caught in the act with a Prisoner not, be it observed, in the Female Ward, but in the open Maidan in broad day light. The result was the child alluded to by the Inspector, as being three years old.
>
> Again this *same Jussia* was suspected of having gone a stray [*sic*] and of having miscarried, and she was punished.
>
> The Inspector mentions the case of the woman Budnee and the discredit of it is laid to the Jail at Sandoway, whereas the real truth is that on the 21 February 1853 this Budnee arrived at Sandoway having been

---

[64] Theodore Walrond, ed., *Letters and Journals of James, Eighth Earl of Elgin; Governor of Jamaica, Governor-General of Canada, Envoy to China, Viceroy of India* (London: 1872), p. 189 (Singapore, 6 June 1857).

[65] John Furnivall, 'The Fashioning of Leviathan', *Journal of the Burma Research Society*, vol. 29 (1), 1939, p. 38.

sent from Akyab and on the 25th of June following she gave birth to a child. The child therefore, if the produce of a Sandoway Jail irregularity must be, what would be called a four months child! Is such a thing possible? I doubt it myself.[66]

Mouat wrote that he would be happy to think that he had been mis-informed,[67] but he clearly did not think he had been. Shortly after-wards he recommended that the transportation of women should cease altogether.[68]

Is there anything further in this 'official transcript'? I believe that there is, and that it can be interrogated to reveal something of the centrality of women to power relations inside the jail. When Mouat arrived at Sandoway, the magistrate had been away for two months. It was, by Mouat's own admission, an extraordinary state of affairs. Indeed, the Commissioner of Arakan wrote that he should not have been so taken aback to find things not quite in order: 'a stranger in a school in the absence of the school master... would not be sur-prised to find the boys enjoying a sort of saturnalia'.[69] James Emerson, his Principal Assistant, admitted that there were problems with jail superintendence, describing the darogah as a 'grinning idiot' and most of his subordinates as 'a discontented ill-paid rabble'. He added that if it were not for the efforts of the Head Native Officer and some of his subordinates, the convicts would be able to do as they pleased. Emerson was keen to know precisely *what* Mouat had heard from *whom*.[70]

Mouat refused to be drawn on the issue, and would only say that he had reached his conclusions by 'personal observation'.[71] He claimed

[66] IOR P/145/44 (31 July 1856): James Emerson, Principal Assistant Com-missioner Sandoway, to H. Hopkinson, Commissioner of Arakan, 13 May 1856.

[67] IOR P/145/44 (31 July 1856): Mouat to Buckland, 10 June 1856.

[68] IOR P/145/64 (25 June 1857): Mouat to Lushington, 13 April 1857.

[69] IOR P/145/22 (31 July 1856): Hopkinson to W. Grey, Sec. to Gvt Bengal, 1 May 1856.

[70] IOR P/145/22 (31 July 1856): Emerson to Hopkinson, 13 May 1856.

[71] IOR P/145/22 (31 July 1856): Mouat to Buckland, 10 June 1856. Mouat added that he had not singled Sandoway out for particular criticism: 'The fact is that the state of the female wards of all the Jails under my supervision is a

that his conclusions had nothing to do with the absence or otherwise
of the Superintendent. Rather, he wrote, he had been told that the
subadar and darogah of the jail had contracted syphilis some years
previously, apparently after intercourse with one of the women still
in confinement. Further, he alleged that 'a quantity of gold and other
expensive personal ornaments' had been removed from the women
before he inspected the female ward, by implication by the darogah
or another guard. Mouat described this as 'most probably the price
of concubinage'.[72] In other words, according to Mouat, women were
engaged in an economy of sexual exchange.

Is it possible that Mouat was correct, and that women were being
paid for sexual services in kind? Two rare photographs of Indian
female convicts in Singapore Central Jail show a substantial amount
of jewellery. Bangles, earrings, rings, and a necklace are all in view.[73]
It is not of course possible to say where the jewellery of these women—or that of the women Mouat described—came from. Mouat
himself might have been drawing assumptions about the provenance
of the jewellery he claimed female convicts possessed, though given
the speed with which it was removed before his visit this seems

---

source of much anxiety and misgiving to me.' He attached an extract from his
report on the Hazareebaugh Penitentiary (n.d): 'The "ward for women" is not
only in the same compound with those of the male prisoners but is otherwise
so accessible that I am convinced that it is the scene of every species of irregularity, whenever the back of the European Jailor is turned. One example
brought to my notice by Sergeant Rix, is so flagrant, that I can scarcely suppose
it to have escaped the notice of the Magistrate. A woman confined for life for
the murder of her husband is employed as the cook of the women's ward. The
paramour for whom the crime was committed is also an inmate of the Penitentiary, and Mr Rix says he cannot prevent their "getting together"': IOR P/145/
22 (31 July 1856): Mouat to Buckland, 24 May 1856.

[72] IOR P/145/22 (31 July 1856): Mouat to Buckland, 24 May 1856.

[73] These photographs are held in the Imperial College Archives, London
(Huxley Collection), and in the collections of the Royal Anthropological Institute, London. I deal with the production of these and other such anthropometric
photographs in *Legible Bodies*, ch. 5. See also Elizabeth Edwards' brilliantly
nuanced discussion in *Raw Histories: Photographs, Anthropology and Museums*
(Oxford: 2001), ch. 6.

unlikely. Neither is it possible to draw firm conclusions about who controlled sexual access to convict women—the prison guards or the women themselves. However, the women's ownership of jewellery is strongly suggestive that, notwithstanding the potential for exploitation, they enjoyed at least some of the fruits of their sexual labour.

Reshaping the Boundaries of Incarceration

Convict women transported to penal settlements in South East Asia during the first half of the nineteenth century only became subjects of concern during the 1840s. Until then, there are fleeting glimpses of them in the archives. The emergence of women in written records at this time is important, for it reflected a fundamental shift in colonial attitudes. During the early part of the century penal administrators had not interfered in convicts' negotiations of relationships and kin networks. Later on, as new discourses of hereditary crime emerged, they began to intervene both in representing women in new ways and in creating separate accommodation for them. There are then important meanings to be attached to the 'silences' of and about convict women during this period.[74]

The agency of convict women in reshaping the boundaries of incarceration can also be read through the written record. From the repertoire of punishments awarded to women and the comments of contemporary administrators it is clear that female convicts engaged in everyday resistance to the prison regime, for instance in refusing to engage in particular types of labour. The economy of sexual exchange that operated in prisons is perhaps the most problematic element of women's agency to interpret in this respect. The exchange of sexual services for cash or other goods was and remains a complex social encounter into which both exploitation and empowerment can be read. In the face of only fragmentary evidence and the silence of convict women themselves, perhaps the best way to reconcile this dualism is to see it as women's deployment of the 'weapons of the weak'. In this sense, convict women were disempowered but not completely powerless.

[74] Prakash, 'Subaltern Studies', p. 1486.

7

THE LITIGIOUS WIDOW:
INHERITANCE DISPUTES IN
COLONIAL NORTH INDIA, 1875–1911

NITA VERMA PRASAD

Historical scholarship on the Hindu widow in colonial India tends to focus on several well-known issues that were embodied in legislative reforms during the nineteenth century. These include the abolition of widow-burning or sati (1829), the Hindu Widows' Remarriage Act (1856), and the Age of Consent Act (1891).[1] Reform of the widow's condition was indeed hotly debated in the nineteenth century, and the ensuing legislation is doubtless worthy of historiographical scrutiny. But too narrow a focus on the reform of textual law and its abuses (many of which occurred mainly among the higher castes) gives us very little insight into how widows actually lived their lives. Moreover, much of this literature is suffused with a victimology approach, stressing crimes committed against

[1] For a discussion of these acts and the debates surrounding them, see Lata Mani, *Contentious Traditions: The Debate on Sati in Colonial India* (Berkeley: University of California Press, 1998); Lucy Carroll, 'Law, Custom, and Statutory Social Reform: The Hindu Widows' Remarriage Act of 1856', in J. Krishnamurty ed. *Women in Colonial India* (Delhi: Oxford University Press, 1989), pp. 1–33; Dagmar Engels, 'The Age of Consent Act of 1891: Colonial Ideology in Bengal', *South Asia Research* 3 (1983), pp. 107–29.

widows as opposed to actions taken by the widows themselves. What we are left with, then, is an overly simplistic story of dwindling rights and freedoms. We know all about the prohibitions and restrictions placed on the widow during the colonial period, but very little has been said about how she adjusted to her losses. This essay will forgo long discussions of nineteenth-century reform efforts and will attempt to look at women, the law, and property rights from the perspective of the Hindu widow: how did she adapt and respond to the changing social, economic, and legal context of her time? How did she, in the words of Charles Tilly, live the big changes?

In tackling such a question, this essay does not dispute the fact that widows in particular, and women in general, did indeed suffer losses on multiple fronts during the colonial period. The tightening of social, behavioural, and economic restrictions is undeniable, and the literature that highlights these trends is both well researched and compelling. It tells us that the consolidation of British rule—or, more specifically, the alliance that was forged between the colonial state and upper-class (Brahmin) men—had the effect of strengthening and disseminating rigid Brahminical behavioural norms. As lower classes pressed for higher status, they too began to emulate traditional high-caste gender norms, a central part of which was hawkish surveillance and control over widows' behaviour. What this meant in real terms was that widows of all castes were now encouraged to remain celibate, shave their heads, dress in plain, unadorned saris, eat bland, unspiced food, and refrain from participating in social festivities.[2] This 'Brahminization' of Hindu society meant that more and more widows would experience widowhood as a state of a 'social death'.[3]

---

[2] For elaboration on these themes, see Dipesh Chakrabarty, *Provincializing Europe: Postcolonial Thought and Historical Difference* (Delhi: Oxford University Press, 2000). Chakrabarty examines the work of Kalyani Datta, a nineteenth-century Bengali woman who documented the suffering of widows. These as well as other restrictions on widows' conduct are described in vivid detail.

[3] This phraseology is widely used in studies of Hindu widowhood. See, for instance, Uma Chakravarti and Preeti Gill, eds, *Shadow Lives: Writings on Widowhood* (New Delhi: Kali for Women, 2001), p. 7.

The economic developments of the time were similarly unfavour-able to women. Scholars generally agree that, under British rule, Indian women suffered losses in inheritance and property rights, as well as access to land. Indeed, women are commonly depicted as eco-nomically dependent and vulnerable, if not entirely propertyless. Veena Oldenburg, for instance, in her exhaustive and illuminating study of dowry murder, identifies a 'masculinization' of the economy: as property was placed in the hands of men exclusively, women were often 'left landless with no legal entitlement to the land their husband or father in-law owned.'[4] Likewise, Lucy Carroll points to the fact that, beginning in the mid-nineteenth century, many lower-caste widows who chose to remarry were disinherited.[5] Shunned by society, and financially dependent on their in-laws for support, Hindu widows often had no choice but to work as domestic drudges in their matrimonial home.

The historiography goes on to detail how the newly-established Anglo-Indian judiciary played an important role in the twin processes of masculinization and Brahminization. This thesis that the courts aided in the social and economic marginalization of women is parti-cularly relevant to my study, and, as we will see, needs to be qualified and nuanced in several ways. The Anglo-Indian High Courts, which were created by an Act of Parliament in 1861, were the highest courts of appeal on the subcontinent and enjoyed wide jurisdiction over all civil matters.[6] It is indisputable that in rendering decisions on personal matters, such as inheritance and property disputes, the High Court

---

[4] Veena Talwar Oldenburg, *Dowry Murder: The Imperial Origins of a Cultural Crime* (New York: Oxford University Press, 2002), p. 15.

[5] Carroll, op. cit.

[6] The Indian High Courts Act of 1861 established High Courts with unprece-dented powers over all civil, criminal and maritime jurisdiction. The first High Courts were established in Calcutta, Madras, and Bombay. In the Northwest Provinces, a High Court came into being at Agra in 1866; it shifted to Allahabad in 1875. The highest court of appeal in the British colonial judicial system was the Privy Council, which sat in London. Many of the cases cited in this paper were eventually heard by the Privy Council. For further details see M.P. Jain, *Outlines of Indian Legal History* (Bombay: N.M. Tripathi, 1952).

and its justices (who were both Indian and British in origin) favoured ancient texts over the more fluid and dynamic local customs. Moreover, the uniform application of orthodox Hindu codes had the general effect of crystallizing into law those high-caste traditions and practices that favoured men, while making women of all classes subject to them.

Traditionally, gender historians have insisted that this Brahminizing tendency, combined with a healthy dose of social ostracism, kept most women out of the courts. Dagmar Engels, for instance, in her study of women and the law, writes that 'law, as an agent of social reform under colonial conditions, almost inevitably favoured religious orthodoxy and male conservatism.' In fact, the juridical process was so thoroughly dominated by men (*Brahmin* men) and their interests that women's appearance in court was 'circumvented at all costs'.[7] Likewise, Janaki Nair argues that the privileging of Brahminic sources (*srutis*, *smritis*, *dharmasastra*) made the courts an unwelcoming environment for women. Even today, she insists, most women do not use the legal system and are not aware of their legal rights.[8]

Thus, studies of women in colonial India stress the losses suffered by women—social, economic, and even legal. This being the general backdrop of South Asian women's history, it must be noted that several scholars have recognized the extraordinary efforts made by a handful of Indian women. Meera Kosambi and Uma Charkravarti, for instance, tell the story of Pandita Ramabai Saraswati, a Brahmin widow who converted to Christianity and spoke out against the treatment of women and widows. They detail the waning freedoms of Maharashtrian women during the colonial period, yet also acknowledge women like Ramabai, who used the tools of reading and writing to 'lay bare the full range of oppressive practices imposed upon all women.'[9] Rosalind O'Hanlon also highlights women's resis-

---

[7] Dagmar Engels, 'Wives, Widows and Workers: Women and the Law in Colonial India', in W.J. Mommsen and J.A. De Moor, eds, *European Expansion and Law: The Encounter of European and Indigenous Law in Nineteenth and Twentieth-Century Africa and Asia* (London: Berg, 1992), p. 168.

[8] Janaki Nair, *Women and Law in Colonial India: A Social History* (New Delhi: Kali for Women, 1996), p. 5.

[9] Uma Chakravarti, *Rewriting History: The Life and Times of Pandita Ramabai*

tance through writing in her translation of the work of Tarabai Shinde, a Maharashtrian woman who angrily protested women's changing status in her 1882 book, *A Comparison between Men and Women.*[10]

Historical scholarship, then, does recognize the exceptional responses and efforts of certain Indian women, but these are always located within a broader picture of maltreatment, oppression, and loss. This essay does not dispute the general plot of such stories. Women were indeed marginalized during the colonial period, and the vast majority of widows suffered in silence. Moreover, it is clear that the newly-established Anglo-Indian legal system and its affinity for the written text had a great deal to do with these changes. But there is more to the story, particularly with respect to women and the law. There is, quite frankly, the story of everyday resistance and adaptation, the story of *doing.* Not every widow published books like Shinde or founded reform societies like Ramabai. Yet these women truly were unique. Many 'ordinary' widows fought their own personal battles in the colonial courts. For such women, Hindu law enshrined in a liberal judicial system represented a new space in which they could speak out, resist, and negotiate the injustices in their lives. Prem Chowdhry is one of the few scholars to document women's use of the legal system for these purposes. In her research on Punjabi widows' battles against forced levirate remarriage, Chowdhry gives widows a firm presence in the colonial courts: she shows how widows used the new legal forum to counter the 'dual control' of patriarchy and the state, 'activate their inheritance rights, assert their preferences in sexual and marital relationships, and make counter-claims.' Even though Chowdhry's widows generally lost in court, they nonetheless made quite a bit of noise with 'prolonged legal battles and open confrontations.'[11]

(Delhi: Kali for Women, 1998), p. 248. See also Meera Kosambi: *Crossing Thresholds: Feminist Essay in Social History* (Delhi: Permanent Black, 2007).

[10] Rosalind O'Hanlon, *A Comparison between Men and Women: Tarabai Shinde and the Critique of Gender Relations in Colonial India* (Delhi: Oxford University Press, 1994).

[11] Prem Chowdhry, 'Contesting Claims and Counter-Claims: Questions of

It is in this direction that the current project will continue. Contrary to the notion that colonial courts were 'for men only', I show that between 1875 and 1911, a significant number of widows came before the Allahabad High Court (HC) in order to secure their rights over their late husbands' estates.[12] What were these women's experiences in court? As plaintiffs, did they manage to wrest more powers over their property than Hindu textual law granted them? Or did they, as much of the literature suggests, merely provide the judges with an opportunity to bolster Hindu orthodoxy? Were they doubly victimized by a colonial judiciary that combined forces with Hindu traditionalism, or did they manage and manipulate the juridical process in ways that suited them?

Before answering these questions, it makes sense to take a brief look at Hindu doctrinal codes governing the devolution of property. The Hindu law of inheritance, as embodied in the Mitakshara school of law, gives the Hindu widow very limited rights over the property of her late husband and the estate of her marital family. Essentially, a widow was entitled to hold her husband's property only under certain predefined circumstances: (a) her husband did not hold his property jointly with other family members; and (b) there were no sons, grandsons, or great-grandsons to take immediate possession of the

the Inheritance and Sexuality of Widows in a Colonial State', *Contributions to Indian Sociology*, New Series 29: 1 and 2 (1995), p. 65. Levirate marriage, known as *karewa*, *karao*, or *chaddar andazi*, involves the remarriage of a widow to one of her late husband's agnates—preferably a brother, but cousins were acceptable as well. This type of marriage, which takes its name from the white sheet (*karewa*) that was thrown over the head of the widow during the remarriage ceremony, was most commonly practised in Punjab and Haryana, and was often forced upon widows. The intention behind karewa was, of course, to keep the property and reproductive power of the widow in the family. See also Prem Chowdhry, 'Popular Perception of Widow-remarriage in Haryana: Past and Present', in Bharati Ray, ed., *From the Seams of History: Essays on Indian Women* (Delhi: Oxford University Press, 1995), pp. 37–66.

[12] A brief note on periodization: the project begins with the year 1875 out of necessity—the records begin in this year. The court system underwent a reorganization in 1911, making it a logical ending point.

estate. If these two conditions were met, then the Hindu widow could take possession of her deceased husband's estate, but only for the remainder of her natural life. During this period, her rights as 'owner' were severely restricted: she was only allowed to spend as much as was needed to support herself and her children, and to perform certain rituals for the benefit of her husband's soul. She was not able to alienate the estate in any way. The widow's tenure really represented a break, or a temporary interruption, in the chain of devolution, and as such cannot actually be deemed 'ownership'. As soon as she died, the property would continue on to the next male heir of her husband—i.e. the period of abeyance would be lifted. The widow's job, then, was to safeguard her husbands' estate until it passed into the hands of its rightful (male) owner.[13]

Clearly, the textual restrictions on a widow's right to inherit were severe. However, even a quick perusal of the records of the Allahabad HC indicates that many widows did not quietly acquiesce to these regulations. This essay relies on the many suits that were instituted by widows because they offer a unique window into the thoughts and conditions of the plaintiffs. Put plainly, these inheritance disputes allow us to see how the widow *herself* viewed her property rights and her place within the legal system.[14] What we find is surprising, particularly given the general consensus on women in colonial India: the widows featured here do not approach their property or the courts in a restricted and encumbered way. Rather, the plaints put forth by widow plaintiffs in Allahabad are imbued with a sense of entitlement. In the first instance, these women displayed a bold sense of ownership

[13] The two schools of Hindu law, Mitakshara and Dayabhaga, differ very little on the widow's rights of inheritance. The Mitakshara school was followed in most parts of North India, with the exception of Bengal, where the Dayabhaga school was applied. See Jain, op. cit., and Bina Agarwal, *A Field of One's Own: Gender and Land Rights in South Asia* (Cambridge: Cambridge University Press, 1994).

[14] Out of 172 inheritance disputes involving widows, approximately 68 were instituted by widows. This essay will focus mainly on suits with widows as plaintiffs. This analysis is part of a larger project that looks at cases in which widows appeared as defendants, or as plaintiffs, and even those where they sat on both sides of the bench.

and entitlement towards their late husband's estates; and second, in an effort to protect these rights, they felt entitled to use the courts in a free and unencumbered fashion. Finally, these disputes show that widows had a heightened awareness of their legal rights and positions and an in-depth knowledge of the judicial system itself.

Let us now turn to the actual cases, which are divided into three broad categories. First, we will look at the most common grievance put forth by our widow plaintiffs, the non-payment of maintenance. The pleas for regular, fixed maintenance payments demonstrate the plaintiffs' awareness of the changing legal, moral, and economic context of the time. Second, these are those suits in which widows tried to manipulate the court: these plaintiffs display an intimate knowledge of the judicial process, and they were savvy and confident enough to abuse the system. Finally, I examine a few cases in which widows tried to enlist the support of the court in the management and oversight of their inherited estates. These disputes feature widows who approached their inherited property with an attitude of total ownership. All of these varied legal battles place a question mark over historiography that renders the widow an inert, passive object doubly controlled by patriarchy and the state. The widows here are an important corrective to a nearly uniform picture of maltreatment and victimization.

Changing Custom: The 'Right' to be Maintained

Widows came to court for many reasons, but they sued over maintenance more frequently than for any other single issue. These suits not only indicate how important maintenance was to them, but also tell us a little bit about widows' expectations and desires regarding this allowance. According to Hindu law, a widow in a Hindu joint family was entitled to receive maintenance from her late husband's estate. The property that her husband had held jointly with other male members of the family would devolve to the next male heir, and the widow's only claim on this property was to be supported out of it.[15] However, it appears that even this right was frequently reneged

[15] The Hindu joint family is legally defined as a coparcenary in which at least three generations of men, all of whom resided in a joint household, were

and scanted on by widows' marital families.[16] By our period, the amount, frequency, and even currency in which maintenance was paid was left to the whims of individual families. In practice, then, maintenance was more a social custom, or a charitable handout, than a firmly defined legal right.[17]

Approximately two dozen widows in the Allahabad region objected to this state of affairs by coming to court to claim their due. Most of them were trying to institute social change through the courts— they were asking the justices to take a vaguely defined custom and make it a fixed and legally enforceable right. Moreover, the majority of plaintiffs argued that the burden of supporting a widow should be shared by the larger society, as opposed to the affinal family. This was a radical request indeed, and it was met with firm resistance by their in-laws, and many times by the justices themselves. Nonetheless, such pleas were consistently and regularly put forth by widows during our period.

The simplest of plaints involved a mere request for a monthly allowance plus arrears. In addition, widows from wealthier families usually asked for a house in which to reside. Even these simple requests, when viewed in the proper context, were quite bold: the demand for regular and fixed payments betrays a desire for a reliable, legally enforceable source of income. Take, for instance, the widow Jamna, who in 1879 sued her late husband's nephew for maintenance. In his will, Jamna's husband had left all his property to his nephew, and he specifically stated that no other relation of his should have any claims over the property whatsoever. In court, Jamna took issue

---

members. Women who came into the household, either through birth or marriage, were not coparceners.

[16] Although no in-depth study on maintenance has been undertaken, the various accounts of widows that have survived make this clear. See Chakrabarty, op. cit., and Chakravarti and Gill, op. cit.

[17] This fact is openly stated by the justices themselves in several suits over maintenance. See, for example, 'Jhunna (plaintiff) *v.* Ramsarup and others (defendants)', *Indian Law Reports*, Allahabad Series (hereafter *ILR All.*), vol. II, 1879–80, pp. 777–8 and 'Sham Lal (defendant) *v.* Banna (plaintiff)', *ILR All.*, vol. IV, 1882, pp. 296–300.

with this directive: maintenance, she argued, was her right—one that could not be rescinded by anyone, not even her late husband.[18] Then there was the widow Bainsi, who in 1890 sued her late husband's uncle for maintenance and arrears, arguing that she deserved to be supported in a lifestyle appropriate to the wealth and status of her affines.[19] Also worthy of mention is the widow Daulta Kuari, who stopped receiving her maintenance of food and clothing after she became unchaste. In court she asserted that, unchastity aside, a Hindu widow should *under any circumstances* be entitled to what she called a 'starving maintenance,' i.e. enough money or food to prevent starvation.[20]

These women were asking the Allahabad HC to sanction an appropriate allowance and fix its payment: they were asking that the heretofore voluntary handouts be recognized as an unwavering legal right. Maintenance, they felt, should not be given capriciously, whenever and however the marital family pleased, but be paid in a precise and timely fashion. The plaints put forth by widows are littered with the concept of entitlement and obligation. Their in-laws, they were arguing, were not just morally, but legally obliged to support them in a suitable manner, or at the very least prevent them starving. And while the plaintiffs were concerned with their own situation first and foremost, there is a sense of generalizing outwards to all widows. Daulta Kuari, for example, was talking about a certain standard that needed to be established and met for *all* widows. Significantly, these women (along with several others whose cases have not been detailed here) turned to the Anglo-Indian legal system to redress their grievances and legitimize their ideas.

Many widows went even a step further than Jamna, Bainsi,

[18] 'Jamna (plaintiff) *v.* Machul Sahu (defendant)', *ILR All.*, vol. II, 1878–80, pp. 315–18. A similar dispute occurred a few years earlier as well: see 'Narhar Singh and another (defendants) *v.* Dirgnath Kuar (plaintiff)', *ILR All.*, vol. II, 1878–80, pp. 407–9.

[19] 'Bainsi (plaintiff) *v.* Rup Singh (defendant)', *ILR All.*, vol. XII, 1890, pp. 558–64.

[20] 'Daulta Kuari (plaintiff) *v.* Meghu Tiwari and another (defendants)', *ILR All.*, vol. XV, 1893, pp. 382–4.

and Daulta: not only did they ask for a fixed sum in the present and backpay from the past, they also looked to the future and asked that their maintenance be made a charge on the estates of their late husbands. This way, if the property were to be sold or otherwise alienated, the purchaser would still be obliged to pay, no matter who he was or what relation, if any, he had to the widow. Thus, the plaintiffs in these suits were seeking to shift the burden of maintenance away from their individual families and attach it to land—a neutral commodity that could fall into anybody's (any man's) hands.

Let us look at the case of Ram Kunwar. This widow fought in the courts for over *fifteen years* for her right to be maintained. Shortly before 1887, she sued her sons for maintenance and was awarded an unspecified sum by the courts. Her sons, however, were quite lax in making payments, and Ram did not receive the total amount due to her. Thereafter, the property was sold to an outsider. The widow Ram then sued the purchaser for back-pay of maintenance and also demanded that her allowance be made a permanent charge on the estate. She argued that, as the property had originally belonged to her late husband, she was entitled to be supported out of the profits derived from it as long as she was alive, no matter who owned it. Despite Ram's prolonged struggle, the court eventually ruled against her.[21]

Unfortunately, this case became something of a landmark ruling: it was cited as precedent in similar cases for many years to come. The following year, for example, the widow Gopal Dei also sued to have her maintenance made a charge on the estate of her late husband. This dispute actually dated back to 1865, when Gopal's husband was still alive. At this time, she sued her husband for a monthly allowance, claiming that the family status merited it. The courts ruled in her favour, and she began receiving Rs 120 per month. Many years later,

[21] 'Ram Kunwar (plaintiff) *v.* Ram Dai (defendant)', *ILR All.*, vol. XXII, 1900, pp. 326–9. This was not the first such case in our period. Several widows had already asked that their maintenance be made a charge on their late husband's estates, and some of them prevailed. It is unclear why the court did not cite these cases as precedent. See 'Raghubans Kunwar and another (defendants) *v.* Bhagwant Kunwar (plaintiff)', *ILR All.*, vol. XXIV, 1899, pp. 183–6.

after her husband died, the family ran into financial difficulties and was forced to sell off most of its property. The widow Gopal's maintenance was subsequently stopped. At this point, she brought another suit, arguing that the previous ruling had established a charge on the estate, and whoever was holding the property was obliged to continue paying her. Moreover, she stated that the buyers were aware of her claim to maintenance before they bought the property. This, in her view, made them doubly liable to remit her monthly allowance.[22]

Several similar suits were heard by the Allahabad HC between 1875 and 1911. Most ended in defeat for the widow; some did not. But win or lose, these widows' plaints are important for a variety of reasons. First, we need to recognize the extraordinary efforts put forth by the widow plaintiffs: many of these disputes lasted for decades, and women like Ram Kunwar and Gopal Dei hung in there until the end. Moreover, some of the plaintiffs had remarried, or had been unchaste, or were childless—they were not in the most ideal position to be fighting with their in-laws. Yet in their eyes, maintenance was a right, despite what Hindu law, society, or the courts dictated. To them, this support should not be haphazard: it should be a fixed sum, paid regularly. Second, the widow plaintiffs clearly believed that the Anglo-Indian courts were an appropriate forum in which to fight their battles. They used the courts freely, and obviously felt comfortable doing so—otherwise they surely would not have brought case after case and appeal upon appeal, for fifteen to twenty years.[23]

Third, a special emphasis should be placed on the fact that the overwhelming majority of widows suing over maintenance requested

[22] 'The Bhartpur State (defendant) *v.* Gopal Dei (plaintiff)', *ILR All.*, vol. XXIV, 1902, pp. 160–4.

[23] That a single case goes through appeal after appeal and remains in the legal system for so long is not extraordinary in the Indian setting. In the past, anthropologists have addressed this phenomenon in an effort to understand why the colonial and postcolonial legal process in India seems to be so incredibly inefficient. What is relevant for our purposes, however, is to recognize that widows were sometimes litigants in these long and drawn out cases—they used the system just like everyone else did. For the major outlines of the anthropological debate, see: Oliver Mendelsohn, 'The Pathology of the Indian Legal

that their allowance be attached to property. Plaints bearing this request were extremely common during our period; this issue must
have been awfully important to the plaintiffs. All these individual
widows, in all their varying circumstances, were essentially speaking
with a common voice: they were saying that adequate financial support should be a legal right that derives from their late husband's
ownership of property rather than their membership in a particular
family. The advantages of this are clear. First, the widow is guaranteed
support for life, as opposed to the duration for which her marital
family owns its property. Second, this support is not dependent on
any particular individual or family. It is not, therefore, subject to the
souring of relations, the changing membership of the coparcenary,
succession, bequest, or any of the other vagaries that can obfuscate
personal relationships. Rather, it derives from the unalterable fact
that the widow's husband had an interest in the property. The
plaintiffs would have a claim on this property, no matter who owned
it. In this way, their support would become a society-wide burden—
anyone who purchased an encumbered estate would be compelled
to pay maintenance.

Finally, the request to attach maintenance payments to land is a
prime example of South Asian women adjusting to 'big changes'. The
commodification of land and the increasingly high rates of land
alienation in the latter half of the nineteenth century must have been
problematic for widows who depended on a family's ownership of
land for maintenance. Fixing the payments to land would have
remedied this problem. The plaintiffs were doubtless trying to adapt,
adjust, and reshape the rules and customs regarding maintenance to
better fit the new policies in land. These women, then, were asking
that their support be made a fixed, systematic legal obligation that
was shared by all society and that withstood both personal and economic caprices. Moreover, they clearly believed that the Anglo-
Indian courts were an appropriate forum in which to put forth this
request.

System', *Modern Asian Studies* 15:4 (1981), pp. 823–63; R. Kidder, 'Courts and
Conflict in an Indian City', *Journal of Commonwealth Political Studies*, XI (1973),
pp. 121–39; Bernard Cohn, 'Anthropological Notes on Disputes and Law in
India', *American Anthropologist* 67: 6, part II (1965), pp. 82–122.

Beating Them at Their Own Game: Manipulation
and the Legal Process

Many of the widows whose stories have been preserved for us not only felt free to enter the judicial arena, they felt free to bend the rules and manipulate the system as well. The shrewdness they displayed and the tactics they employed in trying to serve their own ends indicate that these women knew the system well—they were not outsiders who occasionally ventured in. The widows we will meet in the following pages used crooked arbitrators, negotiated and bargained with their in-laws, and flat-out lied in court to secure their rights over property. Quite removed from the meek, helpless and socially ostracized characters that one might expect to find, these women were on the offensive.

The 1906 case *Ram Sarup v. Ram Dei* offers the most compelling example of this type of behaviour. In this suit, a group of widows banded together and conferred upon *themselves* proprietary rights to joint family property. The persons involved were as shown in Table 1.

The background to the dispute is fairly simple: the last male in the coparcenary to die was Bahadur Lal, and, as is apparent from the genealogy in Table 1, there were no surviving male heirs to take immediate possession of the property. Thus, the considerable estate (consisting of landed property, several houses, and shops) fell into the hands of Ram Dei, who took temporary possession with the limited rights allowed widows. A small number of shares was retained (probably in lieu of maintenance) by her two sisters in-law, Parbati and Kausila. The next reversioner after Ram Dei would have been Ram Sarup.

This case entered the legal system in February 1892, when the widow Ram Dei sued Parbati and Kausila for a declaration that, as the widow of the last full owner, she was entitled to the entire estate. The suit, however, never came to trial, for the three widows, along with Kirpa Dei, struck a compromise whereby the estate would be divided equally among them, and each one of them would hold their portion with absolute title. The agreement was overseen and executed by a (not so neutral) arbitrator—he was the agent of Ram Dei! These

Table 1

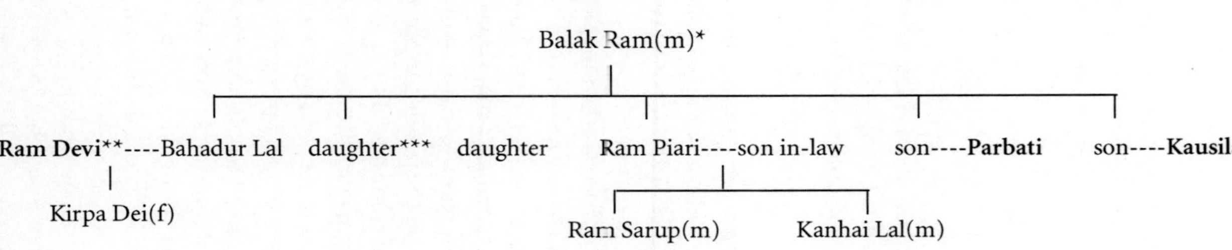

*where the sex of a family member is not obvious, it has been indicated by (m) for male and (f) for female
**widows' names are given in bold
***many of the names of family members are unknown and are therefore recorded in relation to Balak Ram

details came to light only when Ram Sarup objected. At this point, the court launched a detailed inquiry into the goings-on between these women.

Although the widows' agreement was overturned in the end, the implications of their actions are far-reaching. This was an estate in which not one of them held absolute title, and over which not one of them had any permanent rights. Yet they somehow decided to take and to confer on each other full proprietary rights in the said estate. Moreover, their use of a 'neutral' arbitrator is telling. Arbitration was often used to settle cases before they came to court, and many times it was just a ruse; it was a way to have a certain outcome legitimated and stamped by the justices. Ram Dei was most likely aware of this and tried to use arbitration to manipulate the outcome of her suit. This widow, then, was quite familiar and comfortable with the ins and outs of the legal process.

Finally, it is quite possible that not just the arbitration, but the suit itself, was initiated fraudulently. These three widows, seeing a valuable estate and no immediate heir, probably orchestrated the events leading up to the arbitration with an eye to dividing the property among themselves. And their scheme might have worked had Ram Sarup not legally objected. The widow Ram Dei and her cohorts took a proactive stance in securing their financial self-interests. Rather than pinning their hopes on maintenance payments that could be decreased or rescinded at any point, they took steps—albeit dishonest ones—to ensure that they would benefit from the family property.[24]

This type of shrewdness was not uncommon among widows appearing before the Allahabad HC. Hedging, negotiating, bargaining, and even outright fraud were committed by more than one widow. As in the above case, the lines between defendant and plaintiff were often blurred due to collusion—the litigants in these cases were not so much fighting each other as trying to circumvent Hindu laws of inheritance. In the 1870s, for instance, the young widow Jeoni re-married her late husband's cousin according to the *karewa*, or

[24] The justices themselves assumed that all three widows were in on the deal, although there was no hard evidence or testimony to support such a claim. 'Ram Sarup (plaintiff) *v.* Ram Dei and others (defendants)', *ILR All.*, vol. xxix, 1907, pp. 239–43.

levirate form of marriage. She was then 'sued' by her new father-in-law for possession of her deceased husband's estate. This suit was settled out of court: Jeoni relinquished all her rights to her former husband's estate and handed it over to the 'plaintiff'. In other words, she did not try to resist or fight in any way.

Years later, in 1897, the court discovered that the suit and settlement between Jeoni and her father-in-law had been collusive: Jeoni had struck a deal with her father-in-law in order to transfer her late husband's property to her current husband. The court reversed this settlement, arguing that Jeoni's total surrender of the estate, without even a struggle, was tantamount to an alienation by her, and as a Hindu widow this was not in her power to do. But even though her plan was thwarted, Jeoni's story is noteworthy for the effort and creativity that she employed in trying to keep her property intact. By transferring her late husband's estate to her new husband and father-in-law, it was free of all restrictions and could be passed on in full to any sons that she might have. Otherwise, it would have been divided up among a very large family upon her remarriage. Faced with the choice of losing her late husband's property altogether or transferring it to her new husband, she quite reasonably chose the latter.[25]

Once again, then, we see a young widow trying to beat the system in order to secure her hold over property. In this instance, she allied with male coparceners in the family. This case raises a number of important issues. First, we see a widow who had undergone the levirate form of marriage manipulating the system and colluding with her in-laws. Widows generally disfavoured levirate marriage—some even ran away in order to avoid it.[26] Yet Jeoni was trying to make the best of what was most probably a bad situation. If both she and the property had to remain within the family, she at least wanted to keep it intact and retain some degree of control over it.

Second, the fact that Jeoni was in cahoots with her new father-in-law highlights an important possibility. That a member of the

[25] 'Sheo Singh and others (plaintiffs) *v.* Jeoni and others (defendants)', *ILR All.*, vol. XIX, 1897, pp. 524–7.

[26] Chowdhry, 'Popular Perceptions of Widow-remarriage in Haryana', op. cit.

coparcenary (particularly one that occupied such a powerful position) found it beneficial to negotiate and collude with a young widow challenges the thesis that all widows were powerless and entirely dependent in their matrimonial homes. It is quite likely that family members were aware that forging an alliance with a widow in temporary possession of her husband's separate estate could have a huge pay-off. If this estate was considerable, then holding it—even just temporarily—might well have put the widow in a position of power, with her in-laws jockeying for approval and friendship, trying to strike deals, hatch plots, and plan fraudulent lawsuits. If this was the situation in which certain widows found themselves, it would not be the first time in history that such alliances with women were key to gaining wealth and status.[27]

Lastly, this suit exemplifies one of the many ways in which widows got around restrictions on the alienation of property. Here, a phoney lawsuit was staged in order to mask what was essentially the transfer of property by a Hindu widow. This kind of trickery popped up quite

[27] Leslie Peirce, in *The Imperial Harem: Women and Sovereignty in the Ottoman Empire* (New York: Oxford University Press, 1993), documents how alliances with women and between women in the Ottoman household were key to the consolidation of power in the late medieval Ottoman empire.

The fact that there are other ways to look at this case has not escaped my attention. It is possible, though unlikely, that Jeoni had been coerced or manipulated in some way. Clearly, the plan could have been conceived purely by Jeoni's father-in-law. In response to this, I would argue that the lines between agency and manipulation are not always clear cut; neither are the two mutually exclusive. If, however, we assume that the power relations here were unidirectional, that is, *if* Jeoni's father-in-law alone had hatched the plan, and *if* he had forced her to take part, then at the very least, we can say that he needed her to pull it off. The most likely scenario, however, is that the two had colluded: first, because the transfer of property was beneficial to both, and second, because coercion was not mentioned as a possibility, neither by the court nor by the nephew who legally objected. Wherever the justices sensed coercion, they tended to document it, and they have not done that here. Rather, they concurred with the nephew's assertion that 'in order to transfer the property to her second husband, the device to which [Jeoni] resorted was that she got a suit instituted against herself by [her father-in-law].' See 'Sheo Singh *v.* Jeoni', op. cit.

consistently throughout our period, especially with regard to the alienation of property. Indeed, the stipulation against alienation seemed to be highly unpopular among widows. In order to get around it, they would typically try to obtain consent from the next reversioner before gifting, selling, or mortgaging property—in other words, they would try to safeguard their alienations in anticipation of objections from other parties.[28] In certain instances, this tactic worked: the court sometimes ruled that a widow's transfer was valid because it was done with the next heir's approval. The point, however, is that whether they were successful or not, widows like Jeoni did not just throw up their hands in the face of the many restrictions on their tenure. Rather, they found loopholes and clauses in the system and did their level best to use them to their advantage.

But what did they do when there were no clauses, no loopholes, no tangled webs to weave? Many widow plaintiffs resorted to flat-out lies. The widow Dharam Kunwar, for example, first came to court in 1900, swearing that she had validly and legitimately adopted a son, Balwant Singh, as heir to her deceased husband's estate. Eight years later, however, the same widow came before the same court, alleging that this adoption had never taken place. Clearly, Dharam was lying in one lawsuit or the other. Given the voluminous amount of evidence with which she supported her first plaint, it seems highly likely that she was lying the second time around. Her motives here can be surmised with a fair degree of certainty: in the first suit, Dharam was protecting not only her son's right to hold the property in question, but her own control over it as well. At the time, Balwant was a minor, and she would have been appointed guardian of the estate—the sizeable tract of land in question would have been under her complete control.

Nearly a decade later, however, when the second suit was instituted, Balwant had most probably reached the age of majority and Dharam was again in danger of losing control over the estate, this time to her own son. Unfortunately, the record indicates little about the

---

[28] See, for instance, 'Sia Dasi and others (defendants) *v.* Gur Sahai (plaintiff)', *ILR All.*, vol. III, 1881, pp. 362–4 and 'Ramphal Rai and another (plaintiffs) *v.* Tila Kuari and others (defendants)', *ILR All.*, vol. VI, 1884, pp. 116–21.

relationship that existed between mother and son—perhaps Balwant would have granted his mother a generous allowance or perhaps she feared receiving no support at all. One thing, however, is quite clear: by 1908 the tables had turned for Dharam, and it was then in her best interests to argue that the adoption was invalid. In doing so, she put a plain lie before the court. Evidently, this widow was not shy in pursuing her financial goals and using (in fact, abusing) the legal system in the process. Even if this meant presenting a falsified claim and lying before the justices, she was determined and confident enough to do this.[29]

There were, then, at least a few widows who believed that they had every right to throw their hats into the legal ring. They did not behave as though they were at a disadvantage; they did not feel restricted in either access or expression. Not only did they use the legal process, they tried to manipulate it as well. These women knew the internal workings of the system—so well, in fact, that they tried to bend it to suit their own ends. In their eyes, the courts belonged to them just as they did to everyone else.

Court as Partner:
Widows and Property Management

Not every widow came to court in order to get around the laws of inheritance: some came in search of a partner. And the court made an able partner, of sorts, particularly when it came to the efficient management of an estate. Once property passed into the hands of a Hindu widow, the management and oversight of the entire estate, including moveable property, immoveable property, profits, and the payment and collection of debt became her responsibility. Not surprisingly, widows came up against a variety of obstacles in trying to accomplish these tasks, not the least of which was lack of cooperation on the part of business associates and family members. During our

[29] 'Dharam Kunwar (plaintiff) *v.* Balwant Singh (defendant)', *ILR All.*, vol. xxx, 1908, pp. 549–59. This was not the first time a shaky plaint was brought to court over the alleged adoption of a son. See 'Ram Kuar and another (opposite parties) *v.* Sardar Singh (applicant)', *ILR All.*, vol. xx, 1898, pp. 352–4. In this suit, two co-widows tried to deny an adoption nearly twenty years after they were notified of the transfer of property into their adopted son's hands.

period, quite a few widows turned to the legal system in an effort to maximize profits and manage their wealth more efficiently. These suits demonstrate not only how Hindu widows used the courts, they also show the detail and care with which they oversaw their estates.

In February 1878, for example, the widow Ruka Bai sued her husband's sister, Ganda Bai. She did so in an attempt to reduce Ganda Bai's monthly allowance. After the deaths of her husband and father-in-law, the family business temporarily fell into Ruka Bai's hands. In years past, this business had done very well, and during this period Ganda Bai had sued for a portion of the profits. She won her suit, and was granted a monthly allowance of Rs 30 for as long as the company existed. But by the time Ruka Bai took over the business, it was failing. The widow plaintiff then instituted a suit to reduce her sister-in-law's allowance by Rs 10 per month, arguing that the firm did not enjoy enough profits to sustain the current sum. In support of her argument, she produced detailed financial records showing profits and losses, proving that the company could not afford Rs 30 per month. Clearly, Ruka Bai was on the ball when it came to managing the family business: she kept meticulous records and did what she needed to do to protect the assets of the company. This widow looked to the Anglo-Indian courts to secure the cooperation of her sister-in-law and protect the firm from sustaining further losses. This turned out to be a wise decision: she won her case.[30]

Nearly thirty years later, the widow Jwala Dei presented the High Court with a similar request: she asked the justices to protect the family business from loss of profits. As the widow of a pundit, Jwala Dei was severely restricted in her ability to carry on her late husband's business: by virtue of the fact that she was a woman, she could not perform the same duties that he had. She therefore turned her husband's books over to another pundit, and asked that he carry on the business of *purohit* (family pundit). Their agreement was that he would hand the proceeds over to her.[31] The pundit in question, however, refused to pass the profits on to Jwala, and she subsequently

---

[30] 'Ruka Bai (plaintiff) *v.* Ganda Bai (defendant)', *ILR All.*, vol. I, 1876–8, pp. 594–6.

[31] A *purohit's* books, or *pothis*, typically contained lists of his clients, or *jujmans*, along with a short family history and the duties that he traditionally performed for them.

sued to recover the money as well as her husband's books.[32] The court eventually ruled in her favour.

Thus, we see that certain widows used the courts to bring legal action against those that put the family business at risk and threatened their profits. These are not isolated cases: we see widows using the legal system for these purposes throughout our period.[33] In most of them, the widow plaintiffs prevailed. These suits demonstrate the readiness of plaintiffs to turn to the legal system as well as their tenacity as property managers. Hindu law asserts that widows only hold their late husbands' estates temporarily, with little or no rights; they hold it as 'the useless half' of their late husband. One might then expect widows to take little care or interest in maintaining the wealth and profitability of such property. But the widows who came to court approached their property with a sense of responsibility and accountability. In short, they approached it with a sense of ownership.

Widow as Subject: A Postscript on Agency

The cases discussed above illuminate a number of themes and trends. We have seen why widows entered the legal system, how they used the courts and how they perceived their property rights. Their concerns were varied, as were their backgrounds and status. Yet there is one common thread tying all of these widows together: they all displayed a keen awareness of the legal system, and they all acted on this knowledge. In other words, the widows featured here used the judicial process and their knowledge of it to exert power, to a greater or lesser degree. There is no denying that the court did not always side with the widow, and sometimes when it did its ruling may not have been enforced. At the very least, however, our widow plaintiffs were able to delay the goals and complicate the paths of opposing parties.

[32] 'Hans Raj (defendant) *v.* Ratni alias Jwala Dei (plaintiff)', *ILR All.*, vol. XXVII, 1905, pp. 200–3.

[33] For example, see 'Parbati (plaintiff) *v.* Niadar (defendant)', *ILR All.*, vol. XVIII, 1896 pp. 129–31. In this case, the widow Parbati sued one of her late husband's tenants when he refused to pay rent to her. She argued that she had the right to collect rent, even though this had not been specified in her husband's will.

The question of agency looms large here, as it does in most work on dominated groups. It is indeed true that our widows' cases were taken up by male pleaders and advocates (in this they very likely had no choice). Furthermore, lawsuits were sometimes initiated jointly, and in many instances widows acted in conjunction with male family members. However, it would be a mistake to presume that widow plaintiffs were, as a matter of course, being manipulated or used by these third parties. Granted, the legal actions taken by widows, as well the legal awareness displayed by them, is 'shocking', and it is easy to assume that their lawsuits were being orchestrated and instigated by others. After all, the widow plaintiff's proactive and aggressive protection of financial self-interest does not jell with our image of a meek, tonsured, socially ostracized and outcasted woman.

The widow's litigious protests, however, *do* fit in perfectly with the larger legal context of the time. The late nineteenth century in India has been called the 'great age of litigation'. During this period, the incidence of litigation rose dramatically; particularly sharp was the rise in cases concerning landed property. Moreover, the colonial courts proved to be hugely popular with the natives: it was here that these land disputes were brought.[34] While most legal histories do not address women's participation or place in these developments, it stands to reason that women were affected by these trends as well. This presumption is supported by the court records: between 1875 and 1911, the vast majority of cases heard by the Allahabad HC involved landed property, and these suits were instituted by all sorts—disgruntled sons, brothers, sisters, daughters, mothers, and even fathers. Our widows' cases pop up in the midst of these numerous

[34] There is a substantial literature on the legal developments of the late nineteenth century. See: David Washbrook, 'Law, State and Agrarian Society in Colonial India', *Modern Asian Studies* 15:3 (1981), pp. 649–72; Marc Galanter, 'The Displacement of Traditional Law in Modern India', in Rajeev Dhavan, ed., *Law and Society in Modern India* (Delhi: Oxford University Press 1989), pp. 15–36; Nicholas B. Dirks, 'From Little King to Landlord: Property, Law and the Gift under the Madras Permanent Settlement', *Comparative Study of Society and History* 28 (1986), 307–33; Pamela G. Price, 'The "Popularity" of the Imperial Courts of Law: Three Views of the Anglo-Indian Legal Encounter', in Mommsen and de Moor, op. cit., pp. 179–200.

property disputes: they were but a small part of the general rise in litigation.

In this environment, there were various opportunities for widows to familiarize themselves with law and the colonial courts. Some of our plaintiffs, for instance, came from propertied, litigious families and would have been familiar with the legal system and the laws relevant to the protection and possession of landed property.[35] Still other widow plaintiffs had the prior experience of being named as a defendant in a suit, or had been involved in more than one legal action.[36] In these ways, widows would have learned how the judicial process worked as well the many legal positions they could claim. Thus, the widows Jwala Dei, Lachman Kunwar, and Raghubur Kunwar sued over broken contracts; the widows Jamna, Bainsi, and Daulta Kuari fought over what they perceived to be their moral and legal rights; the widows Jeoni, Dharam Kunwar, and Ram Dei had such an intimate knowledge of the system that they were able to manipulate it and capitalize on its shortcomings. Therefore, given both the data and the context, it makes most sense to assume that our widow plaintiffs were not passive and dependent objects who were manipulated by men, but subjects acting in their own self-interest.

Concluding Remarks

The study of women and the law has taken off in recent times, not only among South Asianists but among scholars of other formerly colonized regions as well.[37] The literature produced, while both engaging and insightful, is still in its formative stages: tackling an entity

---

[35] See 'Indar Kuar (defendant) *v.* Lalta Prasad Singh (plaintiff)', *ILR All.*, vol. IV, 1882, pp. 532–46 and 'Raja Rup Singh (plaintiff) *v.* Rani Bainsi and the Collector of Etawah (defendants)', *ILR All.*, vol. VII, 1885, pp. 1–20.

[36] See 'Bhaoni (plaintiff) *v.* Maharaj Singh (defendant)', *ILR All.*, vol. III, 1881, pp. 738–44 and 'Ram Kunwar *v.* Ram Dei', op. cit.

[37] Most notably, social historians of the Middle East have been engaging this topic in recent years. See, for example, Judith Tucker, *In the House of the Law: Gender and Islamic Law in Ottoman Syria and Palestine* (1998). In the Indian context, two significant works are Sudhir Chandra (on the Rukmabai case), *Enslaved Daughters: Colonialism, Law, and Women's Rights* (Delhi: Oxford

as multifaceted and multilayered as 'the law' is a mammoth project. Thus far, however, the study of the interaction between women and the law, particularly as it unfolded on the South Asian subcontinent, has meant studying nineteenth-century legislative reforms. Indeed, to many gender historians, 'law' has become nearly synonymous with reforms such as the abolition of sati, the Hindu Widows' Remarriage Act, and the Age of Consent Act. The end result is that most studies on women's place within the law focus solely on the impetus, effects, and women's participation (or lack thereof) in these reforms.

This is highly problematic, for it ignores the many faces of the colonial legal system, the many levels on which it exercised power, and the many ways in which it was generated and regenerated, incorporating elements of both the 'colonial' and the 'indigenous'. To study a system only in its times of crisis and debate is to understand very little about how it operated, on a daily basis, at the grassroots level. And to do this is to lose women from the picture altogether. For, while the nineteenth-century reforms were significant, they occurred with very little input and participation from the women whom they purported to help. They were, at base, a series of dialogues between the colonial state and the indigenous male elite.[38] Thus, the overemphasis on colonial legislative reforms forces us to look at 'women and the law' from the perspective of the law, as opposed to women—women do not figure in the story.

This project, however, has attempted to tell the story of the Hindu widow in the colonial courts from the perspective of the widow herself: how did she view the legal system? What did she use it for? What property rights did she exercise? While not claiming to offer definitive and comprehensive answers to these questions, this study can provide a preliminary picture. The women featured used and interacted with the law in a very non-spectacular way. They used the legal system—the courts, the pleaders, the arbitrators, the appeals process—for themselves, to redress personal grievances. They did so

---

University Press, 1998); and Meera Kosambi's essay on the same case in *Crossing Thresholds: Feminist Essays in Social History* (Delhi: Permanent Black, 2007).

[38] Lata Mani shows this quite clearly in her study on the abolition of sati. See Mani, op. cit.

quietly and ordinarily, by initiating lawsuits, appearing in the courts, and putting requests before the justices. They were concerned not with legal reform and sweeping changes but with the betterment of individual situations. Clearly, these widows did not see the legal system as out of bounds, or for men only, and they did not behave as though they had been banished from the public sphere. Rather, they demonstrated an intimate familiarity with the workings of the system, and a willingness to use it, not just once, but sometimes over and over again.

Moreover, the women represented in these suits came from all walks of life. Many came from extremely wealthy families, as one might expect. These plaintiffs were often maharanis suing for possession of small kingdoms. The majority of women, however, came from more humble backgrounds—their marital families owned small portions of villages, tracts of land, or maybe a couple of shops. Then there were a few widows who came from very poor families. One widow, for instance, testified that she contributed to the family income by grinding and selling grain; another came from the sweeper caste. There were even one or two suits instituted by widow paupers. The Anglo-Indian courts seemed to welcome all of them, or at least provide them all with a forum for fighting their battles.[39]

But what, if anything, came of all these widows' efforts? Did they win for themselves any rights? Did any meaningful changes come about as a result of their actions? When the cases are examined as a whole, it is apparent that some legal precedents were established by widows. Lower-caste widows in Allahabad, for example, won the right to retain their former husband's property on remarriage.[40]

---

[39] See: 'Harpal Singh and others (defendants) *v.* Lekhraj Kunwar (plaintiff) and Janki Kunwar (defendant)', *ILR All.*, vol. xxx, 1908, pp. 406–21; 'Parbati (plaintiff) *v.* Niadar (defendant)', *ILR All.*, vol. xviii, 1896, pp. 129–31; 'Har Saran Das (plaintiff) *v.* Nandi and another (defendants)', *ILR All.*, vol. xi, 1881, pp. 332–4; 'The Secretary of State for India in Council (plaintiff) *v.* Bhagawanti Bibi and others (defendants)', *ILR All.*, vol. xiii, 1891, pp. 326–30. These cases exemplify the varied backgrounds from which widow plaintiffs and defendants came.

[40] The Allahabad High Court was unique in its rulings on Act XV of 1856, the Hindu Widows' Remarriage Act. The act granted the legal right of remarriage

'Unchaste' mothers (who had already been widowed) won the right to inherit from their sons; 'unchaste' widows won the right to retain their late husband's estate, provided that the 'misconduct' had occurred after their husband's demise. In other words, thanks to the efforts of widow plaintiffs, chastity and fidelity became legal conditions for the *succession* as opposed to the *retention* of an estate. Widows won the right to receive an equal portion of family property if it was being partitioned, and they also won the right to hold this share with absolute title.

With regard to maintenance, widows were able to secure a major victory during our period: they were able to have this moral obligation recognized as a legal right, one which had to be met by their affinal family. All the simple requests for maintenance and arrears were granted, and they formed a string of oft-cited precedents. With respect to having maintenance made a charge on family property, however, widows came up against a brick wall: the Allahabad justices consistently ruled that a widow's right to maintenance must not be allowed to encroach upon the free sale of property. This meant that, for all practical purposes, a widow would lose her maintenance once family property was sold. If, however, family property changed hands through bequest, succession, or mortgage, widows were often able to have their maintenance made a permanent claim on the estate. So women did manage to secure limited gains during our period, and, significantly, they were able to affect the development of case law in the Anglo-Indian courts.

A brief word about widow defendants would be appropriate at this point. Surprisingly, the attitude of total ownership shines through even more clearly in these suits than it does in those instituted by

---

to all Hindu widows, including high-castes widows who previously did not enjoy this right. The most contentious part of the act was section 2, the clause that stipulated that a widow must forfeit her late husband's estate on remarriage. While the other High Courts applied this clause to all widows (even those lower caste widows who traditionally practised remarriage), the Allahabad justices consistently ruled that the act and all its clauses were meant to apply to high-caste widows only. See Lucy Carroll, op. cit., for further discussion of the High Courts' rulings on the Hindu Widows' Remarriage Act.

widows. As mentioned, the scope of this essay does not allow for detailed discussion of suits with widow defendants. But let it be said that when suits were instituted against widows, it was generally due to the 'inappropriately' bold actions that they took with respect to inherited property (usually an alienation of some sort). These disputes over alienation are rich in detail and insight. They display, quite powerfully, the widow's attitude of total and complete ownership of her inherited estate: in them, we see women selling, gifting, and regifting, bequeathing (often to natal family members!), and micromanaging property as though they had absolute title.[41] These widows did not feel restricted by the stipulations of Hindu law, society's expectations, and even High Court rulings. That is the salient point here—not what was *allowed* by society and the courts, but what was *done* by the widows themselves.

This attitude of ownership was also apparent in the suits examined, albeit not so glaringly. Both as defendants and plaintiffs, our widows' behaviour casts a huge question mark over our current notions of the Hindu widow. How do we reconcile the social restrictions on the widow's dress, movements, and sexuality with her regular appearance in court? How do we account for the Hindu widow as proprietor and manager, given the strict Hindu law of inheritance? At the very least, we can say that the prohibitions placed on the widow speak volumes about society's attitude towards the widow while telling us very little about the state of mind and attitude of the widow herself. The Hindu widow was indeed *granted* very limited rights over property, but she *exercised* a great deal of power over the property that fell into her hands. Many widows either paid no heed to social and legal impediments, or they figured out ways to get around them—this is apparent from the handful of cases involving collusion and manipulation that were discussed above.

But, more importantly, the two pictures can be reconciled by bearing in mind the limitations imposed by the historical record. Regrettably, we can only discuss those few widows who came to

---

[41] An excellent example of such behaviour can be found in 'Srimati Prosonomyi Devi and another (defendants) *v*. Beni Madhab and another (plaintiffs)', *ILR All.*, vol. v, 1883, pp. 556–62.

court between 1875 and 1911. And their numbers are extraordinarily small: a couple of hundred-odd widows, out of hundreds of thousands. What we are discussing, then, are exceptions to the norm—it is quite possible, in fact probable, that the majority of widows did not fight and struggle to retain their property, and that most of them never even thought of using the colonial courts. Most widows were indeed financially dependent and helpless. But the widows in this study, while few in number, highlight the complexities and diversities of widowhood in nineteenth-century India. Widowhood cannot simply be dubbed a state of 'social death', full stop.

Although our widow plaintiffs' experiences may not coincide with those of most other widows, their stories are nonetheless important and need to be added to the landscape of Indian social history. In a 1990 article, Judith Tucker reformulated Charles Tilly's well-known thesis on the meaning and purpose of European social history:

> It is the way people lived [the macro] changes—they way they perceived, struggled against, accommodated, or actively encouraged them—that give these changes their content as well as their historical meaning . . . Social historians are bridge builders. Through the investigation of the lives of ordinary people, they seek to span the big structural changes and the human realities.[42]

This, in a nutshell, is what this essay set out to accomplish. We already know about the 'big changes' of the period: the uneven penetration of the colonial state and the opportunistic application of capitalist relations; the introduction of gendered rights in land and property; the favouring of upper-caste men and ancient scriptures—these developments and others like them formed the backdrop, the landscape, of women's lives in the colonial period. However, the details and colours of the landscape are provided by individual women who adapted, struggled, responded to, and accommodated the big changes. Their story is one of doing: what they were doing

[42] Judith E. Tucker, 'Taming the West: Trends in the Writing of Modern Arab Social History in Anglophone Academia', in Hisham Sharabi, ed., *Theory, Politics, and the Arab World: Critical Responses* (New York: Routledge, 1990).

was owning property and using the colonial legal system, despite all of the obstacles that were placed in their path. Without them, the picture remains incomplete.

Finally, the struggles of the individual widows outlined above make an important statement on the nature of power, resistance, and the relationship between the two. The plaintiffs discussed above were hardly self-conscious 'resisters'. They were simply trying to better their lives, and using all the means available to them along the way. The underlying assumption behind resistance is, of course, that it should produce some type of positive sea change for those undertaking it. This, in many ways, has become the yardstick by which we measure resistance. But the women we met here achieved only tiny gains, perhaps because their 'resistance' was expressed only through the tiny cracks *within* the overarching structures of patriarchy and colonialism. What their stories tell us is that systems of dominance contain within them, as an integral part of them, spaces that allow for resistance and input from all levels. Thus, it would be overly facile to define a colonial legal system that was allied with upper-caste men and shut women out completely; it would be incorrect to perceive Hindu law and the Hindu joint family as systems which stripped women of all meaningful power and participation. The Hindu widow indeed laboured under unforgiving structures of power, but these structures—the colonial state, patriarchy—contained within them limited avenues for her agency. It is these avenues that she sometimes availed of in court. So, while the litigious widow's isolated victories and limited gains may seem trivial compared to the widespread maltreatment of women, they are in fact an integral part of the colonial legal system and the patriarchal family structure that it upheld; they are integral to the story of the Hindu widow in colonial India.

8

A WORLD OF THEIR VERY OWN: RELIGION, PAIN, AND SUBVERSION IN BENGALI HOMES IN THE NINETEENTH CENTURY

Anindita Ghosh

The process of rendering women's literary and *antahpur* culture as depraved and in immediate want of correction is apparent in nineteenth-century debates on social reform. Women, in such discourses, appear as a major hindrance to the modernist project by continuing to subscribe to outdated rituals, morally polluting print, and coarse and boisterous entertainment. Implicit in such discursive formulations is also a given consensus on gender issues, not just between men but also among women themselves. The figure of the subservient and passive woman has too often shrouded our understanding of what was a much more varied and heterogeneous response to reformist moves.

While the existing literature on the subject treats this as a realm from which all women sought emancipation, paradoxically in our study this domain of tradition and seclusion emerges as a female haven of comfort and solace on the one hand, and gendered solidarity and struggle on the other. Hidden away in the deepest corners of the inner courtyards was a world of their very own—of religion, superstition, and ritual, resolute domesticity, and sisterhood—where women held their ground and from which they drew daily sustenance. Whether seeking support from female comradeship and a deep personal spiritualism, or surreptitiously contravening unwritten rules of domesticity, or even occasionally rebelling against ritual—we find women in this world challenging the borders of their gendered existence and voicing their disappointment with the surrounding social world.

Unruly Songs and Private Speech: Subversive Domestic Cultures

The image of compliant, submissive wives and daughters composing didactic tracts to further the cause of domestic reform under nationalist male aegis forms the subject matter of much recent scholarship on nineteenth-century Bengal. What is less appreciated is that, despite such strenuous efforts and the censorious frown of the reformist regime, substantial sections of Bengali middle-class women continued to hold on to their cultural preferences. As I have shown elsewhere, much to the agony and consternation of reformers, women were challenging dominant ideas of literary desirability and creating alternative tastes in reading. In patronizing contemporary racy print-cultures—novels, thrillers, and titillating romances—emerging from cheap presses in Calcutta and its suburbs, literate women were implicitly subverting the reformist agenda.[1] The social tensions created by middle-class women participating in particularly bawdy and earthy forms of feminine entertainment in the inner courtyards of the time have been amply documented in other studies.[2] That it required a concerted effort from educated Bengali men, English missionaries, and administrators to eventually put an end to such practices bears testimony to the enduring nature of such cultural traditions.

[1] Anindita Ghosh, *Power in Print: Popular Publishing and the Politics of Language and Culture in a Colonial Society, 1778–1905* (New Delhi: Oxford University Press, 2005), see ch. 6.

[2] Sumanta Banerjee, 'Marginalisation of Women's Popular Culture in Nineteenth-century Bengal', in Kumkum Sangari and Sudesh Vaid (eds), *Recasting Women: Essays in Colonial History* (New Delhi: Kali for Women, 1997).

Basar, or wedding songs, occupy a unique position in the print scene of that period, in that some of the most virulent attacks by critics in the columns of *bhadra* newspapers and journals were targeted at this genre. While novels and related 'useless fiction' were meant to corrupt and waste the female mind, basar songs were looked upon as a veritable source of disruptive and aggressive behaviour among women. These were songs sung by women in the bridal chamber on the wedding night, teasing the groom and engaging in verbal wrangles with him. Inherent in them is an honest admission of love and lust in the physical world, and open enjoyment of it.

Printed collections of these songs were much in demand. While women would have certainly had their own cache of songs from a rich oral folk repertoire, it is very likely that they would have read such works and learnt new, more stylish, songs from them. The title page of one such work carries a little inscription advertising the utility of the work for a basar participant:

> If there is anyone who has to visit a basar at short notice
> It would be useful to buy a copy of *Basarjamini* quickly.[3]

In the absence of a significant body of women writers creating this literature—let alone women writing in a lighter vein—it was male authors who catered to the demand for such works. But in as much as women patronized the genre, they 'authored' it as well. By the simple act of reading and enacting the songs printed, women were 'producing' the texts they consumed.[4] Their prices varied from two

---

[3] See Lalbehari De, *Basar Jamini* (Calcutta: 1886). Women in these works are represented as coming prepared on such occasions, armed with not just specific basar songs, but also a wider collection drawn from medieval romances and the latest dramas available in print. See Nandalal Ray, *Basar Kautuk Natak* (Calcutta: 1877), p. 17.

[4] Chartier's argument that reading is not passive but constituted out of a conscious interaction with the written text, and produces its own meanings, is relevant here. See Roger Chartier, *The Culture of Print: Power and the Uses of Print in Early Modern Europe*, trans. Lydia G. Cochrane (Cambridge: Polity, 1989); *The Cultural Uses of Print in Early Modern France*, trans. Lydia G. Cochrane (Princeton: Princeton University Press, 1987); *Cultural History: Between Practices and Representations* (Cambridge: Polity/Blackwell, 1988).

and a half to four annas, which was very affordable. The popularity of the genre is also evident from the fact that social reformers preferred to table their proposals under the covers of a basar song collection. Thus, Batakrishna Ray presented a collection of debates on widow remarriage in 1875 in the guise of a basar drama. Less than a third of the work deals with a basar, the rest is given over to the debate.[5]

In reformist bhadralok circles basar songs were condemned in no uncertain terms and efforts made to wean women away from the lure of such apparent trash.[6] Writing in the early 1880s Shib Chunder Bose, a Brahmo reformer, recorded his distaste for the practice: 'In the suburbs and rural districts of Bengal, females . . . are tacitly allowed to have so much liberty on this special occasion that they entertain the bridegroom (among other things) . . . with amorous songs . . . Frail as women naturally are . . . [this] has undoubtedly a tendency to impair the moral influence of a virtuous life.'[7] As a staunch Brahmo, Bose was predictably casting his criticism in a religious mould, but in this he was not standing far apart from educated Hindu reformist groups. Basar songs were looked upon as a social disease by the entire bhadralok in nineteenth-century Bengal.[8]

In fictional works, *basarghar* rituals were vehemently deplored. One such composition, *Kaminikusum Natak*, portrayed a bridegroom being smothered to death on his wedding night by revelling women.[9] A play, *Basar Udyan*, offered vicious representations of these sessions,

[5] Batakrishna Ray, *Basarkautuk Rahasya Natak* (Calcutta: Sudharnab Press, 1875).

[6] Not just in Bengal, but also elsewhere in India, in the late nineteenth and early twentieth centuries the singing of such songs was considered a serious shortcoming in women, and lack of proper education among them was held responsible for the evil. See Nita Kumar, 'Widows, Education and Social Change in Twentieth-century Banaras', *Economic and Political Weekly*, 27 April 1991, pp. 19–25.

[7] Shib Chunder Bose, *Hindoos As They Are* (Calcutta: 1881), p. 67.

[8] In fact, even Muslim Bengali gentlemen complained of the practice. See Maniruddin Ahmed, *Samajchitra* (Brahmanberia: 1908), p. 17.

[9] Shyamapada Banerji, *Kaminikusum Natak* (1886). See *Quarterly Reports of the Bengal Library*, Calcutta, June 1886, pp. 8–9.

with the participating women boxing the groom's ears till they turn red.[10] In the Preface to this work its author says:

> Perhaps many of you are aware how village women misbehave with grooms in basars. In particular, their cruel methods of boxing the groom's ears, and unbearably jubilant cries, turn the happy occasion into a prison-house [for the groom]. This work has been presented with the intention of stopping them from perpetrating such excesses, and in aid of the hapless groom. If this is staged widely, [I am] sure people will heed the advice, and mend their ways.[11]

While offering a relatively sober portrayal of wedding-night rituals in one of his social novels, Bankim too warned his readership in his distinct authorial voice.[12]

Newspaper reports occasionally complained of basarghar excesses, such as the following letter written to the editor of a leading paper by a bridegroom, sharing his plight with bhadralok readers: 'There were women all around me . . . Initially I was welcomed by them, but soon they began to use their hands. . . . They slapped me and pulled my ears, and almost tore out my beard and moustache. . . . Then, the ladies asked me to seat my wife on my lap, and began to heckle me. I cannot repeat them. You, and the readers can guess what sort of taunts they were.' The editor took strong note of this letter and warned all male elders of households to discipline their potentially disruptive wives, daughters, and daughters-in-law, advising them to threaten forfeiture of such freedom to their women if they continued to abuse it. [13]

It is, however, easier to see basar songs redefining women's sexuality in playful and mildly combative terms, rather than as posing any

[10] Nabagopal Das De, *Basar Udyan* (Calcutta: Samachar Chandrika Press, 1880), Introduction.

[11] Ibid., p. 10.

[12] That the message was important is evident in the way it is introduced. The intervention is direct and uninvited, and the sombre tones of social responsibility belong clearly to Bankim. See Bankimchandra Chattopadhyay, *Indira*, reprinted in Upendranath Mukhopadhyay, *Bankimchandrer Upanyas Granthavali* (2 vols), vol. 2 (Calcutta: 1909) pp. 405–6.

[13] *Someprakash*, 30 November 1863.

obvious threat to men. The mood on such occasions is normatively relaxed and often bordering on the erotic with rites encouraging the symbolic and literal sharing of bodily secretions between man and wife.[14] Even Bose's diatribes cannot hide the sexual cavorting underlying the depiction of physically abused bridegrooms.

> For the subdued women immersed in the drudgeries of monotonous domestic life this is an occasion of unbridled pleasure. The bride is made to sit on his lap and lie down beside him while he is forced to acknowledge her beauty. The groom is frequently slapped and pinched, and his ears pulled. The attempt is to outwit the bridegroom by their *thatta* and *tamasha* [jokes].[15]

A typical basar song collection would depict women gathering for the occasion on the wedding night and inviting the groom to match his wit with theirs. The groom is coaxed and cajoled into singing, while the women indulge him with flirtatious jokes and riddles. Sexual innuendoes abound in what appears to be an honest celebration of the imminent physical union. Curiously, the bride never speaks, her shadowy and passive presence being accepted as a general fact. Rather than resembling sexually inhibited prototypes of docile and submissive *bhadramahilas*, women on such occasions come across as playful and exuberant, engaging in a frank celebration of bodily pleasures. Culturally imposed modesty is thrown to the winds, for the situation warrants an upsetting of normative sanctions. Women's deliberate advances match masculine desire through delicate poetry as well as undisguised and bold sexual challenges. Disturbingly for the men, the thin line between sexual reticence on the one hand, and aggressive bawdy fun on the other, stands too obviously exposed.

The groom in Shyamacharan De's work is greeted by basar women with amorous songs.[16] One participant, Anjana, is so won over by the

---

[14] The groom was thus expected to chew the same spicy betel leaf that had been chewed by his wife. If he proved obstinate, the chewed betel was 'forcibly' thrust into his mouth by the women. Shib Chunder Bose, *Hindoos As They Are*, p. 69.

[15] Ibid., p. 67.

[16] Shyamacharan De, *Basarkautuk Natak*, p. 2.

groom that others chide her for being too easy with him.[17] Elaborate and aesthetic metaphors of sexual intercourse interlace riddles asked by the women, and the groom's answers match their candour.[18] Vivid descriptions of the general teasing and banter follow. The vocabulary depicted is unmistakably *meyeli*, or 'feminine', in character. The orthography matches the speech style. Informal language and depiction of easy familiarity among the characters make for very engaging reading, even if occasionally bordering on the gently abusive.[19]

The mock combats present the women in assertive positions, while the groom is uncertain and cautious. In this brief ritualistic reversal of roles, the groom surrenders himself to frolicking women. While they move closer and encircle him, apparently blocking any chances of his escape, the scene betrays heightened bodily tensions. The women vie with one another for his attention.[20] Warming up to the session they refer to the groom in familiar (but abusive) terms, generally reserved for partners, like *minshe* and *shala*.[21] They challenge him to match their verbal assaults, in the form of jokes and repartee. If answered well, he is promised rewards in the form of sexual pleasures by one of the participants, the infidelity and promiscuity implicit in the songs seeming to offer titillating possibilities of impending physical experience.

The transgressive roles of apparently meek housewives in basar sessions, I would argue, underwrite an imagined world of sexual autonomy and power that challenges prevailing ideas of gender

[17] Ibid., pp. 5–6.

[18] Thus, e.g. (Q.) 'What hurts the woman most? (*Ans.*) Misunderstanding with her lover; (*Q*) What ensnares the unsuspecting man? (*Ans.*) The female lover's hidden trap between her hips; (*Q*) Who is incapable of pleasing a woman? (*Ans.*) An ugly man.' Shyamacharan De, *Basarkautuk Natak*, pp. 11–14.

[19] Thus, words like *pnod* (arse) and *shala* (literally, a married man's brother-in-law, but often used as an abuse) and *minshe* (derivative of *manush*, man) are used in reference to the groom. Shyamacharan De, *Basarkautuk Natak*, pp. 5, 8.

[20] Ibid., p. 8.

[21] In literary depiction such terms would be generally used in the context of rustic or uneducated women, or women from the lower classes.

hierarchy. Representation of such unharnessed sexuality, not tied to either legitimate procreation or the confirmation of conjugal bonds between husband and wife, is tantamount to virtual rebellion. When viewed in the context of a customary belief in the ability of a married woman, by virtue of her sexuality, to disrupt relations even between her husband and his patrilineal kin, the implication is all the more serious.[22] The songs challenge this devaluation of women's sexuality and articulate a dramatically different perspective on sexual (and implied power) relations between men and women.

Of course, if we are to understand the basar sessions more fully, we need to place them within a tradition of bold and coarse entertainment—such as licentious songs and dances by low-caste occupational groups—believed to be shared by women, which was sought to be systematically stamped out from bhadralok homes in the nineteenth century.[23] Sumanta Banerjee has located a 'dissenting space' in such cultural practices shared by women from all classes against prevailing patriarchal values: 'The mockery of male depravity (as in the barbed shaft aimed at Krishna's promiscuity, or in the more openly bawdy description of old Vyasa), based on a common recognition of

[22] The dangerous sexuality of young wives, and the power that they have over their spouses, it was held, threatened other relationships within the patrilineal household—such as that between older and younger male members, and brother and sister, and senior female affines and young wives. The assumption was that the husband's natal ties take precedence over the conjugal relationship, as testified in contemporary proverbs:

Shuno bhai kolir abotar; koner bouri bole bhatar bhatar.

Oh hail the Age of Kali; the 'cornered' daughter-in-law
[newly-weds being assigned only the corner of any room]
cites her husband in every conversation.

The insolence seemed doubly unbearable as all newly-weds were supposed to be shy and obedient in their marital home. See Sen, *Women's Dialect in Bengali*, p. 60. Lusty wives are seen as suspect in other North Indian traditions as well, as exemplified in a Punjabi proverb: 'A woman who shows more love for you than a mother is a slut.' See Sudhir Kakar, *Intimate Relations* (Chicago: University of Chicago Press,1990), p. 19.

[23] Banerjee, 'Marginalisation of Women's Popular Culture'.

tyrannical husbands or unfaithful lovers, was no doubt popular with female listeners, who found in the songs a symbolic solace or perhaps even a revenge.'[24] Influential opinions like those of Guha would see these more as 'ritual rebellion(s)' that 'reinforce authority by feigning defiance' in a temporary, contained, and innocuous reversal of the otherwise authoritative and unquestioned cultural discourse,[25] while still others might consider it as a 'subordinate discourse' rather than an alternative or competing ideology.[26] But far from confirming social order through mock inversions, as in carnivalesque rituals, Banerjee argues, these traditions allowed women to think and act in ways well beyond their conventional roles, roles that were fearful to men. In fact, the disruptive potential of such seemingly innocent entertainment was given formal recognition when male reformers of the time launched a forceful campaign against them.

As other studies have demonstrated, even carnivalesque 'safety-valve' reversals do not simply confirm authority. Violent clashes during or coincidental with carnivals show how these could be socially dangerous occasions too, with conflict rather than consensus forming the defining moment.[27] To regard this as 'dramatic' and 'occasional' is to miss the point. Ritual is part of the everyday, and struggle exists where we think it is absent.[28] The 'hidden transcripts' embedded in such songs make for veiled but serious communication about the singers' alternative self-perceptions and social perspectives. Even Guha acknowledges elsewhere that women may have special command over knowledge and speech concerning their own bodies, beyond the purview of their male guardians, and goes far enough to

[24] Ibid., p. 140.

[25] Ranajit Guha, *Elementary Aspects of Peasant Insurgency in Colonial India* (New Delhi: Oxford University Press, 1983), p. 31.

[26] O'Hanlon, in Haynes and Prakash, *Contesting Power*.

[27] Nicholas B. Dirks, 'Ritual and Resistance: Subversion as a Social Fact', in D. Haynes and G. Prakash (eds), *Contesting Power: Resistance and Everyday Social Relations in South Asia* (Berkeley: University of California Press, 1992).

[28] See F. Hall, T. Jefferson, and B. Roberts (eds), *Resistance Through Rituals* (London: Hutchinson, 1976); D. Hebdige, *Subculture: The Meaning of Style* (New York: Methuen, 1979).

note that it 'constitutes a challenge which is genuinely dreaded by male authority'.[29]

Oldenburg's study of courtesans in North India thus uncovers 'the invisible activism in the domestic arena where women invent and use covert strategies to resist and undermine the oppression and drudgery of the average patriarchal household.'[30] More recent anthropological writings have also highlighted women's resistance to and negotiation with dominant cultural representations within the constraints set by patrilineal kinships, and indicated the ways in which they articulate subversive moral perspectives.[31] Folk songs by Rajasthani women thus supply many images of women as simultaneously seductive and fertile, erotic and domestic, with no apparent unease or conflict. In highly confident and celebratory songs dealing with women's bodies and sexual desires, they reverse conventional gendered representations, and yet do not seemingly aspire for a fundamental change in their social world.[32] In other performative traditions in North India it is possible to discover women interrogating the precedence that the natal bond takes over the conjugal in their husbands' households, while paying overall obeisance to the dominant discourse on kinship and gender.[33]

[29] Ranajit Guha, 'Chandra's Death', in Ranajit Guha (ed.), *Subaltern Studies V* (Delhi: Oxford University Press, 1987), p. 163.

[30] Oldenburg, in Haynes and Prakash, *Contesting Power*, p. 25.

[31] Gloria Goodwin Raheja, 'Women's Speech Genres: Kinship and Contradiction', in Nita Kumar (ed.), *Women as Subjects: South Asian Histories* (Charlottseville: University Press of Virginia, 1994) and Ann Grodzins Gold, 'Sexuality, Fertility and Erotic Imagination in Rajasthani Women's Songs', in Ann Grodzins Gold and Gloria Goodwin Raheja (eds), *Listen to the Heron's Words: Reimagining Gender and Kinship in North India* (Berkeley: University of California Press, 1994).

[32] Gold, 'Sexuality, Fertility and Erotic Imagination in Rajasthani Women's Songs', pp. 30–72. Reversal of gendered worlds in songs of abuse, some especially reserved for welcoming the bridegroom, also appear to be in vogue among Dalit women in Gujarat. See Fernando Franco, Jyotsna Macwan, and Suguna Ramanathan (eds), *The Silken Swing: The Cultural Universe of the Dalit Women* (Calcutta: Stree Publications, 2000), pp. 201–4.

[33] Raheja, 'On the Uses of Subversion: Redefining Conjugality', in Gold and Raheja, *Listen to the Heron's Words*, pp. 121–48.

The rich repertoire of nineteenth-century proverbs attributed to Bengali women goes some way in uncovering the tense relationship that prevailed between the sexes within a domestic sphere. While it is possible to read some of this as harmless banter, the inherent mistrust and deep contempt for men (usually husbands) that they embody cannot be bypassed. Women's speech practices as sites of struggle about kinship, gender definitions, and power have been identified in recent studies.[34] Such practices, it is proposed, may be seen as resistance to a dominant cultural order when they offer alternative visions of the social world, and when they are practised and valued despite attempts to suppress them.[35] For those like Susan Gal they represent opposition to a dominant cultural order (rather than mere rituals of rebellion). She argues that women's speech genres do not always simply reflect or reinforce an already constituted social order; they may function as strategies in ongoing negotiations and contestations in kinship and gender identities. In fact, the authority of normative discourses begins to disintegrate when juxtaposed with the heterogeneity and resistance often evident in women's speech.[36]

'If songs are confined to ritually marked spheres that are somehow set apart from everyday life', comments Raheja, 'proverbs insert those interrogations into everyday life . . .'[37] Kenneth Burke notes that proverbs are nothing other than 'strategies for dealing with situations'.[38] They present perspectives on the immediate social world and are invoked to represent or make known the discursive positions of the participating group. The implied shared understanding within the group that deploys them, and the communicative function they

[34] Raheja, 'Women's Speech Genres, Kinship and Contradiction', and Minault, 'Other Voices, Other Rooms: The View from the Zenana', in Kumar, *Women as Subjects*.

[35] Raheja, 'Women's Speech Genres', in Kumar, *Women as Subjects*, p. 52.

[36] Susan Gal, 'Between Speech and Silence: The Problematics of Research on Language and Gender', in Micaela di Leonardo (ed.), *Gender at the Crossroads of Knowledge: Feminist Anthropology in the Postmodern Era* (Berkeley: University of California Press, 1991), pp. 175–203.

[37] Raheja, 'Women's Speech Genres', in Kumar, *Women as Subjects*, p. 55.

[38] Kenneth Burke, *The Philosophy of Literary Form* (Berkeley: University of California Press, 1973), p. 296.

fulfil in specific speech situations, help proverbs reproduce social relations in everyday life.

In our case, we find them questioning an oppressive patriarchy which has lost the moral authority to continue. This deeply critical attitude can be read in the ways in which women confront and voice their rejection of unworthy husbands, with implications for male control over women's bodies and lives. The alternative moral discourse comes across in the underlined legitimacy of a husband's principal role as provider. He who is unable to provide, it is offered, should be stripped of his authority over his woman. The lazy and incompetent husband is whipped mercilessly in this undercover world seething with discontent and failed expectations.

> *Bhat dile bhatar, noile gramer chhatar*
> (He is a husband only when he can provide, otherwise he is no better
>   than the village carpenter)[39]

> *Bhat debar bhatar noy, kil maribar gnoshai*
> (Not a husband in giving rice, but a guru in thumping me)[40]

> *Knure bhatarer patkel shitan*
> (A lazy husband gets a brick for a pillow)[41]

By contrast, the housewifely role is much celebrated.[42] A deep sense of betrayal and violation resonates in such proverbs and seeks to undermine the power of the male householder. Inasmuch as the apparent rightful authority of the man is based on his ability to provide and look after his wife, any departure from that trusted role

---

[39] Lalitmohan Ray, *Meyeli* (Mymensingh: 1799), p. 10.

[40] James Long, *Prabadmala or the Wit and Wisdom of Bengali Ryots and Women as Shewn in their Proverbial Sayings* (Calcutta: 1869), p. 91 (original translation); for another variation of this, see Sukumar Sen, *Women's Dialect in Bengali* (Calcutta: 1979), p. 67.

[41] Sen, *Women's Dialect*, p. 66 (original translation). Also, *Kaje knure khete dere, bochone mare puriye puriye* (He is lazy at his job, eats for one and a half, and yet burns me alive with his sharp tongue): ibid.

[42] *Koto dhane koto chal, ginni bine al thal* (The housewife is not missed until she is gone and disorder reigns, just as paddy goes unappreciated until it transforms to rice grains). See James Long, *Prabadmala*, p. 20.

profoundly damages his public self-image.[43] The worthlessness of a husband who has failed to gain recognition in public is brought out sharply when contrasted with his lording over the woman at home:

Darbare na peye thnai, ghare eshe mag kilai

(Not having found a place in the court, I beat my woman when back at home)

Numerous versions of this proverb did their rounds in nineteenth-century Bengal.[44] Tanika Sarkar has observed that the crucial distinction between two forms of subjection—that of the colonized male in the world outside, and the woman in her own home—was needed to bolster the ruined self-confidence of the bhadralok.[45] The helpless surrender to the will of the lord and master—that is, the husband—and the abject misery that follows are also recorded with due frustration and sadness:

Jar kachhe byabostha, shei kore tin abastha
(He who is vested with the powers [to protect me] ruins my life)

Porechhi dojjaler hate, jonjal joray dine rate
(I am in the hands of an unruly lout, trouble manifests itself all the time)[46]

[43] James Scott has shown how public professions of morality and responsibility by the dominant elite render them more vulnerable to criticism from the subordinated. E.g., priestly castes are most brought into disrepute if shown as promiscuous and gluttonous; the benevolent image of the Tsar is undermined if his troops open fire on helpless assemblies of his subjects; and the slave owner's paternal role is shattered if he is shown as whipping his slaves arbitrarily. See James Scott, *Domination and the Arts of Resistance: Hidden Transcripts* (New Haven: Yale University Press, 1985), pp. 105–6.

[44] See e.g. Long, *Prabadmala*, pp. 120, 127; Lalitmohan Ray, *Meyeli*, p. 5; Sukumar Sen, *Women's Dialect in Bengali*, p. 66.

[45] Tanika Sarkar, 'The Hindu Wife and Hindu Nation: Domesticity and Nationalism in Nineteenth Century Bengal', *Studies in Indian History*, 8, 2 (1992).

[46] Sen, *Women's Dialect*, pp. 66–7; *Ami buror ghor korchhi, na kebol tar mon jogachhi?* (Am I the old man's wife, or someone who merely panders to his whims?), Rev. K.K.G. Sarkar, *Prabadmala* (Calcutta: 1894), p. 3.

It is obvious that such proverbs and songs would not have been spoken out or enacted in more open shared spaces even within households. Because power relations prevented most women from speaking in the presence of senior male affines, they had to confine their voices to the antahpur world, within a closed, sympathetic speech community. Moreover, the topsy-turvy social situations we encounter are imagined or wished rather than either deriving from or replicated in real life. But the very existence of such communication, often articulating a contrapuntal reading of gender relations, and implicitly shared gendered meanings, is suggestive of a subverted dominant discourse. Far from treating this as 'ritual rebellion' that leaves 'the dominant male ideology more or less intact',[47] we need to appreciate the multiplicity of strategies through which women made their disaffection felt.[48] As Goodwin and Raheja demonstrate in their study of North Indian women's songs in more recent times, 'Resistance and tradition may not inevitably be at odds with each other. Though the women we know in Uttar Pradesh and Rajasthan do in many ways assent to the dominant ideologies of gender and kinship, they also sing of their resistance to such ideologies . . . [and] insert this stance of resistance into their everyday lives.'[49]

The songs and proverbs analysed above may at times perpetuate gender inequalities, but they also present moral alternatives and arguably nourish prospects of active resistance by women in the future. Through them edgy relationships are opened up and tested, discontent expressed, dominance defied, and the solidarity of the oppressed confirmed. Rather than representing innocuous reversals of a monolithic normative discourse, they powerfully invoke another, also valued, belief system. As Scott points out, it is through such 'hidden transcripts' that the idea of social transformation is sustained

[47] Stanley Tambiah, 'Bridewealth and Dowry Revisited', *Current Anthropology*, 30(4), 1989, p. 418.

[48] It is not a coincidence that the most irreverent of fun among women, and their bawdiest, wildest songs and dances encountered by scholars, have been performed in the cloistered inner courtyards of households, often with the doors safely shut. Gold, 'Sexuality, Fertility and Erotic Imagination in Rajasthani Women's Songs', pp. 44, 46.

[49] Ibid.

in seemingly innocuous rituals, jokes, and songs, until active rebellion realizes that vision.[50]

The *Antahpur* as Refuge: Bonds of Pain

The world of domestic rituals and ceremonies surrounding female bodily cycles, routine housework, and feminine entertainment bound women together in strictly gendered ways which marginalized the men in their lives. Coupled with the apparent unruliness and raillery prevailing in such spheres that allowed the practice of immodest and superstitious customs and beliefs, this posed a direct challenge to the male reformist spirit. However, for women, such ties provided vital spiritual succour and the means to survive in a harsh and hostile environment—a comradeship built on sisterly co-operation. In fact, the practice of establishing sisterly ties among women not related by blood through elaborate customs was quite common and celebrated women in contemporary poems. The important role played by the figure of the *patano bon* (mock sister) or *shoi* (female friend) is palpable in not just fiction and poetry but also women's memoirs and autobiographies.[51]

The emphasis placed by many women writers of the time on childhood is significant. It held a special meaning for them as maturity brought with it a debilitating loss of self, and they were inclined to look back fondly on the relative freedom and power of childhood.[52] The happy past is commemorated with loving care in one such verse collection.[53] Recalling happy times spent in playing with dolls,

[50] Scott, *Domination and the Arts of Resistance*, pp. 37–41.

[51] Such fictive sisterhoods are also evident in other parts of North India in the nineteenth century. See Minault, 'Other Voices, Other Rooms: The View from the Zenana', p. 111.

[52] Patricia Meyer Spacks, 'Stages of Self: Notes on Autobiography and the Life Cycle' in Edward Stone (ed.), *The American Autobiography: A Collection of Critical Essays* (Englewood Cliffs, NJ: 1981), p. 48.

[53] Shoroshibala Debi (Basu), *Pushpapunja* (Calcutta: 1884). Other works written by her include a book of poems, *Pushpaknuri* (1885), and a biography of 107 pages, *Swargiya Mahatma Ramcharan Basur Jibancharit* (1900). See Usha Chakraborty, *Condition of Bengali Women* (Calcutta: Calcutta University, 1963), pp. 176–7.

singing to the tune of birds and playing in the rain in 'The Pleasant Days of Childhood', the author, Shoroshibala Debi, laments the loss of that innocence in her later life.[54] Even when the body matured and the duties of a housewife and mistress of the household took over, the mind held on to pleasant memories of the pre-pubertal carefree world. Many themes pertain to the simple pleasures of life, or yearnings for lost friends and family from childhood days. Thus 'Lonely girl' mourns the loss of the author's mother, while 'Description of my dear friend dying' is an elegy dedicated to a close friend.[55] In the poem 'On meeting my sister after many years' Shoroshibala celebrates the occasion while sketching her heartfelt longing for her sibling.[56] Trivial things in daily life, such as a tailorbird's nest, a rose, and a cricket make up the subject matter of some poems in such collections: they fascinate their authors and fill them with sensuous wonder.[57]

In another such work, published anonymously after the death of the child-author at the tender age of 16, a poem, 'Come, come' (*Ay Ay*), outlines her craving for the carefree and happy days of childhood.

> Oh my girlhood days do return
> Bringing my tender heart with you.
> . . . Oh do return my gem, my young heart.
> Come let us play in the dust
> And build toy temples of clay.
> Oh come, let us sing girlish songs by the river
> And count the boats as they sail by
> Lost to the cares of the world
> . . . Oh please do come,
> My heart yearns to see you again.[58]

---

[54] Shoroshibala Debi, *Puspapunja* (Calcutta: Someprakash Depository, 1884), pp. 33–4.

[55] This friend of the poet died in childbirth aged 18. See ibid., p. 83. Also see e.g., Sri R____Debi, 'On the loss of a Girlfriend' (*Shokhi Biyoge*), in *Bhabbikash*, privately published by Surendranath Bandyopadhyay (Calcutta: 1894).

[56] Shoroshibala Debi, *Puspapunja*, pp.11–25.

[57] Shoroshibala Debi, *Puspapunja*, pp. 48–50, 69–71, 71–2.

[58] Anon, *Akalkusum* (Calcutta: Sanyal & Co., 1896), my translation. Published

The burden of domesticity had been placed too soon on the shoulders of the young girl and she longed for her days of freedom and easy abandon. The crushing weight of housework was multiplied in situations where a stream of constant visitors characterized the daily routine.[59] Images of the caged bird and the mute prisoner are recurrent even in women's autobiographies.[60]

Rassundari Debi (1809–1900), a self-tutored woman of a prosperous rural household in Bengal, thus encountered a tyrannical regime of domesticity from the moment she stepped into her marital household, leading a life of non-existence and hard labour—no better, she felt, than the cow harnessed to the oilpresser's wheel.[61] Vividly described in her now famous autobiography, Rassundari recorded her abject compliance to these household duties—overdone, perhaps, to highlight her victimhood.[62]

As a woman of advanced years, and matriarch of an extended successful family, Rassundari recalls her earlier days with much loathing and grievance. The narrative is based on her experiences in a busy landed family as a young bride and mother, crushed under the burden of domesticity and yearning to read. Driven by the need to read a sacred text, Rassundari ultimately succeeds in teaching herself

---

posthumously by the writer's husband, Indubhushan Mallik, with a short biographical preface. Apparently, most of the compositions in the work were written at the age of 14.

[59] But women could also vent their steam in surprisingly vicious proverbs like the following:

Aisho kutom boisho khate, pa dhuabo pukur ghate; pith bhangbo chela kathe

(Come dear guest, sit on the bed, let me wash your feet by the pond; and break your back with a wooden plank)

See Sarkar, *Prabadmala*, p. 2.

[60] For a general discussion of the predicaments of nineteenth-century young Bengali housewives, see Kalyani Dutta, *Pinjore Boshiya* (Calcutta: Stree, 1996)

[61] Rassundari Debi, *Amar Jiban* (Calcutta: 1898). Reprinted in Nareshchandra Jana, *et al.*, eds, *Atmakatha*, vol. 1 (Calcutta: Ananya Prakasan, 1981), pp. 21–41.

[62] Tanika Sarkar, *Words to Win: The Making of 'Amar Jiban', A Modern Autobiography* (New Delhi: Kali for Women), pp. 225–8.

secretly in the dark corners of her kitchen. In its deep religiosity, un-pretentious glimpses into the humdrum details of a rural household, and a naivete bordering on ignorance, Rassundari's memoirs pose a challenge to the rational, hegemonic, reformist discourse from within the borders of the middle-class educated world.

In that harsh regime of selfless sacrifice and hard labour, younger women stuck together for comfort. Afternoons spent in relaxed needlework, hairdos, and careless conversation are recalled with much fondness in many accounts.[63] Reading was an integral part of this companionate world. Not just epics and religious texts, but saucy and potentially disruptive novels and plays were shared in this exclusive space, hidden from the vigilant eye of male guardians. In some cases, of course, the very act of reading was considered mutinous, for Bengal's wakening to liberal reform and the cause of emancipation for women was slow and grudging. Once she had learned to read, Rassundari organized regular clandestine reading and singing sessions with neighbouring women and her sisters-in-law. Held in a spot rarely visited, with a person constantly keeping watch—lest the forbidden act be discovered—this session embodied a continuous and flagrant violation of household codes within a consensual femi-nine space, just the kind that men most felt threatened by.[64] The perceived self-sufficiency and impenetrability of such cultural spheres that unnerved patriarchies—not just in Bengal but also elsewhere in India in the nineteenth century—has been noted by several scholars.[65]

The numerous *bratas* or household rites for young unmarried girls seeking good husbands and prosperity, arranged round the calendar year, created tightly knit communal networks based on shared experiences of starving, worship, and ritual.[66] In the string of

[63] See e.g. Prasannamoyi Debi, 'Shekaler Katha', *Antahpur*, Jaistha 1308 BS, reprinted in Abhijit Sen and Abhijit Bhattacharya (eds.), *Shekele Katha: Shotok Shuchonay Meyeder Smritikatha* (Calcutta: Naya Udyog, 1997), p. 18; Kalyani Dutta, *Thor Bori Khara* (Calcutta: Thema, 1993), pp. 18, 63.

[64] Rassundari Debi, *Amar Jiban*, p. 37.

[65] See Banerjee, 'Marginalisation of Women's Popular Culture'; Minault, 'Other Voices: Other Rooms'.

[66] One estimate gives 39 such bratas celebrated round the calendar year. See Basantakumari Dasi, *Meyeder Bratakatha Ba Brata Mahatya* (Calcutta: 1937).

chores attending the ceremonies—from picking flowers and fetching water from the river to drawing decorative floor designs (*alponas*)—there was much scope for mutual bonding and dependence in daily life. Pursuing the same dreams and aspirations, united against common evils, and following strict regimes of diet and duty, the girls could nurture deep friendships and even fictive sisterhoods. Images drawn in loving detail—of grain mounds, cows, fish, and ornaments symbolizing prosperity—reflect a profound emotional investment in such acts.[67] The enduring impact that bratas had on the lives of women can also be witnessed in contemporary artwork, including embroidery.[68]

A caveat is in order here. The hierarchy of oppression in the household was obviously not just organized along lines of gender. The position and prosperity of the immediate male relative, the age, marital status, and child-bearing capacity of the woman, the extent of her dependence on familial resources, and her particular location in the family tree (e.g. as wife or daughter)—all contributed to the formation of a strict pecking order. Widows, young wives, and poor relatives were particularly vulnerable. Proverbs of the time, while expressing a gendered disaffection of patriarchal norms, also mirror some of these internal conflicts:

Shashuri nayi nonash nai, kar ba kori dor
Age khayi panta bhat, sheshe lepi ghor

(Neither the mother-in-law nor the sister-in-law is at home,
So I care for no one;
Let me first have some stale rice, and wipe the floor later)[69]

A typical brata would entail starving during the day, and living only on milk, fruits and sweetmeats. Meals could be taken in the evening, but only after elaborate rituals had been attended to and the concerned deity worshipped.

[67] See Abanindranath Tagore, *Banglar Brata* (Calcutta: 1919), for such representative images.

[68] Motifs drawn from the brata rituals can be found on quilts of the time. See Sheela Basak, *Banglar Nakshi Knatha* (Calcutta: Ananda Publishers, 2002), pp. 93–7. For some typical brata motifs, see pp. 61 (Plate 70); 90 (Plate 97); and 115 (Plate 135).

[69] Ray, *Meyeli*, p. 6.

The presumed indolence of the housewife in relation to domestic duties, as witnessed above, is a source of incessant complaint. It is assumed that she is given over to a life of comfort and idleness, and spends her time beautifying herself and demanding more luxuries. Nothing about her is pleasing to the in-laws.

Pan shajte janena, du paye alta porechhe
(She does not know how to prepare betel, and yet can paint her feet
  crimson)

Bouer cholon feron kemon, turki ghora jemon
Bouer golar svar kemon, shalik knekai jemon.

(How is your daughter-in-law's gait? Like a Turkish horse.
How is your daughter-in-law's voice? Like a screeching *shalik* bird)[70]

But such seemingly contradictory positions can be explained in terms of the stresses placed by an oppressive kinship system on married women. The divergent claims and expectations imposed on the woman by dominant norms compelled a struggle for survival within a harsh patrilineal structure in the conjugal household, which split gender identities and pitted one woman against another.[71] Thus, in condoning gendered oppression on the one hand, and challenging it on the other, women can be seen as deploying multiple strategies to negotiate a better position for themselves in an unforgiving and competitive world. Like the lower castes in Guha's study, they both confirm and interrogate, uphold and challenge, submit and rebel.

Devotion and Lament: Escape and Critique

The role of women's religiosity in articulating narratives of resistance is also worth looking at in this context. For many, faith in a personal

[70] Sen, *Women's Dialect*, p. 59.

[71] The implications of such split gendered identities for social relations have been discussed by scholars. See Gloria Goodwin Raheja, 'On the Uses of Irony and Ambiguity: Shifting Perspectives on Patriliny and Women's Ties to Natal Kin', in Raheja and Gold, *Listen to the Heron's Words*; Lynn Bennett, *Dangerous Wives and Sacred Sisters: Social and Symbolic Roles of High-Caste Women in Nepal* (New York: Columbia University Press, 1983).

God offered an escape from the misery of daily enslavement. A precious and acutely humanized relationship with the divine pervades the writing of Bengali women in the nineteenth century. It would be erroneous to dismiss this as mere religiosity. For, beneath the veneer of private piety lay a bedrock of gloom and despondency regarding their earthly existence. Condemnation of their wretched condition and hope of deliverance to a better world in the afterlife are expressed, both through anxious lament and burning indignation, in many compositions. Uttered within the conventional rhetoric of piety, such indictment confounded discrete binaries of pain and anger, submission and resistance, thus eluding social sanction. For women, suffering has always been part of the politics of emotion, which is the strategy of the marginal and the disempowered.[72] Punishing the body and mutely bearing the domestic burden were also tantamount to martyrdom and eventual elevation in the eyes of both society and God.

The peculiar condition of women writing in colonial India has been the subject of many writings. Partha Chatterjee points out that their writings were vitiated by a double subjection, to colonialism and to indigenous patriarchy. In echoing the sensibilities and concerns of a nationalist patriarchy, whether in their literary style or attitudes towards sexuality, or their roles in family and society, women were caught up in the male hegemonic discourse.[73] But Chatterjee's views are derived almost entirely from an examination of the lives of important public figures—famous by virtue of their own activities or those of their partners/sons/fathers.

[72] See Susan Signe Morrison, *Women Pilgrims in Late Medieval England*, ch. 5: 'Performing Margery Kempe'.

[73] Even in fictional autobiographies, rendered as first-person narrative, women preferred to toe the hegemonic line. As pointed out, the problem was compounded in the case of educated Muslim women whose deafening silence is underlined by not only the lack of autobiographies, but also fictional writing in the autobiographical mode. See Sonia Amin, *The World of Muslim Women in Colonial Bengal, 1876–1939* (Leiden: Brill, 1996) pp. 214, 229–30. See also Meera Kosambi's work on the analogous lives of women in nineteenth-century Maharashtra: *Crossing Thresholds: Feminist Essays in Social History* (Delhi: Permanent Black, 2007).

It is far more profitable to turn our focus to the less glamorous lives of small-town, rural, and half-literate figures such as Rassundari Debi. For one, it is possible to hear a softer echo of reformist sentiments in them; and besides, the less exalted social position of the writers allows them to write in a less discursive and more personal and honest style. Indeed, as has been pointed out, it is striking how it is not so much women from progressive reformist circles or great and famous women achievers in the professional world who leave behind accounts of their lives, as women from lesser-known circles—housewives, prostitute-actresses, and so on. Writing for such women constituted social worth, and 'writing self-reflexively both mirrored and made that self.'[74]

Compared to the derivative discursive mode of the didactic tracts written by their more prominent sisters, these deeply personal tales of pain and pleasure are vibrant with a life of their own, and have another story to tell. These are not overtly polemical or confrontational writings by passionate feminists. Instead, these compositions lack both force and agenda. The culture of the antahpur, where women bonded in mutual sisterhood over shared religious and spiritual life, household routines, and exchanges of intimate familial knowledge, oversaw the nurturing of different sentiments and themes. We are confronted with enduring and often touching images of domesticity and a god-fearing world centred on the family and its welfare.

Rassundari's autobiography has been a subject of much discussion. While some see her as a 'traditional' woman appropriated by a modern, male rationalistic enterprise,[75] others object to this 'unproblematic annexation' and 'conclusion' of what is seen as a 'complex, highly individual endeavour to a different master-narrative.'[76] There is a lot going on in the memoir that makes it a perfect counter-narrative of the hegemonic discourse. Her earthy, uninhibited

[74] Sarkar, *Words to Win: The Making of 'Amar Jiban', A Modern Autobiography* (New Delhi: Kali for Women, 1999), p. 131.

[75] Partha Chatterjee, *The Nation and Its Fragments: Colonial and Postcolonial Histories* (Princeton: Princeton University Press, 1993), pp. 140–4.

[76] Sarkar, *Words to Win*, p. 224. Also see Susie Tharu and K. Lalita, *Women Writing in India: 600 BC to the Early Twentieth Century* (New Delhi: Oxford University Press, 1993), pp. 161–4.

narrative, with its belief in the supernatural and indelicate vocabulary, is proof of a problematic 'enlightenment'. And yet, the discursive mode in which she writes, and the absence of the emotional and personal (except in the Divine Presence), is borrowed from the reformist palate. The easy alternation between prose and verse, with frequent and unpredictable transgression of normative speech boundaries; her silent, 'willing', and even smiling shouldering of daily chores contrasts with her deep hatred of domesticity and wifely roles; and the juxtaposition of an unfaltering belief in God with a rationalistic and modern conviction in education for girls—these make any straightforward reading of the work quite impossible.

But let us return to the central subject of this debate, which is Rassundari's acquisition of literacy. As an endeavour pursued independent of her husband and family, and nurtured in the secrecy of her private space, Rassundari's efforts to read constituted an act of conscious rebellion. As has been pointed out, the reformist project was irretrievably subverted 'as she surreptitiously scratched the letters on to the blackened walls of her kitchen'.[77] Most importantly, this desire was prompted not by the need to improve her role as mistress or mother within the household, but to read religious literature. Going against the progressive liberal grain, her work throughout shows a burning passion to read texts like the *Chaitanya Bhagavat*.

Existing writings on the subject, however, fail to make much more of this deep religiosity in Rassundari. I would tend to regard the profession of faith in a personal God, as a cathartic exercise for women like Rassundari, to escape the prison-house of domesticity. For many like her, I would argue, religion offered a deliverance from the misery of daily drudgery and anguish. My starting point here is again Sarkar's work: 'Rashsundari worked out a double-edged stance *vis-à-vis* her *sansar* [household] and her identity. She underlined her submission and her unqualified success here. At the same time, she took care to indicate that a deeper truth lay veiled behind this apparent reality, this partial truth, this *maya* that was her *sansar*. By evoking this contrast, she wrested for herself an interior space which was her faith.'[78] But this faith was not simply a sum total of externally

---

[77] Tharu and Lalita, *Women Writing in India*, p. 164.
[78] Sarkar, *Words to Win*, p. 66.

prescribed regulations. It allowed the individual to inhabit a peculiar autonomous space constituted of an interplay between the everyday and the sacred, the mundane and the spiritual.[79] The long hours women spent in the rooms of worship by themselves perhaps enhanced this sense of virtual liberation.

Women were exposed to a religious environment from a very tender age, much more than their male relatives. Like all young girls of her times, Rassundari's childhood days must have been spent in learning the intricacies of domestic religious rituals and performance. While the boys went to village *pathshalas*, girls learnt to prepare clay shiva lingams and draw decorative and ritualistic designs for auspicious occasions.[80] Ceremonial reading of religious works, or *katha-katas*, was a regular affair both in rural and Calcutta households, as was devotional singing and performance. The earliest texts that young girls were exposed to were, more often than not, religious. Literate at six, Saralabala sought out religious texts like *Sridharma-mangal*, *Manasar Bhasan*, *Ramayana*, and *Chandimangal*.[81]

Religious ritual was an integral part of the daily routine. Worshipping the family deity was often the very first thing that women did on waking up at the crack of dawn, before tending to household chores.[82] The act was doubly liberating. It provided an escape from the mundane and material, a rupture with the everyday. It also helped secure a very private space, sanctified by its sacred alterity—and gave the Bengali woman a 'room of her own'. Women saw themselves here as freed from their quotidian life, in direct and private communion with God, who held the promise of deliverance from earthly misery. It was an empowering self-perception that, by couching dissidence in religious piety, successfully played out the 'hidden transcript' of flight.

[79] Ibid., pp. 65–6.

[80] Prasannamoyi Debi, 'Sekal O Ekal', *Bangalakshmi* (Chaitra 1337), reprinted in Sen and Bhattacharya, *Shekele Katha*, p. 58.

[81] Chitra Deb (ed.), *Saralabala Sarkar Racanasangraha*, vol. 1 (Calcutta: Ananda Publishers, 1989), pp. 739–40, 773–4.

[82] Prasannamoyi Debi, 'Shekaler Katha', p. 17; Mankumari Basu, 'Amar Atit Jiban', *Uttara* (Kartik-Agrahayan 1333), reprinted in Sen and Bhattacharya, *Shekele Katha*, p. 115.

Space and social relations are processes that reinforce one another. Granting or withholding access to social spaces both produces and reproduces power, status, and privilege.[83] Creating gendered spaces, it has been argued, thus helps men secure prevailing advantages.[84] But it would be far more fruitful to view space as a realm of competing ideologies, a discursive territory wrought by the struggle of various groups.[85] Gendered spaces thus cannot simply be imposed on women, who could also subvert and create their own socially specific meanings of that space. The spatial politics of Bengali domesticity I see thus underwritten in the bodily withdrawal of women from an oppressive environment into an unassailable spiritual sanctuary. If it is possible to read space as text, as a transparent representation of the ideologies that produce it, then women were writing their protest within the confines of their room of worship.

The sense of complete abandon and surrender to a personal God, often making use of Vaishnava imagery, permeates the writing of many women of the time. Images of physical deprivation (hunger, thirst, pain) and pleasures (sex, even nuptial bliss) serve as metaphors of craving for, and ultimate union with, the Divine. But then miracles and visions with extremely sexual overtones were not unknown. Mysticism could be a bodily and even highly erotic experience in medieval devotional traditions. The ecstasy of physical union with God was enshrined in the legends of medieval women saints like Mirabai and formed an enduring feature of Vaishnavism. Such fleshly or bodily aspects of piety had become an inseparable part of Hindu religious practice in nineteenth-century Bengal.

For women, in particular, the humanity and immediacy of the Divine were invoked through the images of male lover and child. Young girls would bathe, dress, and play with idols of Krishna as the

[83] Michel de Certeau, *The Practice of Everyday Life*, trans. Stephen Randall (Berkeley: University of California Press, 1984); Henry Lefebvre, *The Production of Space*, trans. Donald Nicholson-Smith (Oxford: Blackwell, 1991).

[84] Daphne Spain, *Gendered Spaces* (Chapel Hill: University of North Carolina Press, 1992).

[85] John Eade and Michael J. Sallnow, *Contesting the Sacred: The Anthropology of Christian Pilgrimage* (London: Routledge, 1991).

boy-child.[86] The ritual worship of Shiva by unmarried girls was embedded in the more earthly pursuit of a suitable groom. While it is possible on the one hand to view this as a continuation of women's nurturing social roles into the religious domain,[87] the intensity and fierce fervour apparent in the daily enactment of such material relationships among the most devout, I would argue, is indicative of something else. It marks the forging of an imagined alternative existence, where there are no impossible demands made on women's wifely or motherly (or for that matter, sisterly and daughterly) roles, where there is a greater appreciation of their worth, where all actions are self-controlled, where they are notionally *free*.

For Bengali women writing in the nineteenth century there seems to have existed an intense and intimate relationship with God, which was much more than a simple literary trope. Pervasive despair and disillusionment, coupled with a deep desire for spiritual communion, resonates in many compositions.[88] For those like Prasannamoyi, married at the age of 10 to a man who would turn insane two years later, her marital home must have signified an abode of terror and oppression.[89] The fears of the young girl are expressed quite poignantly in a poem entitled simply, 'Prayer', published when she was only twelve.

> I am only a weak and dependent woman
> Resourceless as I am, how do I reach you?

[86] Anon, *Akalkusum*, Introduction. Adorable and indulgent images of the young Krishna were often expressed in metaphors of the naughty, playful child. See poem by Girindramohini Dasi, 'Khude Chor', cited in Jogendranath Gupta, *Banger Mahila Kobi* (Calcutta: 1930), pp. 82–3.

[87] Caroline Walker Bynum, *Fragmentation and Redemption* (New York: Zone Books, 1991), p. 198.

[88] For a particularly touching collection of poems, see Subodhbala Debi, *Nirabsadhana* (Calcutta: 1913). Titles of individual compositions in the compilation (e.g. 'In Despair'; 'In Vain'; 'Why this Unreasonable Desire?'; 'Why Sing?'; 'Thirst for Death'; and 'Call Me to Your Abode') are indicative of such moods.

[89] In fact, she was to return to her parental home at the age of 12 and spend the rest of her life there. See Sen and Bhattacharya, *Shekele Katha*, p. 231.

My in-laws are unfavourably disposed towards me
Fear haunts my every moment, oh Lord![90]

For the terrified Prasannamoyi, like the unhappy Rassundari, the Saviour seemed to hold all the answers to her problems. The staunch belief in their family deity, Dayamadhab, entrenched in young Rassundari by her mother from a very early age, stayed with her for the rest of her life.[91] Her uncontested and wholehearted submission to the idea is reflected in an incident from her childhood. When an accidental fire burnt their house down one night, Rassundari, along with her young brothers, were moved to the safer location of the neighbouring cremation ground. Fearful of the eerie surroundings, the siblings prayed fervently to Dayamadhab, and their petitions were seemingly answered for Rassundari when passers-by rescued them and returned them to their family. When the next morning, her younger brother confronted her with the information that they had been saved by an ordinary bearded mortal, so shocked and incredulous was Rassundari that she burst out crying and had to be soothed by her mother.[92]

In the numerous elegies that poured out from the late nineteenth century onwards, on the death of near and loved ones, there is a profound spiritual refrain.[93] But the style is also highly emotional and sentimental, belying the more individual aspect of such writing. The genres of *bilap* and *biraha* (lament and longing) feature pro-minently in these compositions. Women here wrote with a sense of acute vulnerability and of an immediate and special relationship to God. Unreasonable accusations and impossible demands direct-ed at the Divine addressee, made in a tentative, conversational, and

[90] Cited in Gupta, *Banger Mahila Kobi*, p. 58 (my translation). The poem was part of a collection by Prasannamoyi, published in 1879, and entitled, *Adho Adho Bhashini*.

[91] This was also noted by Jyotirindranath Tagore in his introduction to the work. See Rassundari Debi, *Amar Jiban*, Introduction.

[92] Ibid. pp. 10–11.

[93] See e.g., Girindramohini Dasi, *Asrukona* (Calcutta, n.d.), a collection of poems written on the death of her husband; Sarojkumari Debi's poem on losing her son, cited in Gupta, *Banger Mahila Kobi*, p. 212.

self-reflective style, provide touching images of private mystical piety and grief.[94] It is not a coincidence, however, that the Divine refuge was almost invariably male. For typically, acts of rebellion by the 'weak' may also reflect and strengthen dominant structures.[95]

Lament, it has been pointed out, is both a literary and rhetorical device for underlining the misery in women's lives. Through their survey of women's writings in the nineteenth century in English, Gilbert and Gubar demonstrate how, as a materially and culturally disadvantaged group, women learn to circumvent dominant ideologies and offer critical but disguised perceptions of their social world. The literature that they produce works like a palimpsest, where surface designs conceal and obscure deeper, less accessible (and less socially acceptable) levels of meaning and offer strategic redefinitions of the self.[96]

The unexpected and sudden passing away of people women were close to undoubtedly provided occasion for sharing in public emotions that were very private, with expectations of a sympathetic audience. But it could also serve as a deeper critique of this-worldly social relations—like a mother's lament at the maltreatment of her daughter by the in-laws,[97] or the helpless material dependence of women on their husbands and sons.[98] Behind the pain and the grief, thus, there invariably lay a sharp, though elusive, appraisal of social reality. When a grieving mother thus detects unhappiness in the cries of a bird, presumably reminiscing its past life, she succeeds in pouring scorn on prevalent patriarchal narratives of conjugal joy. Addressing the imaginary bird she laments:

[94] See e.g. Sushilabala Debi, *Sadhana* (Calcutta: 1905), especially pp. 48–51.

[95] See Scott, *Weapons of the Weak.*

[96] Sandra Gilbert and Susan Gubar, *The Mad Woman in the Attic: the Woman Writer and the Nineteenth Century Literary Imagination* (New Haven: Yale University Press, 1984).

[97] Sushila Sundari, *Asrumalika* (Calcutta, 1905), thus describes how her young daughter, Charu, died at the age of 16 leaving behind a young child, after being very unhappy in her conjugal household. Apparently, she was oppressed regularly and forbidden contact with her natal family.

[98] Tinkari Dasi, *Amar Jiban* (Calcutta, 1910), narrates the misfortunes of a married, and reasonably prosperous, woman who suffers the successive

Maybe you were a simple and innocent young Bengali girl (in your
      previous birth);
Not able to withstand the daily torture of your husband and mother-
      in-law,
You decided to take your life; and when reborn as a bird, sing to the
      world of your pain.[99]

Most significantly, it offered an opportunity to express unhappiness
within a socially acceptable framework, a legitimation of narratives
of personal sadness. It is no surprise that the autobiography of Binodini, the prostitute-actress and *femme fatale* of nineteenth-century
Calcutta, despite being such a pointed indictment of her social
world, was presented as a *bedona-gatha*, a narrative of pain. Understandably it was an amalgam of both 'an apologia and a defence', and
the literary mode in which it is written throws the serrated edges of
the author's social location and her memories of betrayal into
sharper profile.[100]

Women's devotion in a domestic situation was characterized by
penitential asceticism or suffering. Patient bearing of illness, selfless
service to others, and moderation in consumption were organic ex-
tensions of that role. But paradoxically there comes across an extra-
vagant sense of self-worth and deliverance in such voluntary acts of
abasement.[101] Self-inflicted suffering thus becomes a leitmotif of

---

bereavements of her daughter, mother-in-law, and husband within a very short
time. Believed to be an autobiography of a prostitute's daughter, it tells the story
of a humble and ordinary life, suddenly unhinged and rendered agonizing by
the tragic events. Also see Usha Chakraborty, *The Condition of Bengali Women*,
p. 183. A palpable anxiety in another work, written by a mother on the death
of her young schoolteacher son, is that of care and shelter in her old days. See
Binodini Debi, *Shokshindhu* (Calcutta: 1910), p. 45.

[99] Sushila Sundari, *Asrumalika* (my translation), p. 42.

[100] Rimli Bhattacharya (trans. and ed.), *Binodini Dasi: My Story and My Life
as an Actress* (New Delhi: Kali for Women, 1998), Introduction, pp. 27–32.

[101] Caroline Bynum has shown how medieval women saints could reclaim
the authority that had been denied to them within the institutional Christian
world, by resorting to severe physical austerity. Caroline Walker Bynum, *Holy
Feast Holy Fast: The Religious Significance of Food to Medieval Women* (Berkeley:
University of California Press), ch. 7.

emancipation. Rassundari crops up again. Her vitriolic indictment of her drab life, enslaving domesticity, and exclusion from the world of letters sit uneasily with her abject surrender and almost supine dedication to her family. Even when she recounts the rather pathetic tale of her missing food all day on account of domestic obligations, the narrative remains quite remote and dispassionate.[102] Physical subjugation is obviated by an almost transcendent moral stance on submission to duties and God's will. The relentless affirmation of faith in 'Dayamay' or 'The Merciful' helps redeem suffering and pain, resembling the faith of a saint burning at the stake.

The dream sequences in Rassundari's autobiography are complex in the messages they transmit. The visions involving her sons—Pyari's death, and Bepin's fall from a horse—both apparently proved true in real life immediately afterwards.[103] The recall of such experiences in later life does not invalidate her claims. It is not the veracity of such allegations that is on trial here but a mother's love for her offspring.[104] Rassundari emerges a martyr, a symbol of selfless sacrifice and unquestioning obedience—these no doubt the source of her later position of authority in the family—rather than a whining housewife. Like all other aspects of her self-representation, this too was a 'carefully calibrated and highly controlled strategy' that spoke of conflict, dissidence, and despair.[105]

Towards Reinterpreting Gender and Conflict in the Antahpur

Within the confines of the antahpur, then, women waged their discreet battles, wielding a variety of socially acceptable strategies—from disorderly and raucous ceremonials, acidic proverbs, and sisterly

---

[102] Rassundari Debi, *Amar Jiban*, p. 24.

[103] Ibid., pp. 50–4.

[104] Bynum has shown how the reputation and authority of women saints in medieval Europe was based on visions or paramystical phenomena, and defined women's religiosity in fundamental ways. See Caroline Walker Bynum, *Fragmentation and Redemption: Essays on Gender and the Human Body in Medieval Religion* (New York: Zone Books, 1991), especially ch. 2.

[105] Sarkar, *Words to Win*, p. 12.

bondings, to withdrawn and brooding piety. Shielded from direct surveillance and nourished by oppression, this secluded space proved an ideal breeding ground for gendered social discontent. Its significance is apparent from the unremitting efforts of the bhadralok to penetrate and reform the antahpur as a social site, and the corresponding efforts by women to preserve their cultural order. Undeniably, some sought escape via the 'liberal' route of educational reform under male tutelage, but others resisted such easy co-option. For women like Rassundari, entry to the world of letters had to take place on her own terms. Otherwise, unquestioning surrender to the reforming regime signalled newer forms of enslavement. The general consensus on gendered matters—fed by a rich subculture of restrained but resolute subversion of patriarchal codes—drew women together in tight circles of mutual empathy and solidarity. While not suggesting fundamental change, their thoughts and actions constituted some sharp interrogations of the existing social order, expressed unambiguous discontent, and posed moral alternatives.

It would be useless to continually peg the debate about resistance on a dramatic rupture between unchanging tradition on the one hand and radical social transformation on the other. The tremendous potential of hidden domains of conflict in fostering enduring social opinion and struggle has not been sufficiently appreciated. To regard them as 'occupying merely the social space left empty by domination would be to miss the struggle by which such sites are won . . . and defended' by marginal social groups in the teeth of power.[106] It is only by reclaiming the visibility of such spheres that we can find resistance where we did not see it before, and read conflict in seemingly normative situations.[107]

[106] Scott, *Domination and the Arts of Resistance*, p. 123.

[107] A portion of this essay appeared earlier in my book *Power in Print: Popular Publishing and the Politics of Language and Culture in a Colonial Society, 1788–1905* (New Delhi: Oxford University Press, 2006); my thanks to the publishers for permission to use it here.